Also by EMMANUEL ANATI

CAMONICA VALLEY

(1 9 6 1)

This is a BORZOI BOOK,
published by ALFRED A. KNOPF in New York

PALESTINE BEFORE THE HEBREWS

PALESTINE
BEFORE
THE HEBREWS

A HISTORY, FROM THE EARLIEST
ARRIVAL OF MAN
TO THE CONQUEST OF CANAAN

EMMANUEL ANATI

ALFRED : A : KNOPF

NEW YORK

1963

L. C. catalog card number: 62-12898

THIS IS A BORZOI BOOK,

PUBLISHED BY ALFRED A. KNOPF, INC.

FIRST EDITION

TO

Ariela, my wife,

whose help

has contributed so much

to

the completion of this book

ACKNOWLEDGMENTS

The text of this book was read and criticized by several authorities and fellow archaeologists, to whom I wish to express my deepest gratitude. Their comments and suggestions have been most valuable. My thanks go to:

Professor Carleton S. Coon, University Museum, Philadelphia, for having read and commented on the entire manuscript.

Professor Robert H. Dyson, University of Pennsylvania, Philadelphia, for having read and commented on the section "The Proto-Urban Cultures."

Dr. Kathleen M. Kenyon, Institute of Archaeology, University of London, for having read and commented on Parts Four and Five.

Miss Joan Du Plat Taylor, Insitute of Archaeology, University of London, for having examined the bibliography.

Professor Yigael Yadin, Hebrew University, Jerusalem, for having read and commented on Part Five.

Miss Efrat Yeivin, University of Tel Aviv, for having read and commented on Parts Two and Three.

Finally, I wish especially to thank Mr. Harold Strauss, Editor in Chief of Alfred A. Knopf, Inc., for giving so much of his time and skill to the editing of the text, and for his always stimulating editorial criticism and advice.

CONTENTS

ILLUSTRATIONS

NOTE: *The measurement bars that appear in some photographs are marked off in centimeters*

MAPS

FOR ILLUSTRATIONS and for permission to use them, grateful acknowledgment is made to the following:

Mr. David Allon, Kibbutz Mishmar Hanegev, for permission to take the photograph on p. 301.

Mr. Pesah Bar-Adon and the Israel Department of Antiquities, for permission to reproduce eight photographs from Beth-Yerah.

The British Museum, London, for the photograph on p. 160.

Miss Christine Court, of the Sir William Dunn School of Pathology, Oxford University, for making the drawings on pp. 103 and 152.

Professor Dorothy Garrod, for permission to reproduce the photographs on pp. 148, 160, 163, and 171.

The Israel Department of Antiquities, for permission to take twenty-one photographs of objects from Tell Eli, Shaar Hagolan, Tel Aviv, Beth-Yerah, Kinnereth, Kabri, Tell Assawir, Genosar, Nahariyah, and Affula.

Dr. Kathleen Kenyon and the British School of Archaeology in Jerusalem, for permission to reproduce the illustrations on pp. 245, 255 (bottom), and 353 (top).

Mr. Ezra Mayerhoff and the Beit Willfried Museum, Kibbutz Hazorea, for permission to take ten photographs of objects from Tell Abu Zureiq, Hazorea, and Har Haharuvim.

Mr. Tzvi Ofer and the Beersheba Town Museum, for permission to take the photograph on p. 300.

Mr. Jean Perrot, of the French Archaeological Mission to Israel, and Mr. Arie Volk, photographer, for permission to reproduce eleven photographs of objects from Einan, Azor, Bir Abu Matar, Bir Safadi, and Beersheba.

The Pontificium Institutum Biblicum, Jerusalem, for permission to take eight photographs of objects from Tuleilat Ghassul.

Professor Moshe Stekelis, of the Hebrew University, Jerusalem, for permission to take the photograph on p. 167. Again to Professor Stekelis and the Israel Department of Antiquities, for permission to reproduce eight photographs of objects from Shaar Hagolan.

Miss Olga Tufnell and the Wellcome Trust, London, for permission to reproduce two drawings and two photographs of objects from Lachish.

Professor Yigael Yadin, of the Hebrew University, Jerusalem, for permission to reproduce five photographs appearing on pp. 402, 416, and 425.

Other illustrations are acknowledged in the captions.

ABBREVIATIONS

AA   *The American Anthropologist*
AAA   *Annals of Archaeology and Anthropology,* University of Liverpool
AASOR   *Annual of the American School of Oriental Research,* Baltimore
ADAJ   *Annual of the Department of Antiquities of Jordan,* Amman
AFO   *Archiv für Orientforschung,* Berlin
AJ   *Antiquaries Journal,* London
AJA   *American Journal of Archaeology,* Concord, N.H.
AJSL   *American Journal of Semitic Languages and Literature,* Chicago
ANET   J. B. Pritchard: *Ancient Near Eastern Texts Relating to the Old Testament.* 2d ed. Princeton, N.J.: Princeton University Press; 1955.
AOR   *Archiv Orientalni,* Prague
Archives IPH   *Archives de l'Institut de Paléontologie Humaine,* Paris
ASAG   *Archives Suisses d'Anthropologie Générale,* Geneva
Atiqot   *Atiqot,* Journal of the Israel Department of Antiquities, Jerusalem
BA   *The Biblical Archaeologist,* New Haven, Conn.
BASOR   *Bulletin of the American Schools of Oriental Research,* Baltimore

BIES	*Bulletin of the Israel Exploration Society*, Jerusalem
BMB	*Bulletin du Musée de Beyrouth*, Beirut
BPAS	*Bulletin of the Philadelphia Anthropological Society*, Philadelphia
BRCI	*Bulletin of the Research Council of Israel*, Jerusalem
BSPF	*Bulletin de la Société Préhistorique Française*, Paris
CRAI	*Comptes Rendus des Séances de l'Académie des Inscriptions et Belles-Lettres*, Paris
IEJ	*Israel Exploration Journal*, Jerusalem
ILN	*Illustrated London News*, London
JAOS	*Journal of the American Oriental Society*, Princeton, N.J.
JBL	*Journal of Biblical Literature*, New York
JEA	*Journal of Egyptian Archaeology*, London
JNES	*Journal of Near Eastern Studies*, Chicago
JPOS	*Journal of the Palestine Oriental Society*, Jerusalem
JRAI	*Journal of the Royal Anthropological Institute*, London
JWH	*Journal of World History*, UNESCO, Paris
L'A	*L'Anthropologie*, Paris
PEQ	*Palestine Exploration Quarterly*, London
PPS	*Proceedings of the Prehistoric Society*, Cambridge, England
QDAP	*Quarterly of the Department of Antiquities in Palestine*, London
RB	*Revue Biblique*, Paris
RPI	*Rivista di Paletnologia Italiana*, Florence and Rome
ZDPV	*Zeitschrift des Deutschen Palästina-Vereins*, Leipzig

PALESTINE BEFORE THE HEBREWS

INTRODUCTION

WHO ARE WE? Where did we come from? How did human culture develop so as to bring forth civilizations? These and other probing questions are asked by all of us, both scientists and laymen, who want to know something about ourselves. We want to understand why we are the way we are, and are eager to grasp the meaning of our customs, our beliefs, our behavior. This curiosity about ourselves, and about our own civilization, makes us look back in an attempt to trace cultural processes as far back as possible, as far toward their origins as the evidence allows. In many cases the secret is revealed when we understand how and why a belief or a custom came into existence.

Tracing the history and prehistory of human intellectual adventures, we obtain a general picture of the processes of evolution that have transformed the relatively simple and homogene-

ous beginning into the extremely complex and varied cultural
patterns of today. We can see how early anthropoid beings gradually acquired the qualities and defects of man; how our early
ancestors learned to make tools, to master fire, and to communi-
cate with one another through the use of a complex assemblage
of sounds and symbols called language; how the earliest religious
impulses came into existence and developed; how abstract
thought increasingly occupied an important place in human
minds.

Different experiences and different environments led to cultural differentiation. In the course of millennia culture became
increasingly intricate; each community developed its own kind of
society, its technological devices, its spiritual life, its art, and its
religion. Finally, at the end of the prehistoric age, in some societies, men invented writing and eventually began to record history
fully. Archaeologists, anthropologists, historians, philosophers,
and psychologists are continually working to push back the boundaries of our knowledge, and to understand in more detail, more
deeply, the various processes of cultural evolution; but despite
these constant efforts, we still know very little about prehistoric
men, and whatever we know at present is but an elementary basis
for future research. However, a few shining beams enlighten some
details here and there, some aspects of human prehistory; and it
is with these uneven and fragmentary beams of light that the prehistorian tries to build a bridge to the distant past.

In the frame of biological evolution, man appeared on the
face of the earth very recently, after all the rest of the flora and
fauna of our globe had acquired most of their present characteristics. The earliest signs of life appeared on earth about one billion years ago, whereas the earliest anthropoid beings made their
first appearance less than one million years ago.

When literacy enabled man to enter history a few thousand
years ago, he already possessed all the physical, social, intellectual,
and technological abilities that he has today. At the dawn of
recorded history we discover a man very much like us. All his

qualities, the overwhelming majority of his mental and spiritual abilities and disabilities, are part of his prehistoric heritage, and acquired their shape in the course of the half million years that preceded the beginning of history. We have to look for the answers to our questions about the origins of man and of his culture, his beliefs, and his behavior in this long sequence of millennia.

The present volume is an attempt to trace the prehistoric cultural evolution of the peoples in a small corner of the world called Palestine. In very broad lines, before culture became complex the evolution of mankind was rather homogeneous throughout the world. Until thirty thousand years ago, the culture evolving in Palestine was distributed over other, very large areas. When culture became more specialized and localized, Palestine started on its own way and gradually acquired its distinctive cultural traits, first as part of the Eurasian continent, as a part of the Near East, and then as part of the Mediterranean Levant, and finally as a region with several cultural divisions of its own.

After the Hebrew conquest late in the second millennium B.C., the full historical record of Palestine begins, and from then on we know the names of leaders and kings, the dates of battles, and the details of political and military actions, of social and economic organization, of the intellectual and social problems besetting its population. For the millennium that preceded the Hebrew conquest, written documents from Egypt, Mesopotamia, and other regions provide indirect information about Palestine; further back, in the third millennium, these records constantly diminish in quantity and importance. From about five thousand years ago to six hundred thousand years ago—99.9 per cent of the existence of mankind, in Palestine as elsewhere—all we know about man comes from archaeology.

The only way to get an idea about what happened in human evolution during this enormous period is to study the scanty remains left behind in the caves and the other sites where man lived, and to try to understand their meaning. Skeletal fragments, flint implements, potsherds, architectural remains, graves, art objects, and other fragments of what archaeologists call material culture, help us to uncover some aspects of the behavior, the technology, the beliefs, the economy, the social organization, and other details of daily life of these ancestors of ours who bear in the history of their existence the meaning of our own. I hope the reader will be indulgent with those passages where I found it necessary to explain why and how certain conclusions were reached, and where I devoted perhaps too much of the limited space to the description of remains which led to a historical reconstruction; but I felt it necessary to present these detailed descriptions in order to familiarize him with the available evidence, and to allow him to assume as dispassionately as possible all the privileges and burdens of a critical view. The reader who is not yet adept at analyzing such problems might find it more rewarding to skip these descriptions in his first reading and to go back to them only later.

The reader will probably notice that the raw material at the disposal of scientists for historical reconstruction varies considerably, according to its age. The remains left behind by men become more abundant and more varied the closer we come to the historical age. Conversely, the further we go back in time, the less information we have, the larger are the cultural periods we are able to distinguish, the simpler are the cultural patterns, the vaguer is our picture of man and his life. The chain of history and cultural evolution is complex and heavy in recent times; but going back, the links loosen and gradually become detached from one another, the last ones fading out in the horizon of time.

The role played by Palestine in human evolution was conditioned by the limited size of the region, its geographical location, and by the people who happened to settle there. In the Age of Hunting and Gathering, the people of Palestine went through the general evolution that took place in various other parts of Eurasia. The main distinctions that give an individual character to the cultural sequence in Palestine and the surrounding countries are two: here the material cultures typical of the Upper Paleolithic, known as "blade industries," made one of their earliest appearance in the world; and human beings with characteristics approaching those of Upper Paleolithic Homo sapiens appeared here at a rather early date. The problem of the origin of this being, believed to be the earliest direct ancestor of modern man, arises here in all its fascinating complexity.

During the transition between the Age of Hunting and Gathering and the Age of Early Farming, Palestine gave birth to a unique culture, the Natufian, which seems to have been the earliest culture to produce food on a large scale. In this period in Palestine, as far as we now know, the earliest permanent villages in the world were built. The archaeological findings also enable us to understand some of the psychological and technological processes that led man from his previous custom of gathering food to the custom of producing and preserving his supplies. The Age of Early Farming brought to Palestine the earliest-known city. The city of Jericho, located near the Dead Sea, in one of the hottest spots of the world, was surrounded with a huge defense wall about nine thousand years ago, over three thousand years before the building of other known early cities.

In the Urban Age, Palestine was left behind by the main centers of Urban civilizations in the Near East: Mesopotamia, northern Syria, and Egypt. While kingdoms and empires were flourishing in these countries and their communities were evolving into literate societies, Palestine maintained a political pattern of small feudal city-states, remained illiterate for over one thousand years, and was frequently subdued by one or another of its powerful neighbors. Semites, Hamites, and Indo-Europeans lived in Palestine and in neighboring countries in the course of the Urban Age. The remains of these different peoples help us to trace some details of their origins and their early history.

One of the Semitic tribes that reached Palestine in the Urban Age was the Hebrews. They were of Mesopotamian origin and arrived in the wave of the great ethnic migrations that thrust many other marginal tribes westward. For over five hundred years the Hebrews remained at the periphery; some of them lived in the desert, others were settled in the mountain woodlands. One group appears to have reached Egypt and to have gone through a period of slavery there. The Hebrews who lived in and near Palestine before the conquest maintained their traditional way of life as pastoral nomads, and came into accidental contact with the sedentary populations of the towns; but finally, perhaps together with other groups of nomads, agriculturists, and landless people, they were able to fight and conquer the Urban Canaanites, and to destroy their feudal system, spreading over the country the tribal democratic system of the marginal groups. This revolution marked in Palestine the beginning of the Iron Age and with it full historical records.

A great many cultural changes and a rich intercourse between different human groups characterize the prehistory and protohistory of Palestine. On this natural bridge between Asia and Africa, located between the Arabian Desert and the Mediterranean Sea, many people have left their traces. Some of these human groups still have not yielded the mystery of their origins; we do not know who they were and where they came from. Regarding others archaeologists have been more fortunate, and have been able to trace back their history and to gain some idea of their ethnic affiliations.

The reader will notice how many political and social situations in Palestinian prehistory and protohistory remind us of events in our own epoch, and how much we can learn about ourselves and about the world of today when we look at past events in a perspective of thousands of years. This is perhaps one of the main goals of history: to know ourselves better and to be able to place the life we live within a meaningful framework.

PART · ONE

THE FACE
OF THE LAND

I

Geographical
Setting
and
Cultural Areas

THE BORDERS

"PALESTINE" is a relatively recent geographical term. It came into use when the Philistines, some three thousand years ago, made their appearance on the Levantine coast of the Mediterranean. Since then, it has been used continuously, except for some intervals, by Hebrews, Greeks, Romans, Arabs, Turks, and finally by the British mandatory government, although each gave the term different geographical delimitations. Today, however, this term is somewhat obsolete, since new political boundaries have spread over Palestine, which has become a region in which two major countries, Israel and Jordan, are adjacent to patches of no man's land, to demilitarized zones, and to territories incorporated into the Egyptian province of Sinai and into Syria.

Today's political boundaries, like those at the time of the British Mandate, are not natural borders and they cannot define a geographical or cultural area. What I shall refer to as Palestine is the land between the peninsula of Sinai to the south and the mountains of Lebanon to the north, the Mediterranean Sea to the west and the great Arabian Desert to the east. The main landmarks defining its limits to the south are the Wadi el-Arish, which the Bible called "River of Egypt" and which marked the southwestern border of Canaan; the northern end of the Gulf of Aqaba, which lies at the junction of the Sinai Peninsula with the peninsula of Arabia; and the Jebel et-Tubeiq, in southern Jordan, the northernmost point of the Arabian province of Hejaz. To the west, the border runs over the sands of the desert. A natural limit is marked by the line of hills from the Jebel et-Tubeiq northward, dividing the wadis pointing to the west from those descending eastward to the oases of the Sirhan Valley, the green northern gate of Arabian caravan routes. To the north, the river Yarmuk is the clearest landmark east of the Jordan. It once divided the Biblical provinces of Golan and Gilead, and it marks today the border between Syria and Jordan. The northern end of the Jordan Valley and the southern slopes of 9,232-foot Mount Hermon are other clear landmarks; while, more to the west, the rather abrupt transition from the gentle hills and mountains of Galilee sloping southward to the high plateau of Lebanon sloping northward marks, again quite clearly, another portion of the natural boundary of Palestine.

This area is about 45,000 square miles, roughly the size of Ireland (Jordan: about 35,000; Israel: about 8,000; Egypt: about 2,000), and has 3,500,000 inhabitants; it is part of the 2,500,000 square miles of the Near East, in which live over 94,000,000 souls.

THE TOPOGRAPHY

The deep, broad valley of the river Jordan cuts Palestine in two from north to south. It originates at the foot of Mount Hermon, and after forming the Sea of Galilee ends up in the Dead Sea. Its

continuation to the south is the Araba Valley, which connects
the Plain of Sodom with the Gulf of Aqaba, which in turn opens
out to the south to become the large depression now forming the
Red Sea.

On a topographical map of Palestine, one can see that the area
is naturally divided into four main elongated regions running parallel from north to south. The westernmost is the coastal plain
along the shores of the Mediterranean; next is the central mountain region, including the mountains of Galilee, Samaria, Judea,
and the Negev; next is the Jordan and Araba valleys; and the
easternmost is the Jordanian Plateau. The central mountains are
divided into three chains by two broad valleys which connect the
coastal plain with the depression of the Jordan—the Esdraelon
and Beersheba valleys.

This topography has always had a strong influence on the cultural divisions of Palestine. Each one of the four has developed
from time to time as a distinctive cultural area with its own characteristics. The coastal plain has always been more fertile and
better suited to trade than the three other regions. Because of its
strategic importance, its harbors, and its availability as a highway, it was the one most frequently invaded by Palestine's powerful neighbors. This strip of coastal land was also open to the influence of several ancient Mediterranean cultures.

The central mountainous area has had a much more localized
and autarkic history. In many periods it was a region of secondary
importance; its major economic activities until a relatively late
period continued to be hunting and herding, and its trade has
always been less than that along the coast and in the Jordan
Valley.

More to the east, we come again to a region that appears to
have highly favored the development of early cultures. The
Jordan Valley is in a peculiar geographical situation. Whereas the
coastal plain is connected with Egypt and Syria by its natural
highways on land and sea, and thus was influenced at all times by
other cultures and peoples, the Jordan Valley, surrounded as it is

by high mountains, has always been more isolated, forming a thin unit sixty miles long, with many independent cultural characteristics. In its southern portion natural resources are abundant. They include salt, copper, bitumen, and sulfur. Its northern and central parts are well watered, so that agriculture thrives; the Jordan River is navigable in most parts, and thus affords easy communication throughout the valley.

The Jordanian Plateau was in most periods a peripheral region. There is not much agricultural land, and other resources, including water, are scanty. Hunting and herding have always been the traditional activities of this region.

CLIMATE AND RAINFALL

Most of Palestine is located between the 30th and 33d northern parallels, within approximately the same latitudes as Morocco, Georgia, southern California, and southern Japan. Accordingly, its climate is subtropic, but it varies greatly from one region to another; throughout the country there are wide variations in amount of rainfall, atmospheric pressure, winds, and kinds of soil and vegetation.

Rain is mainly concentrated in the three winter months of December, January, and February, and eight, sometimes nine, months a year are totally dry. The annual rainfall in this small country varies considerably from one region to another. The region of the central mountains is the rainiest. In Upper Galilee an average of 40 inches of rain falls a year; in Samaria about 32, whereas in Jerusalem the average is about 24 inches. These figures are similar to the annual averages in western Europe and in the eastern United States, but they apply only to the rather limited area of the central mountains and are concentrated in three months a year. The coastal plain has a mean annual rainfall of 24 inches in the north and 12 inches in the south. East of the central mountains, only fifteen miles from Jerusalem, in the Judean Desert, the average rainfall goes down to 2 inches, just one tenth

Date palms at Kinnereth

of the rainfall at Jerusalem, while in parts of the Araba Valley the annual average is less than half an inch.

The Near East has three major ecological areas, termed fertile, semi-arid, and arid. They are situated one around another, so that the second usually separates the first from the third. The term "fertile" is applied to good agricultural lands having a mean annual rainfall of over 12 inches. Semi-arid are the regions having a mean annual rainfall between 12 and 6 inches. Where there is less than 6 inches of rainfall—the arid regions—modern agriculture cannot be practiced and the main economic activities must be herding or hunting.

The fertile regions occupy a crescentlike area that covers about one tenth of the Near East. Starting on the northern shores of the Persian Gulf, it follows the Tigris and Euphrates valleys up to northern Syria, swings westward to Cilicia and then southward, thinning down and ending up on the Mediterranean coast of Palestine. North of the Fertile Crescent, as it is called, most of the lands are semi-arid, and two major arid regions lie in the mountainous provinces of eastern Anatolia and in central Persia. South of the Fertile Crescent there is just one thin strip of semi-arid land, and behind it are the great Syrian and Arabian deserts.

In Palestine the northern fertile regions fall within the southern and western strip of the Fertile Crescent, while the Negev, the southern desert of Israel, and most of Jordan are arid. Between the two there is a narrow semi-arid strip, which varies in breadth from ten to twenty miles. The border between the "green land" and the "yellow land" is a very sharp one.

CULTURAL AREAS

Palestine today is divided into three main cultural areas which are somewhat influenced by this ecological situation, among other factors. The Negev and most of eastern Palestine are part of the same arid zone that covers the peninsula of Sinai, most of Arabia, and the Syrian Desert. In this first cultural area the prevailing pat-

Bedouin camp at Abdat, in the central Negev. Building at left is a Roman bath which served caravans on the spice route from Arabia to the Mediterranean

Abu Ghosh, a village in the Judean Hills

terns of life are those of the nomadic pastoral Bedouins and of the oasis dwellers who rely mainly on stock raising and the date palms. The mean density of population here is less than one inhabitant per square mile.

The western part of the Jordanian Plateau, the Jordan Valley, western Jordan, and large parts of northern Israel, together with Lebanon and Syria, form the second cultural area. This area is settled by an Arabic-speaking population whose pattern of life is based upon farming villages and a social structure of "extended families." In the extended family all the offspring of a family for at least three generations—all the cousins, uncles, and aunts—live together as a family unit. The mean density of population here is about thirty inhabitants per square mile.

The third area is that of highly industrialized Israel. Here the majority of the population speaks Hebrew and is concentrated in urban centers, where social organization is very similar to that of American towns, or in villages, or in collective and half-collective settlements. The mean density of population here is over three hundred inhabitants per square mile.

The present situation in the third area is the result of very recent events, and the third of these cultural patterns has come into existence in the last two generations. The other two subdivisions are ancient; throughout history there persisted this cultural separation between northern Palestine, directly connected with cultures centered more to the north, and southern and eastern Palestine, connected with the arid and semi-arid zones of the inner Near East.

BETWEEN THE SEA AND THE DESERT

The location of fertile Palestine, between the Mediterranean Sea and the desert, has always influenced its cultural evolution and its history. Here Mediterranean cultures came in contact with the inhabitants of the desert. Because of its location at one of the extremities of the Fertile Crescent, it has frequently played the role

Egyptian rock carving, showing "eastern invaders" on an Asiatic boat (after Winkler)

of a border land. Here people coming from the lands of the North have repeatedly met with people from peripheral areas and with people coming up from Egypt, the gateway of Africa. Ever since farming life was established, the fertile region has been thickly populated. Raids and invasions have occurred several times, and their aim usually was to conquer and occupy these fertile lands. Conversely, the desert has usually been a land of transit, where people pass from one fertile region to another. For this reason the arid zones have always been an important means of contact, sometimes even between quite distant regions. Before the beginning of farming life, migratory bands could pass freely through both well-watered and drier regions, but when farmed fields came to cover large parts of the fertile regions, life and culture became increasingly localized there, while the arid zones maintained their character of *terra franca*, where even large bands of people could easily move about without disturbing or being disturbed by local populations. Since that time distances in the arid zones have had a meaning totally different from that in the fertile regions.

Ever since the beginning of farming, the desert has been the land into which weaker or technically less-developed human groups have been pushed by stronger groups, but the desert has also been the area from which new ideas and new blood have constantly flowed into the Fertile Crescent.

Contacts between the inhabitants of the fertile lands and those of the desert have always existed, and this constant interaction between the "yellow land" and the "green land" has been an extremely important factor in the cultural evolution of the Near East.

BETWEEN ASIA AND AFRICA

Palestine is the only land bridge from Asia to Africa, a fact which makes the study of its prehistory and early history extremely important. Its fertile region is only 200 miles away from the Nile Valley, from the upper Euphrates, and from southern Anatolia. If any prehistoric people traveled by land from Asia to Africa or vice versa, they must have crossed through Palestine. Of course, seafaring in the Red Sea existed from relatively early times, and transit by water across Bab el-Mandeb to the African coast was naturally possible, but the only land bridge was through Palestine and Sinai.

Undoubtedly Palestine has played throughout history and prehistory its role of bridge. It is the first country encountered when one comes from Egypt to Asia, and we know that in historic times it was regarded by the Pharaohs as the gate of Egypt. Conversely, from Mesopotamia, Syria, or Anatolia, one had to cross Palestine in order to reach Egypt and Africa. For the last eight thousand years we find in Africa continuous signs of the infiltration of Asiatic cultural and physical traits, and most of these must have come through Palestine.

Aerial view of Tell of Beth-Shan in 1950, after it was partially excavated. At top, Lisan lacustrine sediments surrounding an ancient lake shore are visible.

II

Geology
and
the Changing
Environment

"IN THE BEGINNING . . ."

THE DRAMATIC ACCOUNTS of the Book of Genesis and of other early Near Eastern mythologies tell us that in the beginning "the earth was without form and void, and darkness was upon the face of the deep." Three thousand years after these lines were written, they still remain the most vivid and impressive account of what the earth must have looked like several billion years ago. From then to the moment when man appeared, a very long "week" must have passed, a period in which the first and most primitive forms of life started moving and slowly evolved, in which the simple organisms became more and more complex, in which the lands and the seas acquired the general shapes they have today.

The crust of the earth finally attained its present consistency and character in a long sequence of processes which is believed to have lasted over four billion years. During this time the nature of the rocks and soils that were formed, and the kinds of living organisms that appeared on the earth, changed constantly. New types of life evolved and grew. Mollusks, fishes, land plants, and other sorts of already complex organisms appeared during the Paleozoic, or Primary, era, the oldest of the four major eras recognized by geologists in which living organisms evolved; mammals, out of which man was to evolve, made their first appearance in the Mesozoic, or Secondary, era; and Primates, the family of mammals to which man belongs, emerged only in the Tertiary, and are believed to have a history fifty million years long. Man did not show up until the beginning of the Quaternary, or Pleistocene, era.

During the millions of years that preceded the advent of man, large parts of the region today called the Near East were submerged several times under the seas. Palestine has seen many incursions and regressions of these seas, and fossilized remains of sea animals are found incrustated in rocks on mountains three thousand feet high.

When man appeared, the lands had already attained most of their present general shape. The great movements of seas and continents had slowed down, and only minor oscillations of the sea level continued to change the coast line a little.

An ocean called Tethys, which had covered most of southern Europe and Asia Minor, had sometimes penetrated deeply into Palestine. Gradually this ocean became smaller and was circumscribed by the coasts of the African and Eurasian continents, until it acquired the tortuous shape of what we know as the Mediterranean.

PLEISTOCENE CHANGES OF LANDSCAPE

The oscillations of the Quaternary seas are indicated by the remains of ancient beaches found all over the shores of the Mediterranean. The wavy lines of sea-deposited gravel, shells, and

GEOLO-GICAL ERAS	MILLION YEARS AGO	BEGINNINGS OF SOME FORMS OF LIFE

Chart labels, left to right: SINGLE-CELLED ORGANISMS, BRACHIOPODS, MOLLUSKS, FISHES, LAND PLANTS, AMPHIBIANS, REPTILES, MAMMALS, BIRDS, PRIMATES, MAN

Geological Eras (top to bottom): PRE-CAMBRIAN (PROTEROZOIC), PALEOZOIC, MESOZOIC, TERTIARY, QUATERNARY

Million years ago scale: 4,500 — 3,000 — 2,000 — 1,000 — 600 — 250 — 70 — 1

other detritus, and the long streaks of raised beaches—when they are still at ground level—are sometimes visible even from a flying airplane.

Finds of extinct species of shellfish, mollusks, and other animals, help in dating the incursions of the sea which formed these beaches. Sometimes, also, remains of human tools are found, and in these cases they can be dated according to the geological age of the beach.

These incursions of the sea (or transgressions, as they are called by geologists) are accompanied by general climatic changes and usually mark periods of milder and drier climate. Sea regressions, on the other hand, occur in rainy periods. (For this apparent paradox, see page 28.) The study of these climatic changes is very important for the prehistorian, because it helps in placing the traces left by prehistoric men in a framework of time, and gives him an approximate idea of their age and environment.

While the sea level was changing, the surface of the earth was also undergoing some alterations. The surface of the earth is continually changing. In regions like the Near East, two main changes may take place, in addition to those that may be caused by earthquakes and tectonic movements. One is the accumulation of new layers, or sediments; the other is erosion, or the removal of previous layers. Sediments vary considerably according to the manner in which they were laid down, so that a sea sediment can easily be distinguished from a layer transported by the wind or deposited by the action of powerful streams. In periods of heavy rain, layers of gravel were thrust down to the coastal plain from the nearby hills, whereas in drier periods winds deposited much thinner and lighter materials, such as the powderlike loess soil or sand dunes. These various strata are the best evidence we have for tracing climatic mutation.

THE HISTORY OF THE COASTAL PLAIN

By observing the sequence of these strata, one can reconstruct the story of the natural phenomena that caused them. On the coasts of Israel, Lebanon, and Syria, this stratification shows that the Quaternary era began during a regression of the sea. Great quantities of gravel then descended from the mountains, driven by the force of large streams and heavy rainfall. This period is called Grand Pluvial (or Pluvial A). Thereafter a dry period came in which light wind deposits were accumulated. During this drier period the sea advanced inland and retreated several times.

Two important layers of marine deposits show that during the Quaternary era there were two major incursions of the sea. Between the periods when the two layers were formed, another but less important rainy period (Pluvial B) seems to have taken place. The second major gravel deposit marks the last period of intensive rainfall, called Pluvial C.

Most of the rest of the geological cross section of the coastal deposits is comprised of dunes deposited in the relatively dry periods of sea regression, in which the sandy sea floor was exposed to the action of winds.

Through the action of chalk and other materials with which they were mixed, these dunes sometimes consolidated and became a sort of stone characteristic of the Levantine coast of the Mediterranean. This sandstone, called Kurkar, disintegrated again when it was exposed for long periods at the surface, and formed a peculiar sort of reddish sand called Hamra, which is characteristic especially of the Plain of Sharon, the central coastal area of Israel. These red sands and the layers of Kurkar are frequently intercalated with layers of marine deposits and with thin layers of gravel, an indication that the geological history of the Quaternary era was rather complex, with several minor transgressions by the sea and pluvial episodes, or rainy periods, in addition to the three major ones.

The sediments of the coastal plain show that the Quaternary era started with a long period of very heavy rains. It was followed by a gradual drying, during which the first major incursions of the sea took place. Between the first and the second major incursions came a time characterized by several minor rainy periods. At the end of the second major incursion, another important rainy period took place, which, in its turn, was followed by a gradual drying, interrupted by several minor rainy periods.

The reason why these periods of rising sea levels occurred just when the climate of Palestine was drier is today quite clear. The pluvials in Palestine must have coincided more or less with the times at which regions further north were covered with ice. In these glacial periods some Near Eastern mountains, such as the Taurus in southern Anatolia and Mount Hermon in Lebanon, were covered with limited glaciers. In periods of drier and hotter climate in Palestine, the ice sheets melted and their waters flowed into the sea, which then rose. This process was more complex than it would appear, since other agents seem also to have contributed to it, and since a considerable lapse of time must be allowed from the time of a climatic change to that of maximum melting of the ice sheets. Each region must have had its own local variations of these broad climatic changes, but the general connection between the rising sea and the melting ice is today quite clear.

In other parts of the Mediterranean coast, a higher number of sea-level changes have been clearly detected by geologists. The coasts of Italy and southern France in the main have favored accurate studies. The two major incursions of the sea found there seem to correspond to the two main ones of the Levantine coast, and to belong to the two major interglacial periods of the European geological sequence. In the central Mediterranean, the earliest one is called Paleotyrrhenian, and the second, Eutyrrhenian. The first is believed to have raised the Mediterranean between 80 and 65 feet above its present level, and the second between 20 and 30 feet. This may give us some idea of the age of the raised beaches of Palestine and Syria, but as tectonic and other movements of the earth's crust have also contributed to topographical changes, the levels of these beaches today are not always the same as they were at the time when the beaches were formed.

The Mediterranean coast at Ras en-Naqura, near Lebanon

The stratigraphy of deposits on the coastal plain shows that a complex sequence of rainy and dry periods characterized the Quaternary era; these periods roughly corresponded to the glacial and interglacial episodes that had taken place, during the same epoch, in northern Europe, Siberia, and Canada. The major discrepancy of the Palestinian sequence is that here we find three major pluvials, whereas we know of four main glacial periods in Europe. The first pluvial in Palestine was extremely long, so that it seems to correspond to the two earliest glacial periods of Europe (Günz and Mindel) and to have lasted over half of the Quaternary era.

THE MOUNTAINS

The mountains can teach us much less about the Quaternary changes that occurred in Palestine. By the Tertiary era they had acquired the general form that they have today. The main agent that continued shaping secondary characteristics was erosion. In rainy periods, water flowed down from the mountains, carrying gravel, earth, sand, and other erosive materials. River beds were carved to greater and greater depths, and river deposits were transported to the plains. Most of the caves in which prehistoric men subsequently found shelter were washed out by nature in late Tertiary and early Quaternary times.

In heavily rainy periods, water filled up all the interstices and natural holes of the rocks, and penetrated inside the body of the earth's crust. Sometimes it met relatively soft stones, or permeable layers, and penetrated deeper and deeper, until it succeeded in finding an outlet. The erosive process went on, great rivers flowed underground, and caves became broader and longer. Most of these caves remained full of water until the end of the Grand Pluvial, and thus did not become suitable shelters for men until thereafter.

THE JORDAN VALLEY

The Jordan Valley was the last part of Palestine to acquire its present form. Its deep and abrupt canyon, the lowest depression in the world—1,300 feet below sea level—was caused principally by several tectonic movements that totally upset the earlier topography of this region. Most of these disturbances occurred before the start of the Pleistocene, but they continued later on, well into the age in which man was already present in the area.

Thick layers of clay and gravel were deposited in early Pleistocene times in the wide, flat valley in the middle of which the Jordan flows today. The valley was then occupied by a much larger river. These layers were formed at the same time as those found at the bottom of the Quaternary series on the coastal plains. In them were discovered, near the village of Afiqim, the earliest human remains found so far in the Near East. They are believed to go back between three and six hundred thousand years. Above the upper layers of this early clay and gravel one gradually comes to a layer of much thinner material, best visible near the settlement of Mahanaym, in the northern part of the valley. This layer probably represents a relatively rainy period in which the Jordan Valley was sometimes partially covered with lakes, and in which the current of the stream was much weaker than in the previous phase. From this period on, human remains in the upper Jordan Valley have been found in abundance.

A drier period followed, in which most of the water of the Jordan Valley evaporated. During this interpluvial phase, earthquakes and volcanic eruptions again disturbed the surface of the valley, and layers of lava and basalt from these eruptions spread over a wide area.

This interpluvial phase was followed by another rainy period, in which the Jordan Valley was transformed into a large lake. The Sea of Galilee and the Dead Sea were then united into an elongated basin which continued south, into the Araba Valley.

The light whitewashed materials then deposited at the bottom of this sea contain clay and gypsum and are called "Lisan" sediments, after the Arabic name of the tonglike peninsula in the middle of the Dead Sea.

At present we have no clear idea of how long this lake lasted. We do not know exactly when the Dead Sea reached its present level of approximately 1,300 feet below sea level, but this must have happened after the end of the last pluvial. Thus man had gone a long way in his physical and cultural evolution by the time the Jordan Valley attained its present state. Climate in this very deep, salty depression is so hot that the natural rate of water evaporation is probably one of the highest in the world. The Jordan and other rivers transport large quantities of minerals, and while the minerals remain, the water evaporates. Consequently, today the Dead Sea is too salty and too full of minerals to allow any kind of life in it, but many of the fresh-water rivers that flow into it have served as shelter for Pleistocene fishes which still subsist in them, in absolute isolation from other aquatic fauna.

THE PLAINS COMPARED

When we compare the Quaternary levels in the coastal plain and in the Jordan Valley, we see that they show the same climatic sequence. In both, the sequence begins with a long period of heavy rains. On the coast this period is followed by an interval marked by a rise of the sea, and in the Jordan Valley by the beginning of the Naharaym deposits. These deposits were laid down throughout the period of mild, intermittent rainy and dry episodes—marked on the coast by the deposits dividing the two major incursions of the sea. Another drier interval is marked on the coast by the second of these incursions, and in the Jordan River by the period in which the tectonic disturbances took place.

MAJOR GEOLOGICAL AND CULTURAL TRAITS OF THE PALESTINIAN QUATERNARY

YEARS AGO	GEOLOGICAL PERIODS	COASTAL PLAIN	CENTRAL JORDAN VALLEY	UPPER JORDAN VALLEY	ARCHAEOLOGICAL PERIODS	KINDS OF CULTURES
14,000	POST-PLUVIAL	UPPER DUNES (PRESENT CLIMATE)	PRESENT JORDAN RIVER BED	PRESENT JORDAN RIVER BED	URBAN / EARLY FARMING	MODERN / IRON AGE / BRONZE AGE / COPPER AGE / LATE STONE AGE / MIDDLE STONE AGE — BLADE INDUSTRIES / FLAKE INDUSTRIES
70,000	PLUVIAL C (WÜRM OF EUROPE)	UPPER GRAVEL (LARGE RIVERS)	LISAN LAKE	UPPER GRAVEL (JORDAN LARGER THAN PRESENT)	HUNTING AND GATHERING	BIFACIAL AND TABUNIAN INDUSTRIES
120,000	LAST INTERPLUVIAL (RISS-WÜRM OF EUROPE)	SECOND MAJOR SEA RISE (EUTYRRHENIAN)	LAVA BED (SMALL RIVER)	CLAY AND BASALT BED (DRIER PERIOD)		
200,000	PLUVIAL B (RISS OF EUROPE)	ALTERNATION OF DUNES AND MINOR GRAVEL DEPOSITS (LOWER DUNES)	NAHARAYM STAGE (LARGE RIVER AND LOCAL LAKES)	PEBBLES AND BOULDERS WITH BLACK SOIL (NAHARAYM STAGE) (RIVER AND MARSHES)		
300,000	FIRST INTERPLUVIAL (MINDEL-RISS OF EUROPE)	FIRST MAJOR SEA RISE (PALEOTYRRHENIAN)	TRANSITIONAL PERIOD BETWEEN GRAND RIVER AND LAKE	HARDENED BLACK SOIL (DRIER CLIMATE)		
600,000	GRAND PLUVIAL (GÜNZ TO MINDEL OF EUROPE)	LOWER GRAVEL (LARGE RIVERS)	CLAY AND GRAVEL CONGLOMERATES (GRAND RIVER)	LOWER GRAVEL (GRAND RIVER)		PEBBLE CULTURE

PALEOLITHIC (OLD STONE AGE)

The third pluvial is marked on the coast by the upper gravel deposit, and in the Jordan Valley by the Lisan sediments. At the end of this last pluvial period, some fourteen thousand years ago, the climate gradually became drier and then the Pleistocene era reached its end.

MAIN CULTURAL TRAITS OF THE LAST 500,000 YEARS

YEARS AGO	ECONOMIC ACTIVITIES	HABITATS	PROBABLE MAXIMAL UNITS	BEGINNING OF SOME MAJOR CULTURAL TRAITS										
	COMPLEX URBAN	VILLAGES AND CITIES	NATIONS											
	EARLY FARMING	VILLAGES	CITY-STATES											
12,000		HAMLETS AND CAVES												
50,000			TRIBES											
100,000														
200,000	HUNTING AND GATHERING	CAVES AND CAMP SITES	SMALL BANDS	TOOL MAKING	MASTERY OF FIRE	BURIAL OF DEAD	PERMANENT BUILDINGS	TRADE	AGRICULTURE	POTTERY MAKING	METALWORK	WHEEL	WRITING	HISTORICAL RECORDS
300,000														
400,000		OPEN AIR												
500,000														

III

A

Bird's-Eye Look

at

Cultural Evolution

A PERSPECTIVE IN TIME

FROM THE DAY when archaic ape-man made his first tools to the day when man started writing his own history, an enormous sequence of events gradually transformed his life. New experiences continuously came to enrich his heritage, and the accumulation of new cultural traits gradually shaped his character and nature. The small groups of the earliest men became bands, which in turn eventually grew to the size of tribes. By the time of the earliest urban settlement, they had become distinct kindred groups.

For over half of his existence, man did not use even caves for shelter. Many millennia had to pass before he learned how to build a hut or a tent, and many more before he was able to build the first permanent house. Villages and cities are very recent inventions.

Technology slowly evolved. From the time in which man's ancestor started throwing stones and unworked wooden sticks to increase the power of his arm, to the moment in which he consciously shaped his first tool, ages passed. In the course of time man became an increasingly skilled tool-maker, and at a very late stage he even learned how to prepare by himself the raw materials necessary for making his tools and objects. Pottery and metals were added to wood, stone, bone, and the other materials that he could gather on the surface of the earth.

The devices at the disposal of man for making life easier and more comfortable slowly grew in number. Over two hundred thousand years ago some men already knew how to transport fire and how to use it for warming and cooking food. But salt was not added to food until ten thousand years ago, and the earliest saucepan came into use only about eight thousand years ago.

The earliest sure evidence of religious thought found so far is connected with the cult of the dead, and does not seem to date back more than seventy thousand years. But a developed religion, with all its beliefs, rules, and conventional rites, appeared for the first time only thirty thousand years ago, as attested by repeated finds of mother-goddess figurines and by the art in sanctuary caves. The earliest-known proper temple, however, is only eight thousand years old, and the earliest-known monotheistic religion of a modern type, the Hebrew religion, began about three millennia ago.

In its general lines, the slow evolution of human culture in Palestine before the beginning of history is similar to that in several other regions of the world. Archaeologists divide cultural evolution into three major ages: the Age of Hunting and Gathering, the Age of Early Farming, and the Urban Age. The first covers all the periods in which man was unable to produce his food and in which hunting and gathering were the dominant, if not the only, economic activities. In the fertile regions of the Near East this period lasted until about 10,000 years ago. The change took place gradually in the Mesolithic, or Middle Stone Age. The second corresponds to the time in which food production began and in which farming gradually supplanted hunting as the major economic activity. In the fertile regions of the Near East this lasted approximately from 10,000 to 5,300 years ago. The third is the age of complex economy, in which trade occupied a prominent place in daily activities and in which societies of specialists developed large and fortified urban settlements, which they defended with armies of professional soldiers. This ended when nations and full historical records began. In Palestine this happened a little over 3,200 years ago.

THE AGE OF HUNTING AND GATHERING

The Age of Hunting and Gathering covers over 98 per cent of the time since man became a tool-maker. Through the remains man left behind at the camp sites, shelters, and caves at which he stopped, we can trace his first steps in technology and the exasperatingly slow evolution of his way of life and his habits. We can see how he gradually developed new techniques of tool-making, how the first abstract speculations came to his mind, and how he developed new instincts besides those of hunger, reproduction, and defense.

The human remains, the bones of men we find throughout this enormously long period, are fossils: time and natural agents have transformed them into parts of the natural soil environment, in which they have remained buried for thousands of years. Tools and objects made of organic materials, such as wood, skin, and fiber, have usually been completely destroyed by time. In many cases the stone implements left behind by man are the only objects found by archaeologists in sites of the Age of Hunting and Gathering, or the Old Stone Age, as it is also called.

The Old Stone Age came to an end at approximately the same time in the Near East, in Europe, and in parts of North Africa. The stages of cultural evolution, as revealed by the nature of the tools made and used, were quite similar in those distant regions, and so were the physical characteristics of man in each one of the three main phases recognized in the Old Stone Age (currently called Lower, Middle, and Upper Paleolithic).

Our early ancestors had to adjust constantly to the changing climate and environment. Toward the end of the Paleolithic, and in the transitional period called Mesolithic, or Middle Stone Age, some drastic changes took place. By then, about fourteen thousand years ago, a new technique of tool-making abruptly appeared, and with it came other new expressions of spiritual and social life. New kinds of art, new ways of burying and of worshipping the dead, new criteria for choosing habitation sites, show that great changes were taking place in the mentality and the way of life of the people. The new tools had a much richer variety of forms: many earlier tools had several possible uses, but most of the new ones had precise and special purposes. This specialization, revealed by remains of implements found in caves and camp sites, is a considerable revolution in itself. It probably indicates also some drastic changes in the economic organization of the human group.

Shortly thereafter, the earliest stone buildings made their appearance. Men started living in fairly permanent hamlets. The economy of the human unit had grown increasingly complex. Fishing had become a common part of daily activities. The discovery of exotic tools and materials demonstrates that human beings spanned long distances and probably pursued some sort of primitive trade. The harvesting of cereal was quickly evolving into what we may call the earliest phase of incipient agriculture, while the earliest attempts at domestication of animals were opening still another field to human activities.

THE AGE OF EARLY FARMING

All these new technological and conceptual acquisitions were the result of thousands of years of trial and error. The main purpose of these efforts was to give some stability and security to human life, which had been, until then, a continuous day-today struggle for subsistence. The main results were a further and much stronger impulse toward more specialization, and a closer attraction of human groups to those spots found favorable to the newly acquired economic activities. Specialization, and variety of economic possibilities, led to a differentiation of cultural patterns. In regions where farming and fishing could not be carried on, hunting remained for a longer period the main source of subsistence. The shores of lakes and river valleys called for an emphasis on fishing. Sites providing important raw materials furthered the development of trade. Fertile and well-watered lands stimulated agriculture.

The archaic hunting and gathering bands were gradually replaced by much more varied groups. The Age of Early Farming is characterized by many different cultural patterns. Environment and personal experience shaped the economic background of each group in a different way. Also the local patterns of social organization, the religious beliefs, the mythological and imaginary world, the psychology, the art styles, and the nature of the material culture of each group were affected in different ways and took different directions.

In the Age of Hunting and Gathering, the semi-nomadic groups that had inhabited Palestine, in their tool-making, in their choice of habitation sites, and in their religious beliefs and rites, showed a remarkable resemblance to a great many other contemporary groups in various parts of the Old World. With the beginning of incipient farming, cultural differentiation became increasingly strong, and the process of cultural evolution took place in different regions in a very different way. Even within the small area of Palestine we can recognize the development of various patterns, each one acquiring individual characteristics and resulting in different types of settlements and different kinds of material culture. We shall see how different was the evolution of this period in the coastal plain, the mountains, the Negev, and the Jordan Valley.

Occasionally, the disproportionate growth of the wealth

of some groups, owing to peculiar and particularly profitable activities such as trade, brought into being types of societies and settlements which were to become common only several thousand years later. So we find at least one case of centralized leadership, and of a highly stratified, well-organized urban society, as far back as nine thousand years ago. This is what a doctor would call a monstrous case of precocious puberty. Such a cultural and social level was more generally achieved, throughout Palestine, about four thousand years later.

THE URBAN AGE

At the beginning of the Urban Age, late in the fourth millennium B.C., a wave of new cultural elements entered the story of Palestine. Throughout the Fertile Crescent this was a time of the rise of small states. Shortly thereafter some of them were to become powerful empires.

Trade and political and military activities were quickly growing to a large scale. Palestine was located on the main highway along the shores of the eastern Mediterranean, the bridge between Asia and Africa. It was an important source of many necessary materials. Its olives and wines were renowned far and wide, its timber was praised, salt and bitumen from the Dead Sea were in great demand. Sinai and the Negev produced copper and turquoise; Galilee and Lebanon, balsam and perfumes; Jordan, stibium and other coloring products. Trade routes became thronged. Harbors developed. Some towns were being strongly fortified and were growing to considerable dimensions; military activities expanded in size and organization.

Although Palestine was deeply affected by this widespread urban revolution, it did not grow into a powerful centralized state until much later. In the Early Urban Age, three main centers of power developed in the Near East: Mesopotamia, northern Syria, and Egypt. Highly stratified social structures, strongly centralized governments, and extensive slavery permitted these regions to accumulate an enormous surplus of goods, and to maintain regular armies of a size incredible for those times. Strategic and economic attractions drew the eyes of these powers toward Palestine, which repeatedly became a vassal country.

Its northern part was subject to continuous waves of influence from the north. The coast was frequently dominated, or highly influenced, by the Egyptians, while the arid lands of the east and the south belonged to nomadic and semi-nomadic populations. In this period, the predominant political pattern in Palestine became that of city-states, somewhat similar to those we find in Europe in medieval times. Each town was a fortress in which the local kinglet or prince had his headquarters. Around the city there were small hamlets and isolated farms where people kept busy with agriculture and herding, and had to pay tribute to their feudal lords. While literacy was developing in the growing nations of Egypt and Mesopotamia, Palestine was still illiterate, and no local prince was strong enough to extend his hegemony over large territories.

In the third millennium B.C., Palestine witnessed a great many ethnic movements. Continuous waves of different peoples arrived, mainly from the northeast and the east, from the deserts on the edges of the Fertile Crescent. The result was an accumulation of various cultural patterns, which are revealed to us by differences in the material culture found in archaeological layers.

This flux reached its peak at the end of the third and the beginning of the second millennium B.C.; it was during this period, probably, that the country saw its greatest and most numerous ethnic movements. This was also the period in which the Hebrew tribe is believed to have moved from the edges of Mesopotamia and to have reached Palestine.

The most powerful of the invasions, and the one for which we have the most historical records, was led by a mysterious and puzzling people called Hyksos, or "leaders of the foreign countries." In the eighteenth century B.C. they occupied Palestine and Egypt and maintained their empire in these lands for two hundred years. When, in the sixteenth century B.C., they were defeated by the Pharaonic army, Palestine became a province of Egypt, and it remained such until the Hebrew conquest, in the thirteenth century B.C., and the subsequent establishment of their monarchy.

The two hundred and fifty years of the Egyptian rule marked a great flourishing of art and religion. An unprecedented wealth embellished and enriched all the Palestinian cities; palaces and temples were built, goods were imported from far away, and despite the continuous local battles and wars, the country was prospering, and increasing literacy was gradually conducting Palestine into the age of history. In this period, one of the greatest inventions of civilization—the alphabet—was developed in or near Palestine. Earlier writing was pictographic or ideogrammatic, or used other complex methods that required a great number of signs, and thus writing was necessarily an esoteric art. The alphabet appears to have been invented shortly before the middle of the second millennium B.C. and with it literacy became possible for everybody, for writing was now a relatively easy matter.

Fully recorded history started in Palestine with the Hebrew conquest, at a time coinciding with the beginning of the Iron Age. Historical records and annals had become common in Egypt and Mesopotamia almost two thousand years before, and in northern Syria and Anatolia several hundred years before. Palestine was the last strip of the Fertile Crescent to enter history. By then its urban civilization had existed for two thousand years, and the walls of Jericho for six thousand; the earliest ceremonial burials at Mount Carmel were over sixty thousand years old, whereas the first tool-makers had appeared in Palestine a half million years before.

PART · TWO

THE AGE OF HUNTING AND GATHERING

I

Men, Materials, and Remains

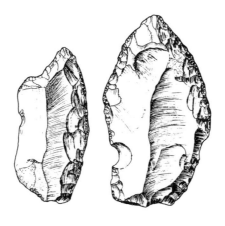

THE REMAINS

HE DISCOVERY of human remains tens of thousands of years old is one of the most exciting experiences a man can have. However, sometimes laymen are bitterly disappointed when they come to visit prehistoric excavations and see that all we discover there are broken pieces of bones and rough flakes of flint. Indeed, these materials, so meticulously collected and measured by prehistorians, do not seem to be so meaningful at first glance.

But these bones and flints form the bulk of the evidence of human evolution during over a half million years, or over 98 per cent of the time that man has existed. These scanty remains reveal a great deal to us. Through them we know how men looked, where and how they lived, how they hunted and what kinds of animals were part of their diet. These remains help us also to estimate how large the human groups were and how long they sheltered themselves in given spots. From this we can sometimes also conjecture about the nature of the unit, its social and family life. Sometimes, chance discoveries enable us to establish the presence of affinities and relations between men who lived far away from one another. When we consider all these elements together, we get a picture of the evolution of man and his culture.

Frequently, prehistoric men have returned for ages, again and again, to the same spots. While living in a cave, or at a camp site, they have made their tools, eaten their food, lighted their fires, performed their rites, lived their lives. The natural sedimentation of dust transported by wind, or of stones fallen from the roofs of caves, is mixed with the remains left by man; thus archaeological layers are formed, and grow with time. When

Cave of Emire at the entrance of Wadi el-Amud

different layers are found on the same spot, the stratigraphy shows us the sequence of cultures, or the succession, from bottom to top, of the remains left behind by the various human groups, in their chronological order.

The shape of flint implements and bones underwent many changes in the course of the Pleistocene era. Changes in climate and ecological conditions had profound effects on fauna. Some animals became extinct, others migrated to new regions, others again underwent extensive physical transformations to adjust themselves to the changing environment. The result is that some kinds of animals are found only in specific periods; and if their bones are found at a particular level, the archaeologist is given some idea of the age of that level and of the natural environment in which man then lived. At the same time, man himself changed a great deal, and the discovery of his bones allows us to follow the steps by which he finally attained his present state. The discovery of human skeletal remains in levels containing animal bones and flint tools, enables us to synchronize the existence of certain animals and the ecological environment implied by them with certain physical features of early man and with tools he made and used at the time.

Besides implements and bones, archaeological levels sometimes contain works of art, evidence of burial customs, or other objects that throw some light on the spiritual life of prehistoric man. But discoveries of this kind have been unevenly distributed in time and space. All of them seem to be associated with a period quite late in the Old Stone Age, and they are not present in all regions. For instance, Palestine possesses a unique group of burials from the Middle Paleolithic period, whereas nothing has been discovered so far to show the burial methods in the Upper Paleolithic period. Up to now at least, cave art has not been found in Palestine, whereas much of it has been discovered in Spain and France.

So far as art is concerned, it is highly probable that most of it was produced on wood that was destroyed by time. In other cases, climatic conditions and the degree of permanence of the coloring materials must have greatly determined the quality of the preservation of a work of art, so that we shall probably never have a clear idea of the distribution and the patterns of art in the Old Stone Age.

When luck does not help the archaeologist in finding remains that reveal the spiritual life of prehistoric man, he has to rely upon the materials which time and nature have been good enough to spare.

THE MATERIALS

Prehistorians use the term "material culture" to designate the assemblages of materials which were left behind by man in the places where he lived and which bear traces of his work or use. This includes tools, weapons, and all the other objects with which man surrounded himself. In order to make his material culture, man used the raw materials that nature offered him, mainly the most common ones, such as stone, wood, and bone, which could be gathered by him wherever he was.

We do not know exactly when early anthropoids helped themselves for the first time by using unworked wooden sticks or stones. But the habit of throwing stones and other natural materials to ward off a dangerous being is present also among apes, so that we may guess that anthropoids had such a custom very early. From this to tool-making is a very long jump. Throwing a stone to keep away an animal could arise from natural instincts, but preparing a weapon, giving it a sharp end to make it more effective, and preparing it in advance while planning its subsequent use—this is a logical sequence of action indicating definite premeditation, and ability which must have belonged only to a developed mind.

Tool-making developed gradually. Probably nature itself taught that a pointed or edged stone is more harmful than a flat or round one. In the course of time man's ancestors realized

Paleolithic site at surface near Kadesh Barnea, in
northern Sinai, with hand axes and flint flakes *in situ*

that a stone could be broken by striking it on another stone and
that flakes with sharp edges could be produced.

Of all the materials used by man for tool-making, stone is
the one that has been preserved best and in the greatest quantities. Stone is one of the most abundant raw materials in nature
and was encountered by early man everywhere. Depending upon
location, various kinds of stones were at his disposal: at times
very hard ones, such as basalt, quartz, granite, and hematite; at
other times softer ones, such as limestone. But everywhere the
most sought-for and utilized stone was flint.

Because of its natural qualities, flint was found to be the most suitable stone for preparing tools. It is a very hard stone, found in chalk levels either in the form of small nodules or in flat layers. The hardness of flint is greater than that of steel, so that a knife blade leaves a gray metallic streak when drawn across its surface. It is brittle, and when hammered it breaks up into a powder of angular grains. When a block of flint is abruptly struck at one point, a flake is detached, its shape varying according to the way in which the blow is given. One side of the detached flake is part of the original surface of the block; the other face is formed by the fracture and therefore fits exactly on the negative flaking surface left on the parent block. This surface usually is concave and the flake convex.

When one knows how, it takes only a few seconds to make a tool. A blow struck with the correct hammering tool, with the right force, at the right spot, produces the desired flake, and an experienced tool-maker could produce hundreds of flakes in a few hours. In places where flint is abundant, prehistoric men made tools on the spot for immediate use, and left them there when they were finished working with them. But flint tools have also been found in regions where the raw material is not available, and from this we learn that tools were sometimes carried a considerable distance.

Tool-making is conditioned by the available raw material, by the technical skills of man, and by his needs. Ancient man learned how to work flint with various techniques and with ever-growing skill. Through the evolution of technology, and through the kinds of tools that man needed for his daily activities, we can follow the course of his intellectual development and indirectly deduce many other details of his progress and his daily life.

Usually certain types of industry, certain tools, and certain techniques used in preparing them are characteristic of definite periods, and enable us to assign discoveries to one time period or another.

After stone, the two principal raw materials used by man for making tools were wood and bone. But the wooden tools, with some very rare exceptions, have been totally destroyed by time. Bone was probably used much less than stone and wood, simply because it is more difficult to shape with accuracy; only the late part of the Old Stone Age has provided enough bone tools to allow a study of their typology and evolution. Hence most of the material culture left by man during the Age of Hunting and Gathering is of stone. Stone implements are in fact the main common denominator of the sites, all over the world, where traces of the Old Stone Age have been found. This is why prehistorians place such importance on the study of flint implements, and collect and observe these little stone splinters with such meticulous attention. To the layman, all these fragments frequently appear similar, uninteresting; but to those who know what they mean in terms of culture, age, and evolution, they reveal their hidden life and explain to us how man made his first steps towards civilization.

MEN AND CULTURES

Prehistorians call the Age of Hunting and Gathering, or the Old Stone Age, Paleolithic. This is the first of the three stages into which traditional terminology divides the "Stone Age," the whole of which in Palestine includes all the periods preceding the Urban Age. The second stage, the Middle Stone Age, or Mesolithic, is a transitional phase between two modes of life, while the third, the New Stone Age, or Neolithic, roughly corresponds to the Age of Early Farming.

The Old Stone Age is further divided into three major periods, called by prehistorians, Lower, Middle, and Upper Paleolithic. In each of them, prehistoric men made a different kind of material culture. In the Lower Paleolithic, single types of material culture are very widespread, and the same industries are found over very large areas. The next two periods see a gradual localization of patterns, and we find that before the beginning of the Mesolithic, types of material culture are confined to relatively small geographical regions. At the same time, the variety of artifacts grows immensely and the length of cultural periods decreases. Already in these early periods we can discern the quickening rhythm of cultural evolution.

The Lower Paleolithic has three major traditions of stone industries, called by prehistorians the Chopper, or Pebble, tradition, the Bifacial tradition, and the Tayacian tradition. The first is characterized by waterworn pebbles or lumps of rock coarsely chipped at one end so as to produce a sharp cutting edge. This tradition of choppers, or "pebble tools," is found in many parts of Asia and Africa but appears less frequently in Europe.

The characteristic tool of the second tradition is the biface, or "hand ax," an all-purpose tool which is believed to represent a further development of the chopper. It is made by retouching or trimming both sides of a flint block, and by working both faces so that they converge at their edges and form a cutting section and sometimes a sharp point at one of the extremities. This tradition of bifacial tools appears to have covered most of Europe, southwestern Asia, and Africa.

The Tayacian tradition, called Tabunian in the Near East, is characterized by the absence or the rarity of large core-tools, and by the presence of crude flakes, and is mainly found in Europe and the Near East. Its earliest-known sites are in western Europe.

Skeletal remains of human beings associated with these three types of material culture in Asia, Africa, and Europe, are extremely rare, and usually very fragmentary, but they reveal a great many differences of features among these archaic men, or Paleanthropi.

It seems that we cannot yet discern at that time one human race, but rather various types of "ape-men" present on earth at the same time. They represent the early childhood of mankind, and many characteristic physical traits of man are found in these Paleanthropi in a formative stage. But in their general features they can already be considered men, and from their material culture we know that they had already succeeded in differentiating themselves from other animals in a crucial way: they were able to make tools and to use them, and, as we have already mentioned, this fact implies a mind which can only be that of a man.

The makers of these three traditions had an extremely long existence. They left traces for over a half million years, up to 60,000 or 70,000 years ago. During this enormously long period bands of them moved about and traveled through various temperate and tropical areas of the Old World. Probably they came into accidental contact with one another, saw tools made by other groups, and learned new techniques and new methods of tool-making. Sometimes traditions mixed, or new kinds of tools appeared, both bearing witness to cultural evolution.

The Middle Paleolithic industries are found throughout most of the regions previously occupied by the Bifacial and Tayacian traditions, but we can begin to recognize several local cultural patterns separated from one another by major natural borders such as seas and high mountain ranges. Tools were made out of better-shaped and thinner flakes, and were lighter, more accurate, and more varied. This material culture, named, like most of the other prehistoric industries, after a French type-site, is called Mousterian. Most of its makers were men who had a physical structure still quite different from that of modern man. The first specimen of this race was found in a cave in the Neander Valley, in western Germany, and was called Neanderthal man. Remains of Neanderthal men are today quite numerous, and are found in approximately the same area over which Mousterian cultures are spread. They appear to have lived between 70,000 and 30,000 years ago. Opinions are divided as to whether they became utterly extinct or were absorbed by other races.

THE AGE OF HUNTING AND GATHERING IN THE NEAR EAST

YEARS AGO	GEOLOGICAL AGES	CLIMATIC CONDITIONS		ARCHAEOLOG-ICAL PERIODS	PREVAILING MATERIAL CULTURES
8,000	FOOD-PRODUCING ACTIVITIES BECOME DOMINANT				
	HOLOCENE	POST-PLUVIAL		MIDDLE STONE AGE	MICROLITHIC INDUSTRIES
14,000	BEGINNING OF FOOD-PRODUCING ACTIVITIES				
	LATE PLEISTOCENE	PLUVIAL C	LATE PLUVIAL C	UPPER PALEOLITHIC	BLADE INDUSTRIES
32,000			GOTTWEIG INTER-STADIAL	MIDDLE PALEOLITHIC	"MOUSTERIAN" FLAKE INDUSTRIES
48,000			EARLY PLUVIAL C		
70,000					
	MIDDLE PLEISTOCENE	LAST INTER-PLUVIAL		LOWER PALEOLITHIC	BIFACIAL AND TABUNIAN (TAYACIAN) INDUSTRIES
120,000		PLUVIAL B			
200,000		FIRST PLUVIAL			
300,000					PEBBLE CULTURE
	EARLY PLEISTOCENE	GRAND PLUVIAL			
600,000					

Upper Paleolithic cultures are characterized by the presence of flint industries in which tools are made out of blades, or thin, elongated flakes, whose length is over twice their breadth. These "blade industries" were created by the true modern type of man, Homo sapiens.

In Europe, Upper Paleolithic cultures replaced the archaic Mousterian culture of Neanderthal man suddenly and abruptly. In the Near East this transition seems to have occurred gradually, in various successive waves; but these blade industries definitely occurred here earlier than in Europe.

The Near East has also produced skeletons of men showing mixed characteristics of Neanderthal man and recent Homo sapiens, and here the mystery of the origins of Homo sapiens arises in all its fascinating complexity.

This enormously long Paleolithic age, in which the economy of man was based on hunting and gathering, came to an end quite abruptly, about 14,000 years ago, and then evolution took a new rhythm, culture became infinitely more complex, and abstract thought increasingly occupied an important place in the human mind. By then man had already gone a long way in his evolution and possessed most of the values that were to lead him to civilization.

The story of all these millennia is told by the broken bones and the rough flakes hidden in the dust of caves, and the only way to understand what happened during this time is to examine archaeological levels, to unearth the remains left there, and to try to penetrate their meaning.

II

The Earliest Traces
of Man
in the Near East

THE PEBBLE CULTURE

I N A PREVIOUS section we looked at the Quaternary
history of the Jordan Valley as revealed by its sequence of geological levels. This valley has yielded several groups of remains
of early man, and its clear stratigraphy is of great help in dating
them. The earliest anthropoid remains known so far in the Near
East come from the Jordan Valley, from a site called Ubaidiya,
near Kibbutz Afiqim. These are two small fragments of a skull
four times as thick as the skull of modern man, and one incisor
tooth. They were found in the levels of clay and gravel which
belong to the Grand Pluvial, the first and most conspicuous pluvial of the Quaternary era, and date back to between 300,000
and 600,000 years ago. In the same levels were found fossil bones

of some forty different species of extinct animals which lived under different climatic conditions. They include elephants, rhinoceroses, hippopotamuses, wild bears, turtles, and large numbers of a catfish called "Clarias." [1]

Ubaidiya was probably located on the shores of the large Early Quaternary lake in the Jordan Valley, and man appears to have lived in this spot and to have left behind bones of the animals he hunted. Some of these bones had been intentionally fractured so that the marrow might be extracted, and a few bore marks of sharp cuts that were probably executed with flint implements. None of the bones showed signs of burning, and Professor Moshe Stekelis, who excavated this site, believes that the makers of the Afiqim culture did not yet know how to master and use fire.

The tools used by these tool-makers were found in the same deposits, and they illustrate the Pebble (or Chopper) culture. The most typical tools are crude, potato-like pebbles on which sharp cutting edges were made by removing flakes in two directions at one of the extremities. The intersection of the flake scars thus formed a sharp edge.

Other characteristic tools are what are called globular cores, spheroid pebbles trimmed all over, which are believed to have served as throwing stones or bolas stones. One very interesting group of implements is believed to represent a crude precursor of the biface. These have an elongated point made by trimming one extremity of the pebble. The point usually has a triangular cross section, while one half of the tool retains the natural surface.

Another Pebble-culture site is known in Israel, at Khirbet Maskana, a hill overlooking the Jordan Valley, not far from Tiberias, where the same kinds of tools are accompanied by a few very crude bifaces. The only other site with pebble tools in south western Asia is Barda Balka, in eastern Iraq. There these tools

---

[1] M. Stekelis et al.: BRCI, Geological Section, Vol. IX, No. 4 (1960), pp. 175 ff.

Front and side views of a coarse bifacial tool, in
flint, from Khirbet Maskana (height, 3.7 inches)

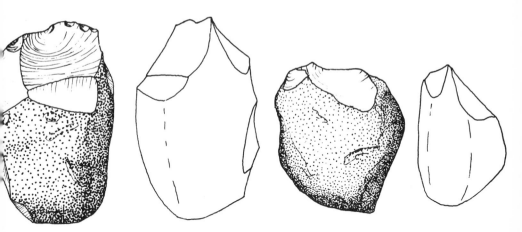

Pebble tools from Khirbet Maskana

are found with a more evolved material culture and seem to be of a much later date.[2]

The Pebble culture had two major areas of development during early Pleistocene times, one in eastern Asia, the other in northern and eastern Africa. It seems that at the beginning the two areas had many similar characteristics, but after a short while they became increasingly different from each other and each one developed in its own way. The Pebble culture persisted for a long time in both regions but became increasingly localized. The Palestinian complex, on the whole, is typologically closer to the African than to the Asiatic group, and bears a strong resemblance to assemblages of early Pleistocene times from northern and central Africa.[3] When we recall that Palestine is the only land bridge between Asia and Africa, we realize how significant and suggestive are these very early remains. If more human remains were found in Palestine, they could probably help to solve the riddle of whether or not the Asiatic makers of the Pebble culture, at the beginning, were related to the makers of the same culture in Africa.

THE TWO TRADITIONS

The Lower Paleolithic cultures which follow the Afiqim Pebble culture show in their general characteristics many similarities with those of temperate Europe. In both areas are found two major traditions of material culture, the Bifacial tradition, characterized by the abundance of tools made on cores, and the Tayacian tradition of flake tools, which, as I have said, is called Tabunian in the Near East.

Some prehistorians believe that these two cultures reflect two different ways of life, the Bifacial reflecting an economy based mainly on hunting, the Tayacian based mainly on gathering. This theory was inspired by the fact that these two kinds

[2] See H. E. Wright and B. Howe: *Sumer*, Vol. VII (1951), pp. 107–18.
[3] See P. Biberson *et al.*: *Bulletin d'Archéologie Marocaine*, Vol. III (1959), pp. 7 ff. Also L. S. B. Leakey: *Olduvai Gorge* (Cambridge: University Press; 1951).

of material culture are frequently found in the vicinity of each other, and sometimes even in different layers of the same site; yet each one maintained its own traditions without mixing with the other. In the Near East, the makers of the Tabunian (Tayacian) culture preferred to live in caves as soon as environmental conditions permitted. They left quite deep deposits of debris, an indication that they were in the habit of remaining in the same spot for long periods. The Bifacial culture is more frequently found near riverbanks and the shores of lakes and in other spots where big game must have been abundant. The makers of the Bifacial industry seem to have become accustomed to living in caves only in later times. When we observe the Tabunian material culture, it is hard indeed to recognize in it any tool that could be used efficiently for hunting. In the Near East, the animal bones found in the layers of this culture usually are extremely scanty.

The theory that these two cultures reflect two different ways of life is quite attractive, but it is far from being universally accepted, for we have very little factual information about these very early people. All we know is that they worked flint, and that these flint tools are found concentrated in open-air stations or sites which must have been suitable spots, for their makers would come back to them again and again or stay in some of them a rather long while. Their traces show that once a region was occupied by them, they stayed there for periods which probably lasted several thousand years.

We know that the people of the Bifacial culture were hunters of very large animals—rhinoceroses, hippopotamuses, elephants. With the tools these people possessed, the only way in which they could kill big game must have been by hunting in some sort of band, in which the able members of the group probably spent several days pursuing and wounding a large animal, until the animal collapsed and could be finished off on the ground. The same method is used today by some bands of South African Bushmen and by other human groups still living in the stage of hunting and gathering.

The flint artifacts reveal a slow technological evolution in which they became increasingly better shaped and acquired new forms. We have already mentioned that flint possesses special qualities and that a sharp blow will detach a flake from it. When the hammering tool is rough and cannot be used with the needed accuracy, the flakes do not come off in the precise shape required by their maker and are simply uneven splinters of the core from which they have been taken. Each flake leaves its other, or negative, face on the core, and additional flakes are obtained by striking the hammering tool on these flat planes in order to obtain more precise results. These flat striking planes, or platforms, were sometimes first prepared by trimming them several times, so that the craftsman could aim more accurately at the spot he wanted to hit, and so that he could adjust the angle of incidence of the striking platform in relation to the dorsal surface. As we shall see, this technique will become much better developed at the beginning of the Middle Paleolithic. In the early phases of Tabunian it is practically absent, but the number of tools showing the use of this technique grows with time, and in Middle Paleolithic times this technique is present on most of the tools.

It seems that hammering tools varied and evolved considerably from the beginning to the end of the Lower Paleolithic. At the beginning they hit a large area of the striking plane. Consequently the impact produced scars and fissures on the splinters, and it was extremely difficult to make thin flakes. In the lower phase of both the Bifacial and the Tabunian culture, flakes are extremely crude and thick, usually having a broad unfaceted striking plane forming an obtuse angle with the dorsal surface of the flake. By degrees they became less massive and the angle with the dorsal surface became less obtuse. Probably man had succeeded in preparing lighter and more effective hammering tools which could strike with more accuracy at the desired point. It is equally likely that the tool-making hand was achieving more skill and experience. We can almost see how the hand of man became more flexible and more clever with time, and how this evolution led it from primitive crudeness to the delicate, well-shaped tools of subsequent periods.

Some of these rough flakes of Lower Paleolithic times were retouched, or trimmed, by very light flaking which produced thin teeth on their edges. In the same way, notches were made, and thus the tool-maker was given the possibility of producing a variety of artifacts.

Flake tools included mainly side-scrapers, or large flakes retouched along one or two sides, and toothed and notched flakes.

All these tools probably had many different uses, and before they developed into a more specialized industry, over three hundred thousand years had to pass—a time span one hundred and fifty times longer than the period separating us from the birth of Christ.

THE BIFACIAL CULTURES

Bifacial cultures are frequently called Abbevillian and Acheulean, after two type-sites in northern France where their artifacts were first observed in significant quantities and at datable geological levels.[4] Until a few years ago these cultures were believed to have first appeared in Europe, and to have spread over Asia and Africa only thereafter; the present evidence, however, shows that their origins must have been roughly contemporary on these three continents. The Bifacial cultures seem to have evolved in

[4] Many prehistorians use the terms "Abbevillian" and "Acheulean" for Near Eastern assemblages as well. But these two terms are presently creating problems even in Europe. For example, prehistorians are engaged in a great deal of discussion over whether certain assemblages should be called "Abbevillian" or "Early Acheulean" and whether assemblages designated variously as "Micoquean" and "Late Acheulean" are actually identical or are, rather, two distinct variants of the same culture. Outside of Europe, these terms create even greater problems, for they are frequently used to designate assemblages that do not correspond with assemblages called by the same name in Europe. For these reasons I have preferred to adopt the more neutral term "Bifacial" for Near Eastern assemblages, or material cultures, characterized by bifacial tools.

a very similar fashion in all parts of this vast area. As I have already mentioned, their typical tools are the hand axes, or bifaces; that is, two-faced core-tools, usually with one pointed or edged extremity.

We do not know how these tools were used at the time, but comparable tools made by primitive people today suggest that they had various uses both as weapon and as working tool. They might have served to open nuts and to cut roots and tubers, as well as for defense and for hunting. It is not unlikely that some of them were used as missiles against game. This possibility is suggested by a type of disk-shaped biface excellently balanced for hurling at nearby targets. Experiments in throwing these disks have shown that they can be effective weapons at up to sixty or seventy yards, but we shall probably never know in exactly what manner these tools were handled and used by their makers.

The Near East, and Palestine in particular, is rich in this kind of artifact. The Palestinian sequence is very similar to that

Late bifacial hand axes from Kadesh Barnea

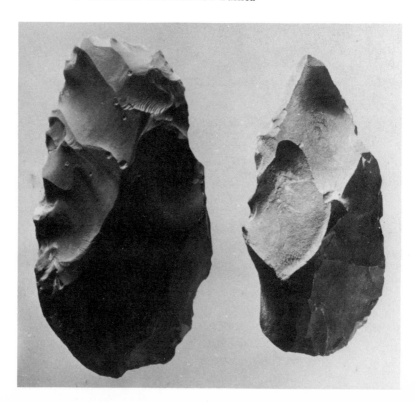

found in other regions of western Asia and Europe. In the earliest phase bifaces were crude, irregular, and thick, with sinuous edges. Probably they were made with very heavy, rough hammering tools, for the places where flakes were removed are large and irregular, with deep waves (or rings) and numerous scars. These Palestinian Early Bifacial implements are of the same type as those found in the Abbevillian and Early Acheulean French sequence. Middle and Late Bifacial correspond to Middle and Late Acheulean of France.

In the Middle Bifacial, hand axes become better shaped and more regular. The retouching is finer and the edges less sinuous. Distinctly different forms of bifaces can be recognized. With time sharply pointed bifaces increased in quantity. In the sites along the Jordan River, mainly at Jisr Bnat Yaqub [5] and at Mayan Baruch, cleavers, or bifaces with a transverse cutting edge, dating from the Middle Bifacial are common. They occur together with heart-shaped, pear-shaped, and lanceolate hand axes. These last two types become more common in the Late Bifacial and are frequently found in caves.

In the Late Bifacial, which in Palestine has many affinities with French Late Acheulean, particularly Micoquean—a type of Late French Acheulean named after its type-site, La Micoque,

[5] M. Stekelis: BRCI, Geological Section, Vol. IX, Nos. 2–3 (1960), pp. 61 ff.

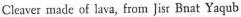

Cleaver made of lava, from Jisr Bnat Yaqub

Hand ax made of basalt, from Jisr Bnat Yaqub

in the Dordogne—bifaces frequently become very sharply pointed and very thin; and sometimes small well-retouched ones are found in large quantities. In the cave of Yabrud, on the eastern slopes of the Anti-Lebanon Mountains in Syria, this kind of biface is found together with artifacts considered to be Mousterian, or Middle Paleolithic (Shelter I, Layers, 11–12); at Yabrud it seems that the transition from Bifacial to Mousterian was gradual.[6] Professor Raymond Vaufrey found similar evidence in France, in the rock shelter Peche de l'Aze, in 1929. Since then evidence gathered in many other places has attested to the gradualness of the transition from Late Bifacial to Mousterian as a widespread phenomenon in some Bifacial cultural areas.

[6] A. Rust: *Die Höhlenfunde von Jabrud, Syrien* (Neumünster: Wachholtz; 1950). Although this site is spelled Jabrud in most of the literature, the more accurate spelling is Yabrud.

Principal types of bifacial tools in outline: 1, oval; 2, pear-shaped; 3, triangular; 4, lanceolate; 5, limande; 6, cleaver; 7, Micoquean; 8, cordiform; 9, disk

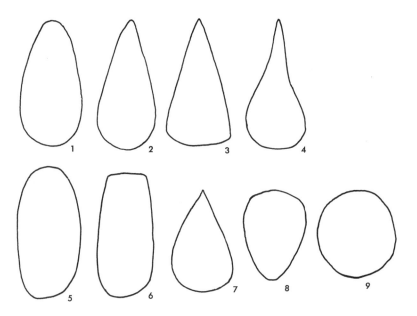

In Palestine, the two most important excavations that have revealed Early Bifacial tools are at Jisr Bnat Yaqub, in the Jordan Valley, and at Rephaim-Baq'a, Jerusalem.[7] At Jisr Bnat Yaqub bifaces of various phases show different degrees of sharpness and have different shades of patination. At these sites the bifaces from early phases have sinuous, S-shaped edges and rough retouching, and are associated with heavy flakes of the Tabunian (or Tayacian) type. At Jisr Bnat Yaqub, among some bifacial tools made of lava are a small number of choppers and some primitive cleavers which might be the descendants of the Afiqim Pebble culture.

Middle Bifacial artifacts are best represented at the two major sites of the upper Jordan Valley, Jisr Bnat Yaqub and Mayan Baruch, and in the cave of Umm Qatafa, in the Judean Desert. Umm Qatafa has yielded the earliest-known cave deposit with bifacial tools in the Near East. The levels at which these tools were found have also revealed traces of fireplaces: hearths with burned earth, stones, and bones, around which sometimes were found larger stones in a circle, probably used as seats around the fire. These are the earliest evidence we have of man's mastery of fire in the Near East. The evidence dates from the Pluvial B period (Riss of Europe) and is probably almost 200,000 years old.

The Middle Bifacial culture is still very sparsely represented, and it is known in Palestine so far only through the artifacts from six or seven sites. Late Bifacial implements are much more abundant. They are found all over the northern Jordan Valley, the northern coast of Israel, the Negev, and the Jordanian Plateau. They were also found in stratified sequences in three of the major caves excavated in the Levant: at Umm Qatafa; at Tabun, on Mount Carmel; and at Yabrud.

The age of the Bifacial culture has been established by these

[7] Both excavated by Professor Moshe Stekelis. See QDAP, Vol. VI (1939), pp. 214–15; Vol. VII (1940), p. 45; JPOS, Vol. XXI (1947), pp. 80–7; *Proceedings of the International Congress of Prehistory*, Vol. IV (1956), pp. 386–9.

various discoveries. So far the most important site for dating purposes is Jisr Bnat Yaqub, where Professor Moshe Stekelis was able to relate the various cultural phases to the geological sequence of the Jordan Valley.

The Quaternary geological series starts here, as elsewhere in Palestine, with the traces of the Grand Pluvial, the rainy period which corresponds to the two early glaciations of Europe. The earliest Bifacial tools were found at the level showing these traces. The Middle Bifacial tools were found throughout most of the next two layers, counting upward; these layers reveal, respectively, a drier period and a second rainy period, and represent the first interpluvial (second interglacial of Europe), and the second pluvial (Riss of Europe). The Late Bifacial was found in two higher levels, both of which indicate a drier climate and represent the second interpluvial (Riss-Würm of Europe).

This chronology has been confirmed by evidence at several other sites. At Umm Qatafa the Early Bifacial is absent, but Middle Bifacial is found at levels which must belong to the second pluvial period. Late Bifacial material also occurs at Umm Qatafa and at Tabun at levels belonging to the last interpluvial. At Yabrud, Late Bifacial seems to have persisted into the early part of the last pluvial.[8]

This chronology shows the enormous persistence of the Bifacial tradition, which lasted through a considerable part of the Pleistocene era—at least from the later part of the Grand Pluvial to the end of the last interpluvial period. In terms of years, this probably means about 300,000 years.

[8] This chronology is based on a reanalysis of the available data. A considerably different view was recently put forward by François Bordes (L'A, Vol. LIX, 1955). Other views were also presented by Alfred Rust (*Die Höhlenfunde von Jabrud, Syrien*) and F. Clark Howell (*Proceedings of the American Philosophical Society*, Vol. CIII, No. 1, 1955).

Cave of Tabun, Mount Carmel

Tabunian flints from Umm Qatafa, Level G-2 (after Neuville)

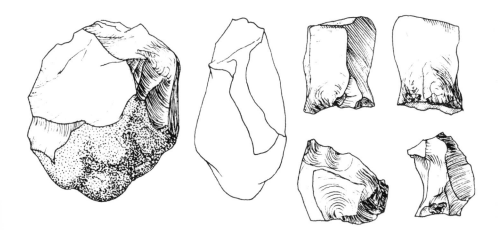

THE TABUNIAN CULTURES

The Tabunian culture of the Near East was until recently labeled with the names of the Clactonian and Tayacian cultures of Europe, which it resembles in its tools and techniques. It was given its new name by an American scholar, F. Clark Howell, after the cave of Tabun, in the lowest level of which the Tabunian is found. This culture is characterized by rough, crude, thick flakes with few faceted striking platforms and by a very low percentage of core-tools, and it is more limited in its geographical distribution than the Bifacial cultures, being found mainly in the Near East and in Europe.

In the Levant, the three type-sites for this culture are the caves of Umm Qatafa, Tabun, and Yabrud, and they seem to represent the three major phases of development of the Tabunian.

Umm Qatafa has produced three levels of Early Tabunian, which were tagged by the excavator René Neuville with the European names of Tayacian I, II, and III. At the earliest level only 5 per cent of the flakes had secondary retouching; at the second level 15 per cent and at the third 25 per cent of the flakes were retouched. Very few of the implements showed a faceted platform.

In these early phases, it is not yet possible to speak of typical tools. The few retouched implements can be defined as notched and toothed flakes, or very primitive side-scrapers. A carinate (keel-shaped) heavy scraper and a very crude, irregular, small biface are the only core-tools present.

At Tabun, the excavations of Professor Dorothy Garrod have uncovered, at the lowest level of this cave, a layer with more evolved and better-shaped Tabunian artifacts.[9] The percentage of retouched tools is much higher, and so is the number of those having a faceted platform. Some tools begin to show a certain recurrence of types and repetition of the same form.

[9] D. A. E. Garrod and D. M. A. Bate: *The Stone Age of Mount Carmel,* Vol. I (London: Oxford University Press; 1937).

Notched and toothed tools are still common, but the scraper becomes the dominant tool, and over 10 per cent of the total number of artifacts are side-scrapers. A few of these are déjété-scrapers, or scrapers continuously retouched on two convergent sides. Another tool, which makes its earliest appearance at Tabun, is the burin, a flake tool with a chisel-like working edge formed by trimming the point or the thin edge of the flake. This tool became well shaped and typical only much later on, in the Upper Paleolithic; but after the Tabunian it was constantly a part of the material culture.

The tool assemblages at Yabrud that have been given the name Yabrudian have been regarded as a separate culture, but they are probably a further evolution of the Tabunian culture. They are found there at several levels, intercalated with Bifacial and other industries. One of these is the so-called "Pre-Aurignacian," one of the earliest-known blade industries in the world, which some prehistorians believe to be the precursor of the Aurignacian, an Upper Paleolithic industry of Europe. The evidence at this Syrian rock shelter shows clearly that several different cultures existed contemporaneously in the Levant. Yet each one of these cultures was probably fashioned by a different people having its own traditions and techniques of tool-making; each maintained its own characteristics without mingling the characteristics of other traditions.

This Late Tabunian (or Yabrudian) culture shows the continuation and development of the types of tools found at the lowest level of Tabun, but the later implements acquired much better shapes, and the quantity of side-scrapers became even greater. The characteristic tool of this phase is the déjété-scraper, which is frequently found in large quantities. In no other material culture of the Near East does this tool represent over 5 per cent of the artifacts. Occasionally a few bifaces of Late Bifacial type occur at Yabrud. At first the percentage of tools with faceted platforms is the same as at Tabun, but at later levels it grows considerably. Here new tools occur in incipient forms. A few pointed tools appear, which seem to be prototypes of Mousterian points, a characteristic tool of the Middle Paleolithic.

There are very strong similarities between the tools of the Late Tabunian of Yabrud and Tayacian artifacts found at La Micoque in the Dordogne and at other sites in France; in both regions it seems that the Mousterian culture originated in the Tabunian or Tayacian cultures of the Lower Paleolithic.

At Yabrud, the transition between Yabrudian and Mousterian—between Lower and Middle Paleolithic—is gradual, and the sequence of cultural levels allows us to follow the slow development of one into the other. Tabunian culture was contemporary with Bifacial culture. The three levels of Early Tabunian at Umm Qatafa are earlier than the levels of Middle Bifacial. The lowest Tabunian level is found in the middle of a geological deposit indicating a rather dry climate that occurred immediately after the lowest sediments of the caves were deposited at the very end of the Grand Pluvial. The earliest Tabunian level at Umm Qatafa apparently must belong to the first interpluvial (Mindel-Riss of Europe). The second level must belong to the end of the same geological period. The third is found in a different deposit, one showing a wetter climate, and must belong to the beginning of Pluvial B (Riss of Europe). Thereafter, in the same geological period, this cave was occupied by makers of Middle Bifacial material culture.[1]

In the course of Pluvial B another deposit of Tabunian

[1] The chronology proposed here differs from that suggested in the 1930's by Dorothy Garrod. It is based on a new analysis of the available evidence, and includes most of the basic views of René Neuville. See Archives IPH, No. 24 (1951).

Yabrudian tools from Level 25 at Yabrud (after Rust)

occurs on the Mediterranean shore of Lebanon, at Bahas, near Tripoli.[2] The layer of red sand in which this industry is found belongs to what geologists call the Middle Dunes levels; it was deposited between the two major incursions of the sea during the Pleistocene era, apparently just after the raised sea beach was formed at the 180-to-200-foot level by the Paleotyrrhenian transgression in the first interpluvial.

The Middle Tabunian at Tabun seems to be contemporary with the Middle Bifacial at Umm Qatafa. It is found in the lowest geological deposit of that cave assigned to the later part of Pluvial B.

The Late Tabunian of Yabrud spans most of the sixteen feet of geological deposits which filled up the shelter in the course of the last interpluvial (Riss-Würm of Europe), and it continues in the wetter deposits of Early Pluvial C (Early Würm of Europe). In the course of this latter period it slowly acquired the tools and techniques of the Mousterian, and it came to an end in levels of mixed Moustero-Yabrudian characteristics.

THE LOWER PALEOLITHIC SEQUENCE

The remains we have described, scanty as they are, form the evidence we possess for the story of man in the Near East from his earliest detectable appearance over a half million years ago to about seventy thousand years ago. What we have learned of the beginning of tool-making, of the first mastery of fire, of the changes and evolution in material culture, gives us some idea of the extremely slow and rather simple dynamics according to which men lived and evolved during all this time.

Men lived in small bands, and sometime during this period, probably at the end of the Grand Pluvial, they learned how to use

[2] E. de Vaumas: *Bulletin de la Société Royale de Géographie d'Egypte,* Vol. XXII (1947), pp. 21 ff. See also R. Wetzel and J. Haller in W. L. Thomas: *Man's Role in Changing the Face of the Earth* (Chicago: University of Chicago Press; 1956), pp. 278 ff.

YEARS AGO	GEOLOGICAL PERIODS	JORDAN VALLEY	UMM QATAFA (JUDEAN DESERT)	YABRUD (SHELTER I) SYRIA	TABUN (MT. CARMEL)	QAFZE (GALILEE)
32,000	INTERSTADIAL (GOTTWEIG OF EUROPE)			1 2 3 4 5 6 7 8 9 } MOUSTERIAN	B MOUSTERIAN	F MOUSTERIAN
48,000		MOUSTERIAN		FAUNAL BREAK	FAUNAL BREAK	
	EARLY PLUVIAL C (EARLY WÜRM OF EUROPE)	MOUSTERIAN	B } STERILE C	10 11 } MOUSTERIAN 12 13 BLADE INDUSTRY 14 TABUNIAN 15 BLADE INDUSTRY "PRE-AURIGNACIAN" 16 TABUNIAN 17 18 } LATE BIFACIAL	C } MOUSTERIAN D	G H I J K L } MOUSTERIAN
70,000						
	LAST INTERPLUVIAL	LATE BIFACIAL	D₁ } LATE BIFACIAL D₂	19 LATE BIFACIAL 20 21 } TABUNIAN 22 23 LATE BIFACIAL 24 25 } TABUNIAN	E } LATE BIFACIAL F	M STERILE
120,000						
	PLUVIAL B (RISS OF EUROPE)	MIDDLE BIFACIAL	E₁ } MIDDLE BIFACIAL E₂ E₃ } EARLY TABUNIAN F		G MIDDLE TABUNIAN	
200,000						
	FIRST INTERPLUVIAL	EARLY BIFACIAL	G EARLY TABUNIAN H } STERILE I			
300,000						
	GRAND PLUVIAL (MINDEL TO GÜNZ OF EUROPE)	PEBBLE CULTURE	J STERILE			
600,000						

LOWER AND MIDDLE PALEOLITHIC IN SYRIA-PALESTINE

caves as shelters and began to leave in them traces of their life and daily activities.

We have seen how the earliest anthropoid beings in Palestine, in the Early Grand Pluvial, were the makers of the pebble tools, and how their material culture is typologically related to the culture of beings who lived at the same time in eastern Asia (in areas of India, Java, and China) and in northern and eastern Africa. These are the two regions of the world in which the earliest and most primitive relics of "ape-men" were found, and probably were the homelands of the earliest human beings. In all the vast expanse between eastern Asia and northeastern Africa, the Jordan River valley is so far the only area to have produced what might turn out to be the "missing link."

Some time must have elapsed between the period of the pebble-tool makers and the following, more sophisticated Early Bifacial culture, of which the earliest evidence dates from the Late Grand Pluvial period. During the first interpluvial another culture appeared, the Tabunian, and thereafter these two traditions coexisted in Palestine and produced their evolving phases for over two hundred thousand years, until new factors changed the character of material culture and marked a new period which archaeologists call Middle Paleolithic. Through the Bifacial and the Tabunian cultures, the Near Eastern traditions of tool-making are connected with those of large portions of the Old World. Palestine is located in the geographical center of the area of Bifacial tradition, which is a triangle whose corners are central India, southern Africa, and eastern Europe. This enormous cultural province is well defined, and no Bifacial industries have so far been found beyond its boundaries. The Tabunian-Tayacian province is narrower, and is limited to the temperate zone of Europe and to the Levant.

Traces of human artifacts became more abundant in later prehistory, while periods became shorter and the rhythm of cultural change accelerated. Significantly, from the 250,000-year period in which the Pebble culture must have persisted (approximately between 600,000 and 350,000 years ago), we know of only two sites in Palestine. Early Bifacial and Early Tabunian artifacts have been found so far at five sites; they represent a period of about 130,000 years. Middle Bifacial and Middle Tabunian are known from ten or eleven sites, and they represent a period of about 100,000 years. Late Bifacial and Late Tabunian are known from over forty different sites, and they represent a period of about 60,000 years.

Flint tools are classified into about ten different kinds each for the Pebble culture, the Early Bifacial, and the Early Tabunian. For the Late Bifacial and the Late Tabunian over seventy different types of tools are recognized, and the inclusion of subtypes more than doubles this number.

During the Lower Paleolithic tools became better shaped. New techniques were invented to produce more effective implements, to reduce the effort in making them, and to exploit better the raw material at man's disposal. All this is evidence of cultural evolution and shows us how man took his first steps in the conquest of nature.

Pebble tools from Khirbet Maskana

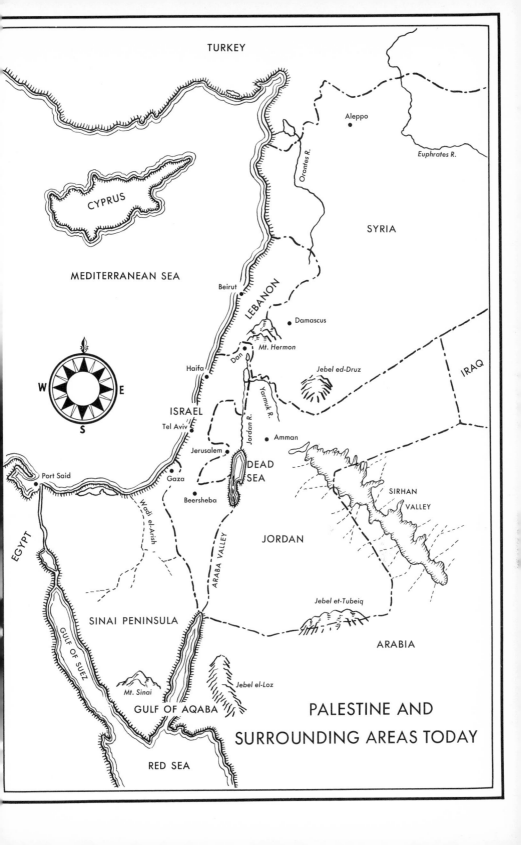

TURKEY

CYPRUS

MEDITERRANEAN SEA

SYRIA

Aleppo

Euphrates R.

Orontes R.

Beirut

LEBANON

Damascus

Mt. Hermon

Dan

Jebel ed-Druz

Haifa

Yarmuk R.

IRAQ

ISRAEL

Jordan R.

Tel Aviv

Amman

Jerusalem

DEAD
SEA

Port Said

Gaza

SIRHAN
VALLEY

Beersheba

JORDAN

ARABA VALLEY

EGYPT

Wadi el-Arish

Jebel et-Tubeiq

SINAI PENINSULA

ARABIA

GULF OF SUEZ

Jebel el-Loz

Mt. Sinai

PALESTINE AND

GULF OF AQABA

SURROUNDING AREAS TODAY

RED SEA

W E
S
N

III

The Middle Paleolithic

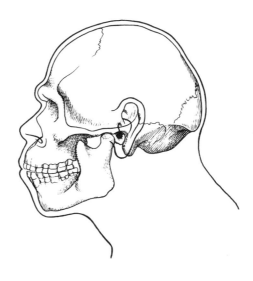

THE MOUSTERIAN CULTURES

THE MATERIAL CULTURE of Middle Paleolithic times is called Mousterian, after Le Moustier, its type-site in southern France. This culture is found over most of the region in which the Bifacial and Tayacian traditions were present during the Lower Paleolithic. However, some basically different traits enable us to distinguish three major regions in which this material culture evolved quite separately, though along similar general lines. One of them is Europe and the Near East, the second is Africa, and the third is south-central Asia.

A typical Mousterian tool or flake, besides being much thinner and better shaped than the previous Tayacian-Tabunian flakes, possesses some new and peculiar characteristics. Very careful and minute retouching is frequently found all along the edges of the tools. This fine trimming had two main purposes—

one to make the edges of the tool stronger and more efficient, the second to give the tool a more regular shape. This secondary finishing of the tools enabled their makers to produce very fine artifacts.

The striking platform of the tool was prepared with great care so that the tool-maker could adjust the angle of incidence in relation to the dorsal surface and thus could give the tool the exact thickness and shape he wanted. We have already mentioned that in the Tayacian tradition the striking platform frequently was a simple large, flat plane produced by the removal of a single flake. Sometimes the presence of several scars shows that the striking platform had been prepared more carefully; however, these preparatory flakes were apparently removed without a very precise technique, and the scars are large and quite irregular. The striking platform of Mousterian flakes was thoroughly prepared by fine and regular trimming, an indication of precise methods.

Sometimes a sharp blow on this striking platform produced a flake with a wavy edge having a large bulge in the center which turned down toward the extremities and then rose into two smaller bulges. This shape reminded French archaeologists of the past century of the policemen's hats of that time, and they called it "chapeau de gendarme."

The most important tool that appears in large quantities in the Mousterian cultures is a characteristic triangular point. This probably served as a point for spears and daggers; in other words, it was the operating part of a composite tool that must have had a handle of wood. Here for the first time is proof for the extensive use of composite tools and weapons. These new instruments were convenient to handle and much more efficient than whatever had been used previously. Hunting was becoming a relatively easy task, and enemies could more easily be kept at a respectable distance.

Until a few years ago it was believed that the Middle Paleolithic was characterized by two cultures, the Mousterian and the Levalloisian (this name was taken from the site of Levallois, near

Paris, in France). The main characteristics of Levalloisian were defined by its discoverer, the Abbé Henri Breuil, as follows: "The flakes are obtained from nuclei prepared in a special manner; the flakes are rarely retouched and transformed into points or side-scrapers." The flakes are prepared on the core before being struck off; the core is roughly trimmed at various angles and given a turtleback shape. The resulting flakes may have a turtleback surface, or if a previous flake has been struck along the same axis, a concave surface.

For many years "Levalloisian" was considered an independent culture differentiated from contemporary "Mousterian." According to this view, highly retouched Mousterian tools were generally found in caves, and less retouched Levalloisian in open-air stations and river terraces.[1] When a few years ago it was observed that such a differentiation did not exist in Palestine, where Middle Paleolithic industries in caves usually show a mixture of characteristics from these two patterns, it was proposed to call the Middle Paleolithic industries of Palestine, and subsequently of southwestern Asia, by the composite name of Levalloiso-Mousterian.

Since then, however, French prehistorians have noticed that in Europe, also, Levalloisian flakes and cores are frequently found in Mousterian layers. It appeared, therefore, that the argument

[1] H. Breuil and L. Koslowski: L'A, Vol. XLI (1931), pp. 449–88. See also L'A, Vol. XLII (1932), and Vol. XLIV (1934).

Levalloisian flake from Site 5, central Negev

for cultural differentiation between Levalloisian and Mousterian was as little justified in Europe as it was in the Near East.

In 1953, the French prehistorian François Bordes was able to clarify this point further.[2] Subjecting "Levalloisian" and "Mousterian" assemblages to a statistical analysis, he found that the principal difference between the two was a changing percentage of the "Levalloisian flakes" among the total number of artifacts. Disregarding this difference, the two industries show very similar quantitative and typological characteristics. Bordes also pointed out that the faceted platform, which was previously considered to be typical of the Levalloisian culture, was in fact common to the artifacts of both cultures. The main conclusion was that "Levalloisian" and "Mousterian" represented two patterns of the same tool-making tradition.

Three main factors are regarded by Bordes as most significant in distinguishing various patterns of Middle Paleolithic assemblages: (1) The number of bifaces in relation to the total number of tools; (2) the percentage of flakes with a faceted platform; and (3) the percentage of Levalloisian tools and flakes.[3] Bordes devised a number of indices to illustrate various peculiarities of an assemblage; through them, different levels of the same spot, or similar levels in different spots, can easily be compared in a visual, graphic manner.

The index for a particular tool is determined by multiplying the number of times this tool occurs in an assemblage by 100 and dividing the result by the total number of all tools. In other words, the index is the percentage of a given kind of implement in the totality of the tools at the level to which it belongs. For each of these indices Bordes established the point, or the significant percentage, that marks the transition between two patterns of material culture, and in this way he was able to establish the existence of various types of industries and to show that in France

[2] F. Bordes: BSPF, Vol. L, No. 4 (1953), pp. 226–34.
[3] F. Bordes: L'A, Vol. LIV (1950), pp. 393 ff. Subsequently Bordes improved this scheme, adding new elements and new indices (L'A, Vol. LIV, 1955, p. 508).

there had existed at least eight main types of Middle Paleolithic industries. The principal ones are the Mousterian of Acheulean tradition (Peche de l'Aze type), the Mousterian of Tayacian tradition (La Quina type), and the Mousterian of Levalloisian tradition (Le Moustier type). The evolution of these different types appears to be simultaneous. Bordes observed in Late Mousterian a higher ratio of blade-tools and of several implements that are found in greater numbers in the Upper Paleolithic. The artifacts of the Near East have a composition very similar to that of tools of the contemporary cultures of Europe, and indicate a similar evolution of material culture, the differences being purely secondary. Bordes, analyzing the material from Yabrud and comparing it with European types of cultures, found that quantitative and typological conclusions indicated the presence here of the three major European types.[4] What I shall refer to as Moustero-Bifacial is a material culture of the same kind as the Mousterian of Acheulean tradition of Europe. The Moustero-Yabrudian is a Mousterian of Tayacian tradition, whereas the most common kind of Middle Paleolithic culture in the Near East is the Levalloiso-Mousterian. An examination of Mousterian sites in Israel, Jordan, Lebanon, and Syria suggests that several other minor local patterns were also present in this area at the same time; nevertheless, the major and dominant types of Mousterian are very similar to those that existed in Europe at the same time.

Prehistorians have frequently debated the possibility that there were actual connections between temperate Europe and the Near East in Middle Paleolithic times. What is the significance of the striking similarities between the material cultures of various groups in Europe and southwestern Asia? And is there any particular meaning in the fact that different cultural patterns are found near one another throughout these areas? We do not know to what extent connections actually existed, and it seems unlikely that regular contacts were kept up between the peoples of the two areas, but we have to consider that we are dealing here with

[4] F. Bordes: L'A, Vol. LIX (1955), pp. 486 ff.

an age that lasted fifty thousand years, and during such an enormous period of time many men could have wandered at random.

It is worth while remembering that temperate Europe and the Near East are less than fifteen hundred miles apart, almost the same distance as from one end of Saudi Arabia to the other. In protohistoric and early historic times, migrations and cultural elements in the Near East spanned similar distances in less than two or three generations. As we shall see, we have today clear proof of the wandering of later hunting and pastoral bands over very large areas. Some groups of rock pictures in the deserts of the Near East and in the Sahara show that extremely homogeneous cultural and conceptual patterns were spread over areas of several thousand miles. At least one people today, the Bedouins, have well-established cultural traditions throughout their domain, which spreads over vast regions of North Africa and the Near and Middle East. It is an area almost as large as that of the Euro-Near-Eastern Mousterian tradition. For hunters, food gatherers, and other nomadic and semi-nomadic populations whose whole life is spent in wayfaring, distance has a totally different meaning than for us sedentary city dwellers.

One of the most puzzling problems of the Middle Paleolithic sequence in the Near East was presented by the discovery of levels containing artifacts of an entirely different kind intruding between the Mousterian levels of caves and shelters. These artifacts are blade-tools, and apparently they indicate the sudden arrival in the area, and subsequent sudden disappearance, of this distinctive tradition of tool-making. These blade-tool levels, which show all the characteristics of an Upper Paleolithic culture, undoubtedly are much earlier than any of the European blade industries, and seem to show that this tradition already existed in other areas while Neanderthal man was still producing his Mousterian tools. At least two levels of these tools have been discovered in the Near East; both belong to Mousterian times, but we have no idea of whether this tradition is local or exotic, or of why it appeared and ended so suddenly. The evidence of these traditions

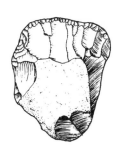

Pre-Aurignacian scrapers from
Level 15 at Yabrud (after Rust)

Pre-Aurignacian core from Level
15 at Yabrud (after Rust)

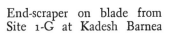

Mousterian flakes from Site
1-G at Kadesh Barnea

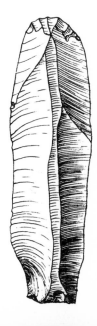

End-scraper on blade from
Site 1-G at Kadesh Barnea

is definite. At first they do not seem to have interfered much with the local evolution of other types of material culture. As they belong typologically to the Upper Paleolithic, I shall discuss them more in detail in the following chapter.

According to our present knowledge of Middle Paleolithic material culture, it seems that Mousterian traditions persisted for a long time in the Near East. They probably still persisted among certain human groups even while, in fertile Palestine, Upper Paleolithic blade industries were already well established.

In the caves of Abu Sif and Sahba, in the Judean Desert, René Neuville, the late French prehistorian, who was also the French Consul General in Jerusalem, found late layers of Mousterian together with large quantities of blade-tools.[5] The same intermingling occurs in the cave of Karain in southern Anatolia.[6] This mixture is even better demonstrated by materials from the Negev. It is not yet possible to establish the steps and the development of these mixed cultural patterns, but it seems that they disappeared slowly from the major caves, leaving little trace in typical Upper Paleolithic levels.

In the areas which are today covered by deserts, the situation appears different, and the Mousterian traditions there seem to have been more persistent. In inner Syria, in the Negev, and in Sinai, several sites have been found where blade-tools occur abundantly in the context of unquestionably Mousterian-like industries.

This late local development of Middle Paleolithic traditions is representative of a rather common phenomenon which occurred, probably independently, in other areas as well. The unusual thing here is that in this period Palestine-Syria seems to have become, for the first time, the border land between two cultural areas which today are distinguished as two major ecological

[5] R. Neuville: Archives IPH, Vol. XXIV (1951), pp. 57–8.
[6] See Kilik Kokten: *Belleten Türk Tarih Kurumu Basimevi*, Vol. XIX, No. 75 (1955), pp. 271–93.

regions, one arid and one fertile. While the Mousterian tradition persisted longer in the "arid zones," the people of the blade-tools of Upper Paleolithic times occupied caves and terraces (the open space in front of caves) in areas which, no matter what climatic changes took place, always were relatively wetter and had more vegetation than the regions covered today by deserts.

This cultural partition, defined by ecological areas, was to become more and more marked with time. The differences during the Upper Paleolithic are visible, but they are not as sharply marked as in later periods.

TIMING AND CULTURAL CHANGES

The earliest occurrence of Mousterian in the Near East seems to be represented by a single short level, from a time when, both in Europe and in the Near East, typically Lower Paleolithic industries predominated (in Pluvial B). This early Mousterian find may have been exotic in the Near East at that time, representing a tradition already well developed elsewhere. In Europe, in the late phases of the Tayacian (or Late Clactonian), and the Bifacial (or Acheulean), in the last interglacial, the Mousterian traits increased gradually, so that with the beginning of the last glaciation, Mousterian became the dominant culture. It became dominant in the Near East at the same time, but its replacement of the old traditions had been more abrupt.

In both regions Mousterian was replaced by blade industries as the dominant culture at the end of the major interval of the last pluvial, the Gottweig Interstadial phase. In Europe this was a sharper change. In the Near East, the makers of blade-tools first arrived in small waves during Early Pluvial C, but the Mousterian culture persisted as the dominant one until well after the end of Early Pluvial C.

It seems that the blade tradition began to evolve early in Pluvial C and was, from the beginning, markedly differentiated from the Mousterian tradition. The brief early occurrences in the Near East of this blade tradition had some influence on the local culture, and for the period of the Gottweig Interstadial, Mousterian industries are found here with a relatively large number of tools typical of the Upper Paleolithic. But the final overtaking by the blade industries in this region occurred at about the same time as in Europe.

The mechanism of cultural evolution and cultural transmission does not abide by absolute laws. Men moved about, carrying with them their own traditions; they came into accidental contact with other people having different traditions. Ideas sometimes were diffused by the slow, random process of hand-to-hand, hill-to-hill communication; at other times more directly by movements of people over longer distances.

During the periods called Pluvial in the Near East and Glacial in Europe, northern Europe, northern Asia, and large parts of central Asia were covered by an enormous ice sheet running from England to Siberia. Despite many ecological differences, all the regions in the territory bounded by this ice sheet on the north, the Himalaya Mountains on the east, the Red Sea and the Mediterranean on the southwest, and the Atlantic coast on the west, were a single large area in which no major natural frontiers existed and where migratory groups could wander in all directions. This means that for hundreds of generations bands of hunters following their game could travel great distances and still maintain their traditional pattern of material culture.

A distinguished prehistorian, Dorothy Garrod, once emphasized that the European sequence of material cultures "is the result of successive immigrations, superposed on a certain amount of local variation and development in place." [7] The same seems to be true for the Near East, and, indeed, for many other areas of the world.

[7] D. A. E. Garrod: "The Near East as a Gateway of Prehistoric Migration," *Bulletin of the American School of Prehistoric Research*, No. 13, pp. 17 ff.

THE LOCAL CHRONOLOGY

I have already mentioned that dating Quaternary cultures demands a consideration of several factors. The main working scheme is based on climatic fluctuations as defined by geology, and these can be detected through variations of the sea level and subsequent changes of the coast line, through changes in natural sedimentation and changes in the fauna, and through various other considerations.

There are two more recent means of dating, palynology and Carbon 14, which so far have not been used very much in the Near East, and therefore, at the time this book is being written, they are of little help. The first is concerned with the study of pollen, microorganisms produced by the millions by every plant or vegetable. Each floral species has a different kind of pollen, so that specialists are able to identify the plant from which a given sample of pollen came. Pollen is composed of an extremely hard organic substance that is practically indestructible, and it is so light that it is blown in great quantities by the wind. Pollen grains are contained in all soils upon which some vegetation grew, and the study of them enables us to identify the flora which existed at the time when a particular layer was deposited, and eventually to know what sort of climate nurtured such vegetation.

The second method, Carbon-14 dating, will help us a great deal in later periods. This method, following recent discoveries in radioactivity, is based on calculating the specific ratio of the carbon isotope 14 to the total amount of carbon in a once-living object. Dating is possible because Carbon 14 is produced by cosmic rays at a fixed ratio in the carbon consumed by and incorporated into all living things. After death, Carbon 14 transforms itself into ordinary carbon and loses its radioactivity at a known rate.

By calculating its present specific radioactivity one can determine how long ago the organism in question was alive. This method is useful for dates up to a limit of about 70,000 years ago.

Bone, teeth, and ivory, carbonized wood, and other organic materials are the objects used in this test.

Science has not yet been able to find a method of dating flint artifacts except through their association with other objects datable by these various methods. In order to establish the age of a culture, prehistorians examine all the factors and try to combine the results from each of them in a conclusion consistent with all the data.

In the Near East, information on the geological age of the Mousterian is provided by numerous sources. This culture is abundant along the Mediterranean coast, and it is frequently associated with levels which can be fixed in the geological sequence. Its earliest occurrence seems to be in Lebanon, near Beirut, in alluvial deposits laid down after the Paleotyrrhenian rise of the sea (first interpluvial), deposits dating from Pluvial B.[8] It is not yet clear whether this industry represents true Mousterian, or whether it was Tabunian with incipient Mousterian characteristics; but according to the excavator of the site, Father Henri Fleisch, it already possessed all the requisites of a Middle Paleolithic industry. If this is correct, the coast of Ras Beirut has disclosed the earliest-known Mousterian in the Near East.

However, the bulk of the Mousterian industries, both at Ras Beirut and at other sites along the coast, appears to be connected with later climatic episodes. The great majority of coastal sites disclosing Mousterian industries are found in the levels of red sands (Hamra) which were formed in the course of Early Pluvial C, and the Mousterian seems to have continued through a smaller sea incursion which was probably connected with the interstadial episode at the end of Early Pluvial C (Gottweig Interstadial). This chronology corresponds to that revealed by the Jordan Valley. Mention was previously made of the stratigraphy at Jisr Bnat Yaqub, where Mousterian appears only at the very beginning of Pluvial C. From the sequence on the Mediterranean coast, it

[8] H. Fleisch: *Quaternaria*, Vol. III (1956), pp. 101 ff.

seems that while Mousterian-like industries appeared sporadically
in earlier periods, typical Mousterian assemblages occurred mainly
during Early Pluvial C, and ceased in the course of the major
interstadial which separates Early from Late Pluvial C (Gottweig
Interstadial of Europe).

More precise details on the age of each Mousterian level are
provided by the major cave excavations. Men had returned again
and again to caves, each time leaving their indestructible artifacts
at a different level. The levels also offer evidence of the sequence
of climatic change, so that the two records, cultural and climatic,
can be matched together and synchronized.

In a newly excavated section of a cave, the color of the earth
can be seen to change at different levels. In a spot where man has
lived, such changes in color and formation are the result of two
major factors—human and natural. It is frequently very easy to
distinguish a layer at which man has lived from a sterile layer, for
man leaves in the soil not only flint implements but also a great
deal of organic material, such as the remains of his meals, which
disintegrate and sometimes give the layer a darker color and a
softer texture. Furthermore, in spots where fires burned for long
periods, the ashes give a characteristic color and texture to the
layer. Generally, after a long period of inhabitation, a cave has
many of these traces of fireplaces in its layers, and the ashes are
spread around and make the layer even more distinctive. For some
unknown reason, these human leavings in the sediment are much
better preserved and more evident in the Near East than in Europe. Probably climatic conditions have helped to preserve them.
The much wetter climate of Europe, the frequent heavy rains
and frost in winter, must have contributed to a more thorough
destruction or distribution of the organic materials.

The second factor, the natural one, is the more important
for purposes of dating. The debris in caves and at open-air sites
has accumulated to a height of many feet, and human factors
have contributed only a small part. Most of the sediment has
been deposited by nature, through wind, rain, disintegration of

rocks, and various other factors. The variation in the color and texture of a natural sediment is due mainly to variation in the kinds of raw materials deposited. Obviously wind and rain bring two totally different kinds of sediment. In wet periods there is a greater chance that part of the rock ceiling of a cave will collapse and that smaller stones together with various kinds of heavy earth will be washed in, whereas dry wind generally deposits dust and the lightest kinds of earth. In some cases heavy rains and subsequent floods may erode or even sweep away existing layers. When this happens, the last flood leaves on the surface the heaviest stones and gravel, which remain as evidence of what has happened. These in turn are covered by the subsequent layer. The result is a stratigraphy of different kinds of soil whose origins we can identify; we can, as well, come to some conclusions about the climatic milieu in which they were laid down.

In regions where Pleistocene was characterized by glacial and interglacial periods, sediments show extremely important variations which make the determination of climatic conditions fairly easy. In the Near East, variations are not as sharp, but they are nonetheless a very precious tool for the study of climatic fluctuations.

In the Near East, two excavations have provided so far the most important clues to the chronology of the Mousterian. They are the cave of Tabun and the rock shelter of Yabrud. In both, the Mousterian is preceded by older deposits and is located in a good framework of cultural and geological sequences. As already noted, at Yabrud the geological strata can be divided into three major levels. Starting from the bottom, there are a series of layers deposited during a relatively dry period (Levels 25–19). This series is about sixteen feet deep, and at the bottom of it there are what seem to be signs of a slightly wetter climate. Some minor fluctuations have given this sequence a few secondary variations. At the center there is a thin layer of desertic sand indicating the period of maximum drought in this age. This first stratum seems to have been deposited throughout the last

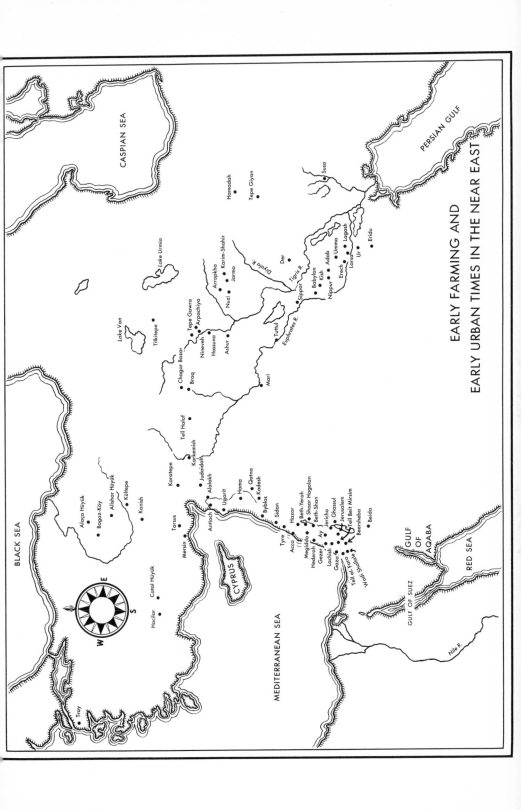

EARLY FARMING AND

EARLY URBAN TIMES IN THE NEAR EAST

CASPIAN SEA

PERSIAN GULF

Hamadan
Tepe Giyan
Susa

Arpakha
Karim-Shahir
Jarmo
Nuzi
Der
Logash
Umma
Adab
Larsa
Babylon
Kish
Ur
Eridu
Nippur
Erech
Sippar
Diyala R.
Tigris R.
Euphrates R.

Lake Urmia

Tell Halaf

Lake Van

Tilkitepe
Tepe Gawra
Chagar Bazar
Nineveh
Arpachiya
Hassuna
Ashur
Tuttul
Braq
Mari

Karkemish
Karatepe
Judaidah
Alalakh
Ugarit
Hama
Qatna
Kadesh
Byblos
Sidon
Beth-Yerah
Shaar Hagolan
Beth-Shan
Tyre
Hazor
Ghassul
Jericho
Jerusalem
Tell Beit Mirsim
Acco
Megiddo
Ay
Hederah
Gezer
Gaza
Lachish
Beida
Tell el-Fara
Wadi Shallale
Beersheba
Antioch
Tarsus
Mersin

Alaça Hüyük
Boğaz-Köy
Alishar Hüyük
Kültepe
Kanish

Çatal Hüyük
Hacilar

Troy

BLACK SEA

CYPRUS

MEDITERRANEAN SEA

GULF
OF
AQABA

GULF OF SUEZ

RED SEA

Nile R.

N
W E
S

interpluvial period. In it are found Bifacial and Tabunian cultures. Mousterian remains are not yet present.

The second stratum is about ten feet deep and indicates a much wetter climate, again with minor fluctuations. This apparently represents Early Pluvial C (Levels 18–10). Its artifacts trace the transition from Tabunian and Bifacial to typical Mousterian, and in the course of it the early blade industry called Pre-Aurignacian appears.

The third stratum comprises the last six feet of deposit (Levels 9–1). It reveals another shorter, drier period, which probably represents the major interstadial found in the Near East, contemporary with the Gottweig Interstadial of Europe. At Yabrud, the Mousterian sequence continued throughout this period.

At Tabun, the geological stratigraphy is quite complex, but it can be classified into four major strata. Starting from the bottom, a level almost thirteen feet thick bears signs of a damp period which slowly became drier (Level G). The level probably dates from the end of Pluvial B, and in it were found Tabunian remains. Thereafter the climate became hotter and drier. The second stratum, which was deposited during the last interpluvial, is very deep both here and at Yabrud. Here it is over thirty-six feet deep and shows several climatic fluctuations (Levels F–E) similar to those of the same period found in Yabrud. In this stratum the Bifacial culture is dominant. Above it the start of a wetter period is indicated in the third stratum, which is chiefly characterized, as at Yabrud, by a hardening of the deposits into what geologists call breccia and into other conglomerate rocks (Levels D–C). The third stratum is about sixteen feet deep, and throughout it are found Mousterian levels. Most of it seems to date from Early Pluvial C, with some parts reaching the beginning of the Gottweig Interstadial. The last stratum, about eleven feet thick, is composed of sandy earth, and a large proportion of it was blown in by the wind. It seems to be the product of a drier climate which probably corresponded to the major interstadial found everywhere in the Near East and was contemporary with the Gottweig Interstadial of Europe. This level also is characterized by Mousterian cultures. Comparing the sequences at Tabun and at Yabrud, we can see that Mousterian, as the dominant culture, appeared first at Mount Carmel, on the coast, and then at Yabrud, in inner Syria. At Tabun, Mousterian was present from the very beginning of Early Pluvial C, whereas at Yabrud it appeared in the same period, but slightly later. At both sites it persisted well into the Gottweig Interstadial, and perhaps until its end. This chronology is fully consistent with that of the open-air sites on the coast and in the Jordan Valley.

It is interesting to note how the faunal sequence corresponds to these climatic changes. The most complete series comes from excavated caves at Mount Carmel, and has been reported by Dorothea Bate. The series of fossil bones from Tabun together with the series from the neighboring cave of El-Wad gives a good picture of faunal changes during Mousterian times.[9] Two major changes took place, one during the period and one at the end, and they seem to correspond to the beginning and the end of the Gottweig Interstadial. Up to the beginning of the interstadial, an archaic sort of fauna prevailed, among which were elephants, rhinoceroses, hippopotamuses, and other large animals which disappeared thereafter from Palestine. Some of these animals require a damp climate and an open environment of bushes and low vegetation, which is their chief source of food. These animals disappeared when the climate became drier and when the environment changed considerably. In an early phase of the Gottweig Interstadial, between Level C and Level B at Tabun, a sharp faunal break reveals a change in the kinds of animals hunted by the Mousterians. For a short while the prevailing fauna was that characteristic of grasslands. Wild oxen, wild horses, gazelle, and deer

---

[9] After thirty years, new methods are now available, and the work done on the Carmel fauna, though excellent for its time, is today somewhat obsolete. However, no recent excavation has yet supplied a similarly rich collection of faunal remains.

were abundant. The predominant animal was the fallow deer. New species of wolf and hyena made their appearance. On the whole, the fauna was less varied than both earlier and later fauna. It persisted until the beginning of the Upper Paleolithic, and then (El-Wad, Level F) a whole new series of forest animals suddenly made its appearance. Foxes, hares, bears, wolves, wild boars, wildcats, and squirrels seem proof that the environment changed again and that forest came to cover large parts of Palestine. One gets the impression that all these animals came down from the north, looking for a milder climate. At the same time, the climate of Palestine was becoming wetter and cooler, the interstadial was over, and another rainy period had started.

The recent radiocarbon analyses of this sequence have provided dates that agree well with the geological chronology. At Ras el-Kelb, near Beirut, Dorothy Garrod and Germaine Henri-Martin, were able to date an early phase of Mousterian "before 52,000 years before present." Several radiocarbon datings from the cave at Tabun establish a date of 39,500 years B.P. for Level B, and "circa 41,000" years B.P. for Level C. This latter date if substantiated by additional evidence, would indicate that the faunal break (between Level C and Level B at Tabun) occurred after the Gottweig Interstadial had already begun. The last Mousterian levels at Kebara date to the very end of the Gottweig Interstadial, to about 35,000 years B.P.[1]

These dates agree roughly with the results obtained by Carleton Coon at Jerf Ajla, near Palmyra, in Syria, where a date of about 43,000 years B.P. (± 2,000 years) was established for an evolved Mousterian phase.[2] Farther to the east, in the foothills of the Baradostian Mountains, the site of Shanidar has provided

[1] D. Garrod and G. Henri-Martin: BMB, Vol. XVI (1961), p. 66; Kenneth P. Oakley: *Advancement of Science*, No. 75 (1962), p. 425.
[2] Carleton S. Coon: *The Seven Caves* (New York: Alfred A. Knopf; 1957), p. 315.

a date of about 50,000 B.P. for a Mousterian level.[3] The climatic changes under discussion have been thoroughly studied in Europe, where they have been dated by many Carbon-14 tests.[4] Pluvial C is believed to have begun about 70,000 years ago, and the Gottweig Interstadial to have lasted 15,000 to 16,000 years, from about 48,000 to about 32,000 years ago. Mousterian culture seems to have lasted about 40,000 years, from the beginning of Pluvial C to the end of the Gottweig Interstadial.

THE BURIAL CUSTOMS OF THE MIDDLE PALEOLITHIC

The sudden extinction of a human being whose life one has shared for a long time has never ceased to be a shock. Fathers and mothers who brought up a new generation and guided their sons toward independence, individuals who wove a net of affection between themselves and people close to them, older men and women whose wisdom increased with age and to whom society entrusted more and more power and influence—all were one day annihilated emotionally and intellectually by death. But the physical body remained before the mourners. They saw the person they had known, motionless, bereft of all attributes except the lifeless flesh. What had happened to the powers that had lived until then in that corpse, and had suddenly abandoned it? Was that lump of flesh and hair all that remained of a powerful man?

Neanderthal man had enough self-awareness to begin asking himself questions. His ritualistic behavior toward the dead indicates his belief that a motionless corpse still possessed some

[3] 50,300 ± 3,000 B.P. Another sample has yielded the date of about 46,000 B.P. (R. S. Solecki: "Early Man in Cave and Village at Shanidar, Kurdistan, Iraq," *Transactions of the New York Academy of Sciences*, Series II, Vol. XXI, No. 8, pp. 712–17). See also R. J. Braidwood and B. Howe: *Prehistoric Investigation in Iraqi Kurdistan* (Chicago: University of Chicago Press; 1960), p. 149.

[4] H. L. Movius: "Radiocarbon Dates and Upper Palaeolithic Archaeology in Central and Western Europe," *Current Anthropology*, Vol. I, Nos. 5–6 (1960), pp. 355 ff.

powers of life and deserved care and attention. If power was still present, perhaps it could be used for either good or evil deeds. Dreams and other phenomena probably shaped more precisely man's concepts of the powers to be attributed to a corpse. Some authors believe that the early cult of the dead had its origins in fear. Guilt feelings and other feelings of responsibility toward the dead were, according to this view, the main forces that inspired ritualistic performances around the dead. These performances were meant to appease the corpse's anger or to neutralize it. Other authors are more inclined to see in burial and in the worship of the dead signs of veneration and love for the deceased. Probably the mind of prehistoric man worked much the same as our own, and there was an interplay of both fear and veneration in what became an ambivalent feeling toward the dead.

Burial methods are quite similar throughout the Eurasian area of the Mousterian cultures. This shows that uniform traditions of ritualistic behavior toward the dead, of which the burials are evidence, were widespread. Judging by his burial customs, Neanderthal man's concepts of death were highly complex and sophisticated. The deceased was buried in the floor of the cave, and thus remained in the same habitation he had shared in his lifetime with the members of his group. In some cases he was buried in a special cave in the immediate vicinity of the living-cave. All this seems to imply that the dead were believed to need a shelter, just like living people. In a few instances, grave goods were buried with him. This custom persisted for an extremely long time, until very recently, and was abandoned only by the monotheistic religions of the modern type. Indeed, several modern peoples still perform this ritual. Grave goods consisted mainly of food, to make pleasant the journey to the "other world." The presence of such goods implies in itself the existence of some sort of primitive mythology and of beliefs much more complex than the simple imagining of harmful or beneficent powers.

Mousterian men usually buried their dead in a pit excavated for that purpose. Sometimes the corpse was covered with a few stones in addition to the local earth. It was laid on its side, with knees slightly bent, in a posture reminiscent of sleep. Its hands were usually placed on or near its breast.

In Palestine there is a unique group of Mousterian burials in the Skhul cave at Mount Carmel. At least ten burials were found there, and the rites revealed by them are highly interesting.[5]

At Skhul most of the skeletons were lying on one side, in the same contracted position typical of Neanderthal burials elsewhere, the knees drawn up and the hands near the breast. One of the individuals held between his arms the jaw of a large wild boar, which, like similar grave goods in other regions, had been buried with the corpse. This custom existed from central Asia (Teshik-Tash) to western Europe (Le Moustier and La Chapelle-aux-Saints, France). Another of the skeletons had an ox skull between his arms, but the excavators are not sure whether it was a part of the burial. Another corpse seems to have been surrounded with stones, another practice found in other Mousterian burials.

At Skhul, all the dead were not buried at one time. On the contrary, there was over four feet of accumulated debris between the lowest and the highest skeletons, which, considering the time it took for the deposit to form, certainly indicates a long period.

When we compare the situation at Skhul with the nearby cave of Tabun, where Mousterian levels are much thicker and where only one skeleton and several bone fragments have been found, it appears that Skhul was used as a burial ground, perhaps by some of the inhabitants of Tabun. The tradition of burying their dead here persisted for many generations, and this is probably the most astonishing fact of all, if we consider that many

---

[5] D. A. E. Garrod and D. M. A. Bate: *The Stone Age of Mount Carmel*, Vol. I (London: Oxford University Press; 1937). See also T. D. McCown and A. Keith: ibid., Vol. II (1939).

Bedouins of today have no regular cemeteries and that all this happened some fifty thousand years ago.

In Europe, Mousterian burials have a similar pattern and character. In the rock shelter of Le Moustier, the type-site of the Mousterian culture, the French prehistorian Denis Peyrony discovered a very interesting burial. The body had been deposited in a pit, and near it several charred bones of animals were discovered. These are the remains of pieces of meat that were put near the deceased as grave goods. A similar case was reported at La Chapelle-aux-Saints, where, interestingly, a small cave which apparently was never used as a habitation shelter was dedicated to the burial. This is reminiscent of the special burial cave of Skhul. At La Ferrassie, another French site, several kinds of burials were found, along with a series of pits. Peyrony believes that these pits are related to the burials and thus to the cult of the dead. The pits also contained some animal bones. One of the La Ferrassie burials was that of a child whose skull seems to have been removed from the body, as it was found some distance away. The grave was covered by a flat stone into which small cuplike carvings known as cup marks had been bored. The Neanderthal burial rites appear to have been very widespread throughout the area where Mousterian industries are found in Eurasia. At Kiik-Koba, in the Crimea, another pit burial was found,[6] and at Teshik-Tash, in central Asia, the Soviet prehistorian A. P. Okladnikov discovered the burial of a Neanderthal child, laid on one side and in the same posture as most of the European and Near Eastern examples, surrounded by five pairs of mountain-goat horns, which again seem to be grave goods.[7]

In each burial there are slight variations, but we can recognize a common burial pattern which was in use throughout a

[6] G. A. Bonch-Osmolovski: "Grot Kiik-Koba," *Paleolit Kryma*, Vol. III (Moscow; 1954).
[7] A. P. Okladnikov *et al.*: *Teshik-Tash: Paleolithichesku Chelovek* (Moscow; 1949). See H. L. Movius: *Bulletin of the American School of Prehistoric Research*, No. 17 (1953).

very large area over many millennia. This suggests that the similarity of material culture throughout the area was paralleled by a similarity of spiritual attitudes, beliefs, and ritual practices.

WHO WERE THE MAKERS OF NEAR EASTERN MOUSTERIAN?

A certain number of Mousterian men were buried in graves prepared for them by their fellows or relatives, but sometimes prehistorians have been unable to find traces of inhumation. Skeletons sometimes have been discovered with no signs of special care given to them after death, and frequently they are fragmentary. In some cases the failure to discover a grave may be the result of careless excavation, but elsewhere human corpses indeed seem to have been abandoned on the floors of caves. For some unknown reason not every corpse received after death the care given to those ritually buried.

In Palestine an unusual quantity of human skeletal remains from the Middle Paleolithic has been found, most of them in the caves of Mount Carmel excavated by Dorothy Garrod. But

Skhul V: a man from Mount Carmel in the
Middle Paleolithic

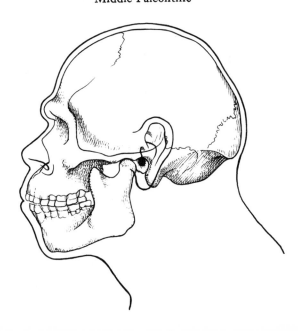

others have come from Mugharet ez-Zuttiyeh, in Wadi el-Amud, in which the famous Galilee man, one of the very few complete Neanderthaloid skulls ever found, was discovered,[8] and from Jebel Qafze, near Nazareth;[9] and fragments have been found in other spots.[1] In the Middle East, two more sites have produced important additional skeletal remains of the same age: Shanidar, in southern Kurdistan,[2] and the cave of Bisitun, in western Iran.[3] When we look at the number of ancient skeletons found in the Near East in relation to the number of excavations, and compare this ratio with the one obtaining in Europe, we realize that Near Eastern archaeologists have been very lucky.

The fact that has most puzzled the scholars who have studied these human remains is that these men are different from the classical Neanderthal men of Europe, and also that they show characteristics of Homo sapiens as well as some traits of their own.[4] Some have argued that the two different races hybridized; others, that a race unknown in Europe was present in the Near East; still others have assigned these individuals to either Neanderthal or Homo sapiens physical types, stating that the slight individual differences from the other known skeletons of these groups were immaterial. These men were the makers of

[8] F. Turville-Petre: *Researches in Prehistoric Galilee*, 1925–6 (London: The British School of Archaeology in Jerusalem; 1927).

[9] Neuville: op. cit.; see F. Clark Howell: *Neanderthal Centenary* (Utrecht; 1958), pp. 185–98.

[1] A. Keith: *New Discoveries Relating to the Antiquity of Man* (London: Williams and Norgate; 1931).

[2] R. S. Solecki: "Shanidar Cave, a Palaeolithic Site in Northern Iraq," in Annual Report of the Smithsonian Institution, 1954, pp. 389–425.

[3] Carleton S. Coon: *Cave Explorations in Iran*, 1949 (Philadelphia: University of Pennsylvania; 1951).

[4] The term "Homo sapiens" has been used with different interpretations. Certain human skeletons showing particularly evolved features, and belonging to the Middle and Lower Paleolithic, have sometimes been included under this label. At other times they have been called "Prae-sapiens," whereas some scholars class them with the Neanderthaloids. The term "Homo sapiens" is used here only for the Cro-Magnon and the other human types associated with the Upper Paleolithic blade industries.

the Mousterian culture, the same culture that in Europe was produced by Neanderthal and Neanderthaloid men.[5] The age of these skeletal materials from Palestine is the same as that of the Neanderthal men who lived in Europe.

The oldest human remains found in a Mousterian complex in Palestine probably are those of the Galilee man of Mugharet ez-Zuttiyeh. Its dating has been much discussed, but it seems to belong to the very end of the last interpluvial. It was found in the earliest Mousterian level of its site, immediately beneath the Bifacial culture. The man found in the cave of Jebel Qafze comes next. He was found in the lowest of seven Mousterian levels (Level L), and it is generally agreed that he dates back to the beginning of Early Pluvial C. At Tabun, remains of two individuals were found in Level C; they belong to the end of Early Pluvial C or to the very beginning of the Gottweig Interstadial. The series of burials in the cave of Skhul probably belongs to this same period. A few isolated bones were present in Level B at Tabun, and they seem to date to the middle of the Gottweig Interstadial.

Among the skeletal remains from Mount Carmel, some differences were recognized between the men from the Skhul cave and those of Tabun, found at a distance of less than 400 feet from each other, both in levels of similar Mousterian industries and not very different in age.

---

[5] Several paleontologists make a distinction between "generalized Neanderthals," or "Neanderthaloids," and "extreme Neanderthals." The latter show more marked Neanderthal characteristics and are mainly concentrated in Europe. Neanderthal skulls are characterized by an exaggerated development of a massive supra-orbital torus (swelling); the absence of a vertical forehead; a relatively high position of the external occipital protuberance and the development of a strong occipital torus; a massive development of the naso-maxillary region of the facial skeleton; a heavy mandible lacking a chin eminence; a pronounced tendency of the molar teeth to taurodontism (enlargement of the pulp cavity with fusion of the roots); a relatively wide sphenoidal angle of the cranial base (about 130 degrees); a slightly backward disposition of the foramen magnum and a large cranial capacity (1,300 to 1,600 cubic centimeters). See W. E. Le Gros Clark: *The Fossil Evidence for Human Evolution* (Chicago: University of Chicago Press; 1955), p. 57.

In Level C at Tabun, the skeleton of a small woman and a male jaw were found. In the nearby cave of Skhul were found ten individuals and some additional fragments.

On the whole, the two individuals from Tabun possessed more marked Neanderthal characteristics than those of Skhul. The man had a robust jaw, similar to those of Neanderthal men, except for a rather marked chin. The woman, short-statured, with a strange long and flat pubic bone, had a low skull, arched brows, and the broad mouth of European Neanderthals. Her head was somewhat more rounded than that of her European relatives.

At Skhul, the cranial cavity, the space in which the brain and the pituitary and pineal glands are contained, was about 1,600 cubic centimeters, which is greater than that of most living men and is rather exceptional for either a Neanderthal or a fossil Homo sapiens. The heavy brow ridges, the large face, the robust jaw, and the over-all thickness of the bones are characteristics found in Neanderthal men. The foramen magnum, the cavity in the skull at its junction with the vertebral column, is long and narrow like that of Neanderthals. The forehead is higher, rounded, and more vertical than that of Neanderthals. The height of the cranial vault, the developed mastoid process, and the incipient chin, present in some mandibles, revealed features more similar to those of the Homo sapiens of the Upper Paleolithic than to the Neanderthals of European Mousterian.

The stature of these Skhul men was similar to our own. Men ranged from 68 to 71 inches, whereas the Tabun woman was shorter, with a height of about 62½ inches. The bones of the limbs of the Skhul people were long and slender; femora were heavily pilastered, in contrast with the thinner Neanderthal forms. The bones of the arms, the radii and ulnae, were straighter and lacked the bowed shape typical in Neanderthal man. The vertebral column of Skhul men had a lumbar curve similar to that of Homo sapiens, whereas the shortness of the cervical region is a Neanderthal trait.

These details suggest a man quite different from both the typical Neanderthal of the Middle Paleolithic and the Homo sapiens of the Upper Paleolithic. He was able to stand very solidly on his feet, in almost the same erect position as modern man. Typical Neanderthal men of Europe had, as a whole, a more crouched posture, with their knees pushed slightly forward, their legs slightly bowed, and their vertebral column a more marked S shape, which pushed the heavy bones of the face forward. Their contemporaries of the Near East, though having many features in common with the Europeans, presented a few characteristics that are common in evolved Homo sapiens.

Skeletal remains from the same general period bearing more "sapiens" features than the extreme Neanderthals, have also been found in various places in Europe.[6] Some scholars believe that the "extreme Neanderthals," who have been found mainly in Europe, are the result of local evolution, whereas in western Asia other Neanderthaloid people evolved into Homo sapiens. Both in Europe and in the Near East, the number of individuals found in association with Mousterian industries is not yet sufficient for a full description of the common characteristics and the differences of the people of these two areas, but the available information seems to be quite consistent with the evidence of the material culture.

Western Europe in prehistoric times was a cul-de-sac where human bands arriving from the east had to halt at the shores of the Atlantic Ocean. The culture cycle there was conditioned by this geographical situation. The evolved Homo sapiens arrived in Europe with his blade industries quite abruptly, and thus the Mousterian culture of Neanderthal men came to an end.

The Near East had seen a richer variety of movements of human groups. We have already noted that early waves of blade cultures reached there a long time before these cultures pene-

[6] H. V. Vallois: JRAI, Vol. LXXXIV (1954), pp. 111–30; see also L'A, Vol. LIX (1956), pp. 555–60.

trated into Europe. Thereafter we find, in the Near East, that Mousterian industries possessed a higher percentage of blade-tools than the contemporary European cultures. Though Europe was part of the same general cultural area, it appears that its cultural patterns were more conservative because of its peripheral location and the consequent poverty of its contacts.

The first evolved Homo sapiens, the maker of the blade-tools, was not born in Europe. When he arrived there, he already possessed all his characteristic traits, and was markedly different from the more archaic Neanderthals. In the Near East, makers of blade industries similar to those of Homo sapiens had paid several visits in the course of the Middle Paleolithic. It is impossible to tell at present to what extent this brought about the mixture of two different races, but it certainly influenced the local evolution of material culture. In the light of available skeletal evidence, it seems that a Neanderthaloid people distinct from Homo sapiens evolved in the Near East without ever passing through a stage of extreme Neanderthal characteristics.

The makers of the Mousterian cultures in Europe and the Near East probably were near cousins, but different environments and different contacts shaped their respective evolutions in different ways.

In previous sections we have seen that in the Lower Paleolithic very large areas had similar cultures, but in the Middle Paleolithic there begin to be some signs of differentiation between the major regions of the large Eurasian Mousterian area. The whole area was still generally united by the same type of culture and also by similar traits in religion and ideology. But in Palestine and in surrounding countries various subtypes of material culture emerged, and each one maintained its own identity for long periods, despite its proximity to others. This shows that the external contacts of these groups must have been extremely poor. However, they started appearing, and succeeded in influencing the local cultures.

The evidence at our disposal—through material culture,

dating, burial customs, and the skeletal remains—help us to compose a general but still extremely fragmentary picture of the makers of the Mousterian culture.

We know that they were hunters of big game, that they lived in small bands and sheltered themselves in natural caves. They fueled large fireplaces with wood from nearby trees and in them they roasted their meat. In the place where they lived, or near by, they used to bury their deceased fellows. They developed rituals connected with the dead, and had their own imaginary world and their irrational beliefs. Physically, these men were already quite similar to some modern races, although some archaic traits still persisted; but they were as tall as we are, they could walk and stand just the way we do, and their hands were refined enough to produce excellent tools. Their language was probably developed enough to enable them to exchange thoughts and feelings.

In the Near East, from Middle Paleolithic times on, the population became quite large. Palestine alone has provided several hundred sites with Mousterian industries, and the far fewer sites provided by the much longer Lower Paleolithic suggest that the population increased greatly in the meanwhile. Between thirty and thirty-five thousand years ago, groups of new people more numerous than the groups which had brought in the very early blade culture, arrived in the area, and they carried with them the fully evolved blade industry. We do not know what happened then to the makers of the Mousterian culture. Their tradition continued into the early phases of the Upper Paleolithic, but very quickly decreased in importance, and after a short while the blade industries totally dominated the caves and the other suitable shelters. In all the archaeological sites of the period, Mousterian culture was covered by the levels of this new cultural tradition.

IV

The
Upper Paleolithic

THE NEW CULTURE

THE PROGRESSION of ice sheets and the cooling of the climate in the course of the Early Würm glaciation probably influenced the concentration of men in milder regions and abetted the relative isolation of human groups which found themselves in regions partially surrounded by ice sheets. Chains of mountains such as the Pyrenees, the Alps, the Caucasus, the Hindu Kush, and the Tien Shan had snow lines between three and five thousand feet lower than those of today, and they formed massive natural barriers. Inland seas, such as the Caspian and the Aral Sea, were fed by the snow and ice surrounding them and covered much larger areas than they do today. Some rivers then had beds almost as wide as lakes and formed impassable barriers. Since then, many mouths and deltas of rivers have advanced a considerable distance seaward as a consequence of the constant depositing of silt by the streams. Rivers such as the Tigris and Euphrates, the Indus and the Ganges, then met the sea many miles up from their present mouths. For these reasons the regions where both men and animals could live were more circumscribed than they are today. (On the other hand, there were also coastal regions that today are submerged in the seas, but on the whole, the outline of the land in these areas was much more sinuous and created a greater number of natural barriers.) The different environment met by man in each of these areas probably was an important factor in the incipient cultural differentiation I have described.

Though most prehistorians agree today that the blade industries originated in Asia, the exact area is not yet known. In the Near East, from their first occurrence they indicate the sudden start of traditions unknown to the Mousterian cultures. The short distinct waves of Upper Paleolithic cultural traits in the Near East during Early Pluvial C seem to have been merely pioneer precursors of a more massive flow of the same traits which reached the area later on.

Most of these Upper Paleolithic traditions appeared, both in Europe and in the Near East, in the late part of the major interstadial of the last glaciation, the Gottweig Interstadial. In this period of milder climate, a temporary but substantial shrinkage in the mountain glaciers had opened new highways to human groups and to their ideas. Traditions that had evolved outside Europe and the Near East during the first climax of the last ice age could then reach these areas in abundance.

The people of the new tradition are of a new physical type, with more refined features and with skeletons very similar to those of modern men. Their hands had unprecedented skill, and were able to make much finer and more delicate artifacts than those of Neanderthal and Neanderthaloid men.

Their elongated and elegant flint blades were the products of a new and highly sophisticated technique. The archaic hammering tool was replaced with a delicate punch that was struck with a mallet. If we can judge from the techniques of primitive peoples of our own time, the elongated blades with almost parallel sides were usually fashioned with a punch of antler, bone, or wood, the point of which could be accurately placed on precisely the required spot. Similar blades were still made less than one hundred years ago by American Indians. The work was usually done seated. The core was held between the feet of the tool-maker, or was bound between strips of wood, and the artisan was free to work with both hands.

The technical achievements of Upper Paleolithic men reveal an intelligence, a skill, and an imagination never recorded before. Indirectly they increased the food supply. "Light missiles tipped with penetrating points made from flint blades or polished bones must have enormously increased the productivity of the chase." [1]

These people have also left behind traces of the earliest man-built habitations. These were huts or tents set over an excavated floor or banked in by stones or small mounds of soil, and they seem to have been roofed over with animal skins supported by slanting poles, in the manner of American Indian wigwams.

But probably the most important achievements of Upper Paleolithic men are revealed by their unprecedented intellectual qualities. They appear to have been the earliest artistic-minded human beings. They had a marked aesthetic sense and used to perforate shells and carve ivory, and make of these materials beads, pendants, bracelets, and other personal ornaments. Coloring materials such as ocher were extensively used by them for painting their dead, and we can assume that living men also decorated their bodies in various ways. This novel concern for ornamenting their bodies has some very interesting psychological implications, an acute self-awareness, for one. Another is the effort to embellish one's own body to please and to attract other people or to prepare oneself for special occasions, with all

---

[1] V. G. Childe: *Prehistoric Migrations in Europe* (Oslo: Institutet for Sammenlignende Kulturforsking; 1950), p. 14.

the social development that such behavior implies. It is also quite probable that body adornment had at that time, as it has today, some connection with the need for attracting the other sex. Thus life was enriched with new values, as man emerged from the primeval mists of his childhood and started on the road to becoming the being we know.

From a few human figurines found in Europe and central Asia we learn that men clothed themselves at this time, and that fashion changed according to the requirements of climate and environment. We also learn that man decorated garments as well as his body.

As far as we now know, men had never before used their imagination and their powers of observation to the extent of creating art. These "sapiens" men were the earliest artists, in the full sense of the word. The lack of artistic objects in association with some Upper Paleolithic cultures may be due to many diverse factors. The different raw materials at the disposal of men in different environments has certainly had an effect upon both the production and the preservation of works of art. Wood was presumably the most important of all materials, and probably durable materials such as bone and ivory were substituted when wood was scarce or of poor quality. The use of different kinds of coloring materials must have greatly determined the quality of the preservation of paintings. Thus the lack of art in some regions does not necessarily mean that these regions did not have prehistoric artists. Most of the known Upper Paleolithic art is concentrated in Europe. Some of it is found in central Asia. In the Near East, artistic finds are very scanty. In fact, the only works of art in the Near East showing strong Paleolithic traditions are a few rock engravings, which will be described in a later chapter. The Mesolithic art of Palestine shows the presence of traditions which must go back to the Paleolithic (see page 159). Beads, pendants, and other body ornaments, in shell, bone, ivory, and stone, are present in the Near East, though they are not very abundant. Despite this uneven distribution, however, the makers of the blade industries possessed the mental ability to be artists.

In Europe they left in their caves paintings, carvings, and high reliefs which mark one of the highest peaks ever reached by art. They also created a mobiliary art—that is, small art objects, easily transportable—decorating objects for practical and magical purposes. They represented not only the creatures of the animal world upon which they depended for their livelihood, but also human figures and abstract signs that suggest a highly sophisticated symbolism. This art points to the growing self-awareness of man, to his sense of being an integral part of the living world.

These Upper Paleolithic men also created a feminine figurine apparently representing a goddess or a being of fertility, and probably involving a religious concept which Homo sapiens has retained ever since: a pregnant goddess or a mother-of-man (or mother-of-god) in whom he exalted the mystery of his own creation. After man had become aware of the enigma of the end of life through the phenomenon of death, his imagination was drawn to the riddle of the beginning of life. This indicates that he grasped the full dimension of time, and that he could think in the past tense, the most abstract one. He was now able to think in terms of present, future, and past. The psychological implications of the mother goddess are therefore of tremendous importance. They mark a new and considerable step in the evolution of the human mind. Here undeniably is a picture of a thinking man, of a man with intellectual as well as material achievements.

The cultures of the Upper Paleolithic spread over Europe and the Near East, and later reached as far east as China, and penetrated into India to the south and into Arabia and North Africa to the southwest. Probably, too, the Upper Paleolithic men were the earliest to reach the American continent.

In the Old World, evolution was beginning to accelerate and cultural patterns were becoming geographically more distinct. The large Eurasian area of the Mousterian witnessed, in the course of the Upper Paleolithic, the localization and increasing isolation of four major regions—western Europe, eastern Europe, the Near East, and central Asia. Africa probably was slightly affected by external influences coming mostly from Asia, across Palestine, but until the beginning of farming life, the development of Africa was to become increasingly separate from the rest of the world, and only the Nile Valley was to maintain relatively steady contact with the Near East.

In the Near East, a great deal of contact and intermingling took place between the new and the old traditions. Not only did early Blade cultures mingle with Mousterian during Early Pluvial C, but when advanced blade industries achieved predominance at the end of the Gottweig Interstadial, Mousterian traditions persisted to a small extent, and the gradual acculturation of some archaic groups seems to have continued after the first massive introduction of the new cultures. The sudden change in Europe probably indicates that events had been quite different there; in Africa, conversely, the slow evolution of earlier patterns shows that, though processes of acculturation actually took place, the archaic men were never totally replaced by new ones.

The powerful expansion of the new culture had as its main result the establishment of technologically more evolved areas in the regions influenced by it in Europe, in western and central Asia, and in parts of North Africa; the expansion also pushed to the periphery those people who maintained older traditions and thus had less economic strength and less powerful weapons. In the course of time acculturation spread, but even so, from this time onward major differences of culture in these peripheral areas developed. Gradually, human bands living in dead-end regions such as southern Africa, Arabia, southern India, and southeastern Asia became isolated, and the tempo of their evolution did not keep up with that of the more vigorous populations inhabiting the regions where, several thousand years later, food-producing economies were to open to mankind the gates of civilization.

THE BLADE INDUSTRIES

In its areas of distribution in Eurasia, the Upper Paleolithic started about 35,000 years ago and lasted between 20,000 and 25,000 years; the main process of localization, which is at the root of the cultural diversity of different regions, took place during this time. Despite this, all blade industries were characterized by some major similarities. The same flint-working technique remained dominant everywhere, so that very similar tools were produced in the various regions. Many of the specific tools even appear to have been produced in similar relative quantities. This fact probably indicates not only similar achievements in technology but also similar daily occupations and a similar way of life.

The principal flint tools of the Upper Paleolithic are pointed blades with a blunt side; end-scrapers, or blades having a terminal and usually rounded retouching; and burins, chisel-like tools made by delicately trimming the point of the artifact on the thin edge of the flake. Each one of these three major types of tool had a great number of variations, and probably each one of these had specific uses. It is believed that some of the blunt-backed blades served as spearheads and that others probably served for cutting various materials. We have only a very vague idea of the use of all the many varieties of "scrapers." They must have been tools of daily use, and among other things might have served for scraping and cleaning animal skins, for cutting hair, for stripping bark from wood, and for other similar work. The chisel-like burin is well adapted for fine work on wood, antler, bone, and soft stones. Some artifacts look like borers, drills, and other instruments which might have been used for various work on skins, wood, and other raw materials.

In its general lines, the classical western European sequence of the blade industries shows at first the development of two parallel traditions, called Aurignacian and Perigordian. These are followed by a culture called Solutrean and then by the Magda-

Upper Paleolithic end-scrapers from Site 1, Kadesh Barnea

lenian culture. All these have been named by French archaeologists after localities where these cultures were first excavated or studied.

The Near Eastern sequence of blade industries starts with the early, thin (and therefore briefly occupied) layers which appeared in the Middle Paleolithic. These, believed by some prehistorians to be the precursors of the Aurignacian culture, were first called "Pre-Aurignacian" at Yabrud, where they were first identified. A considerable lapse of time passed between the "Pre-Aurignacian" and the phase marking the transition from the Mousterian. This "Transitional" phase shows several divergent but probably contemporary patterns.

Upper Paleolithic steep-scrapers and
core-scraper from Site 1, Kadesh Barnea

The "Transitional" is followed by various subsequent phases of a culture showing several similarities to both Aurignacian and Perigordian of Europe. This culture has been frequently given the French name of Aurignacian, but the term has created some confusion, as the Near Eastern culture differs considerably from the typical Aurignacian cultures of Europe. I shall refer to it as "Ahmarian," a name taken from the type-site of Erq el-Ahmar, in the Judean Desert, where this culture is best represented. (Some years ago the term "Antelian" was proposed for this culture. The name was taken from Antelias, a site near Beirut, on the Lebanese coast. This site has never been fully studied, and we do not have precise knowledge of its material culture. It seems therefore more suitable to name this culture after the site where it is best represented.) The Ahmarian is roughly contemporary with the Aurignacian and Perigordian of Europe. It is followed by two other cultures, the Atlitian, named after the locality of Atlit, near Mount Carmel, and the Kebarian, named after the Kebara cave on Mount Carmel. They are roughly contemporary with the Solutrean and Magdalenian of western Europe, though they are very different from them.

The Upper Paleolithic sequence of material culture is known in the Near East from several archaeological excavations. Most of them are in Palestine or near by. The most important are the rock shelter of Erq el-Ahmar in the Judean Desert, the caves of El-Wad and Kebara at Mount Carmel, the caves of Jebel Qafze and Emire in Galilee, and two of the shelters at the Syrian site of Yabrud. In Lebanon, recent excavations at Ksar Akil have revealed the best stratified sequence of this period in the Near East. Over fifty feet of levels were found in this site, an indication that it remained uninterruptedly inhabited from the Transitional phase up to the end of the Ahmarian.[2] After it has been fully studied, a great deal more will be known about the evolution of the blade industries in the Near East.

[2] J. F. Ewing: BPAS, Vol. IX, No. 1 (1955), pp. 6–7.

As already explained, quantitative analysis of tool-types helps to determine the character of a flint industry and the stages of cultural change. In Near Eastern Middle Paleolithic industries, over 70 per cent of the tools and flakes were made with Mousterian (and Levalloisian) techniques. Some of these tools may have been fashioned on elongated flakes, or even on blades, though they still show the use of Mousterian methods of tool-making. In evolved levels of Mousterian some tools of the upper Paleolithic type were fashioned by means of methods typical of blade industries; these usually run lower than 15 per cent and never over 25 per cent of the industry. Between 5 and 15 per cent of the tools show no definable technique. At the beginning of the Upper Paleolithic the nature of the whole flint industry changed quite drastically, and the quantity of tools made by Mousterian techniques sharply decreased from 70 per cent to no more than 30 per cent of the total industry in the Transitional phase, and to no more than 15 per cent thereafter. Conversely, the tools made by the methods of the blade industries increased as sharply, immediately rising from a previous maximum of 25 per cent to 50 per cent of the industry, and to over 80 per cent of the industry after the Transitional phase.

The Transitional phase is known mainly from the caves of El-Wad and Emire, the rock shelter of Yabrud, and Ksar Akil.

Large retouched blades from Early Upper Paleolithic station near Kadesh Barnea

It was described by Dorothy Garrod [3] as being characterized by
the Emire point: a triangular flake with the bulbous end thinned
by clipping upward from the base of the flake. In recent diggings,
however, this implement was also found in layers belonging to
the late Mousterian, and seems to have been made for a longer
time than was previously believed. In Levels F and G at the
cave of El-Wad, considered by Garrod as typical levels of this
period, six of these tools were found among a group of more than
three thousand implements, thus constituting 0.2 per cent of
the total. The levels are characterized by the presence of a certain
number of flake-tools of Mousterian tradition such as side-
scrapers and points. Mousterian points formed 6.5 per cent of
the industry in Level G and 4.7 per cent in Level F.

One of the tools typical of this Transitional phase is a sort of
small knife made on a relatively large and usually pointed blade
and having a bowed cutting edge. This tool, called the Abri-Audi
knife, after a French type-site, is found in both Europe and the
Near East in late levels of Mousterian and in the earliest phases
of Upper Paleolithic. Another characteristic tool of the Transitional phase is a slightly curved point on a more elongated blade
continuously retouched on one side. This tool also is common
in both Europe and the Near East, being particularly abundant
in the earliest phases of Upper Paleolithic. This is called the
Châtelperron point, again after a French type-site. In the Near
East, it continues to be common up to the end of the Ahmarian
but gradually decreases in quantity.

The locality where the Ahmarian industry is best illustrated

[3] D. A. E. Garrod: JRAI, Vol. LXXXV (1955), pp. 1-2.

Emire points from Qafze, Level E (after Neuville)

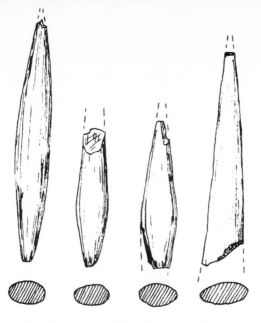

Bone points from Middle Ahmarian level at
Yabrud (Shelter II, Level 4, after Rust)

is the rock shelter of Erq el-Ahmar.[4] This culture is abundantly
represented in Palestine at El-Wad, Jebel Qafze, Kebara, and
elsewhere. It is found in Lebanon and Syria at Yabrud, Ksar Akil,
and Antelias, and quite similar material cultures occur also in
Anatolia, the Caucasus, and the Crimea, and thus it appears to
have spread widely all over the Near East and the surrounding
regions.

The most characteristic tools of this industry are two sharply
pointed blade-tools. The one is usually very thin, and one of its
sides has a continuous retouch. This is believed to have evolved
from the Châtelperron point, and was also given a French name,
the Gravette point. The second tool usually has slightly more
curved sides, and retouching is frequently found on both of
them. Sometimes the bulbous end also is retouched, and the
result is a very delicate and elegant tool, probably representing a
sort of spearhead. This tool is known by the French name of
Font-Yves point.

Burins became very abundant during the Ahmarian period.

[4] R. Neuville: Archives IPH, Vol. XXIV (1951), pp. 57-8.

Many of them are of the types called prismatic burins and angle burins. Scrapers have a rich variety of forms. Scrapers on thick blades (steep scrapers) are rather numerous; others are end-scrapers on thinner blades or finely retouched, rounded scrapers on small flakes.

These tools distinguish the Ahmarian culture even when it is found at the surface and not in a stratified site. They are products of the Ahmarian culture almost exclusively, and markedly diminished in quantity with its end, disappearing shortly thereafter.

Both the Atlitian and the Kebarian are known chiefly from their type-sites, El-Wad and Kebara. Several surface stations at Mount Carmel and in the immediate vicinity seem also to derive from these two phases, but they have not yet been properly excavated.

Other stations in the same area and more to the south, along the Sharon coast, show several other patterns of material culture which probably were roughly contemporary with the Atlitian and Kebarian levels of Mount Carmel.

These periods can be regarded as contemporary with the Solutrean and Magdalenian of France, and some parallel changes in material culture took place in both areas. One of them was the increased percentage of lamelles, or small blades, and other small tools.

The Atlitian is very different from the phases previously described. What characterizes it is the wide use of tabular flint as raw material. This material, very common at Mount Carmel, consists of thin layers of flint sometimes less than a quarter of an inch thick which have been bared on the surface because the softer limestone and chalk that once surrounded them has been washed away by rain and other natural forces. This flint was broken up on the spot, and tools could be made from it without any need to flake pieces out of larger cores. The use of this kind of flint is practically limited to burins and steep scrapers, which are in fact the most abundant tools in these assemblages. This obviously gives the Atlitian a very singular character. An industry with some similarities to the Atlitian, but not identical with it, was found at El-Khiam, in the Judean Desert.[5]

The following stage, the Kebarian, begins to show transitional patterns, and some Mesolithic features begin to appear in quantity amid the Upper Paleolithic tradition. Thus there is an abundance of the Microlithic tools, or very small flint implements, which characterized the Middle Stone age. As described by F. Turville-Petre, the British archaeologist who excavated the cave of Kebara and first recognized this culture, "Microliths greatly predominate over normal-sized implements in this industry, and the characteristic Microlithic form is a much elongated triangle retouched along the back and at the top." [6] Small blades, with retouched backs, obliquely truncated, predominate. A certain quantity of middle-sized implements occurs, including end-scrapers, steep scrapers, and some angle, bec-de-flûte, and prismatic burins.

This period, which immediately precedes the flourishing of the Mesolithic "Natufian" culture, shows increasing cultural differentiation. Sites which probably were roughly contemporary with one another and are located only a few miles away from one another have their own distinctive traits. Most of these sites are concentrated along the Mediterranean coast of Israel, at Tsofit, Kfar Vitkin, Jaffa, Askalon, Bat Yam, and Umm Khalid.

[5] J. Perrot in Neuville: op. cit.
[6] F. Turville-Petre: JRAI, Vol. LXII (1932), pp. 271–7.

Atlitian flint burins from El-Wad, Level C (after Garrod)

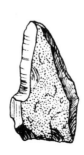

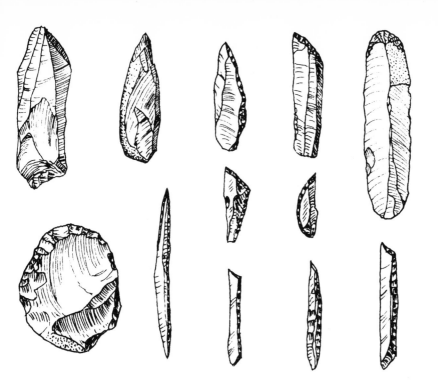

Kebarian flint implements (after Turville-Petre)

Very large sites occur amid recently formed dunes overlying red sands. During this period local variations developed in the interior of the country; the "Nebekian" culture of Yabrud is probably a variant of the Kebarian, and so are some sites on the Jordanian Plateau.[7]

At all these various sites Paleolithic tradition was mixed with the new tradition of the Middle Stone Age, from which the Natufian culture was subsequently to emerge.

With the start of the Atlitian, the long, slow process of cultural differentiation had definitely reached a culmination. The Ahmarian of the Near East and the Aurignacian of Europe were still related cultures, but when they came to an end, cultural patterns had become largely localized, with regional traits. The enormous Eurasian area, where cultures had so homogeneously

[7] J. d'A. Waechter and V. M. Seton-Williams: JPOS, Vol. XVIII (1938); see also D. V. W. Kirkbride: *Man*, Vol. LVIII (1958), pp. 55 ff.

evolved for hundreds of millennia, could not be identified any longer. Further localization of cultures cut up into progressively smaller areas the four major regions that could be distinguished at the beginning of the Upper Paleolithic: western Europe, eastern Europe, the Near East, and central Asia.

Increasing localization was accompanied by faster cultural change. The Lower Paleolithic had lasted hundreds of thousands of years, the Middle Paleolithic about 40,000 years, the Upper Paleolithic 25,000 to 20,000 years. Within this last period, the subdivision into different cultures is sharper and much more evident than ever before. The Ahmarian probably lasted between 12,000 and 14,000 years, the Atlitian between 3,000 and 4,000 years. All the different patterns of material culture that are found in the Kebarian period probably did not exist for a total of more than 2,000 or 3,000 years. Periods had become increasingly shorter, because cultural evolution had become faster and faster.

The Upper Paleolithic in western Europe had been a time of artistic glory. Cave paintings and art objects reveal a marvelous world and a profound artistic and aesthetic sense. Later I shall discuss some desert art from the Near East. Nevertheless, none of the types of art found in the Dordogne has been discovered so far in this region. In Europe, the Upper Paleolithic, mainly in its later phase, possessed a highly skilled bone industry in addition to its flint industry; but in Near Eastern caves bone tools are extremely rare.

The end of the Paleolithic has different meanings in the Near East and in Europe. In Europe, the Magdalenian marked the end of a period of a very rich material culture and of a great art cycle; it was followed by one of the darkest periods in the history and prehistory of Europe, the Mesolithic, which frequently had a degenerate and impoverished material culture. In contrast with this, in the Near East, and in Palestine in particular, nothing has yet been found from Paleolithic times which might equal the richness of expression and the creativity of Mesolithic times. Then the extremely rich variety of flint tools included, for the first time in human history, sickle blades, picks, and other significant tools belonging to incipient agriculture. A bone industry was developing, and grindstones, pestles, and mortars were being produced. Natufian art and the variety of beads and pendants made this complex very different from all other Mesolithic complexes. The end of the Paleolithic seems to mark in this area the start of a new rhythm of life, the turning point of man toward civilization.

HABITAT AND THE HUMAN UNIT

At all times man's choice of habitat has been conditioned by the availability of natural resources. Places lacking fresh water could never be inhabited for long. In prehistoric times the quest for food probably was the main motive for moving about or stopping in one place. Localities in which game or edible plants were abundant obviously must have attracted human beings more than desert regions. Men likewise needed raw materials for their daily activities. Wood was required not only for making tools, weapons, and other objects of daily use, but also for fires, which were probably needed for defense against wild animals as well as for cooking and for warmth. Variations in the natural environment certainly must have influenced the degree of localization of the human unit.

Paleolithic men lived in two kinds of sites: in caves and shelters, where they found natural cover from rain, wind, sun, and other inclemencies of nature, and in open-air camp sites. Because of the special convenience of caves and shelters, men returned to them again and again, whereas camp sites generally were inhabited for shorter or less frequent periods. Obviously, unless an open site was specially suitable, it was unlikely that many different groups would settle at it.

These two different patterns of habitation were customary throughout the world for people living in a hunting and gathering economy. To the archaeologist both are interesting, but each for different reasons: caves and rock shelters accumulate deep layers of residue which are of great help in studying the evolution of material culture and its chronology. The open-air camp site, when it is closely studied, is frequently better suited to isolating single periods and for understanding a particular way of life.

In the Near East, especially in Palestine, caves with very deep man-made deposits are usually found in fertile or semi-arid regions; the caves of the truly arid regions have revealed, so far, much thinner deposits. The arid regions have yielded a great many Paleolithic open-air sites which contained prehistoric remains, but most of them suggest only occasional and temporary use by nomadic and semi-nomadic bands.

It is not yet clear to what extent the Quaternary climatic changes observable in the fertile regions affected the Near Eastern deserts; but in Palestine, the farther north we go, the more clearly are pluvial and interpluvial episodes marked by differences of sedimentation. In the Negev and in Sinai, climatic changes seem to have left less conspicuous traces than in the northern regions.

Some sites, particularly the caves of the fertile regions, leave the impression of having been inhabited for very prolonged periods. Homogeneous layers are sometimes several yards thick, and we can obtain a vague idea of the period of time that this must represent when we count the thousands of tools that were left in these layers by the prehistoric inhabitants, and when we try to estimate, also in a vague way, the amount of time needed for other debris to accumulate to that depth.

In some caves it has been possible to distinguish rather thin homogeneous levels. A good example is Yabrud, where the German archaeologist Alfred Rust was able to differentiate twenty-five levels of habitation in one of the shelters. The thinnest levels were one or two feet thick, and this depth is unlikely to indicate a period of settlement of less than several years.

Where various distinctive, isolated cultural patterns exist

side by side in different archaeological levels belonging to the same period, an extremely significant conclusion must be drawn. If these layers are homogeneous, and if each represents a rather long period of settlement, we can conclude that the same human group, or the same type of human group, had the habit of living in this cave, or at least of constantly coming back to it, while other caves in the vicinity were simultaneously inhabited by groups with a different material culture. This, in turn, would imply property rights in the cave or shelter to a certain degree, an institution that seems to have existed not only in Palestine but in all the regions where different patterns of material culture coexisted and are found in rather thick levels indicating a long time span.

The idea of cave ownership seems to have arisen very early in the Paleolithic. In the middle of the last interpluvial, at Yabrud, Yabrudian culture (or Late Tabunian) persisted for a very long time, while in the cave of Umm Qatafa and in the upper Jordan Valley, Bifacial culture was uninterrupted. In Early Pluvial C, the "Pre-Aurignacian" blade industry is not found in every excavation. At Yabrud two distinct main levels of it are found, dating from a time when Mousterian and other cultures were prospering not far away. We have seen that, in Middle Paleolithic times, various types of Mousterian could evolve side by side though each one kept its own peculiarities. Again, in the late Upper Paleolithic, when various patterns of culture developed near one another, the idea of cave ownership is even more evident. In the desert regions, thickly stratified sites are very rare and seem to be found only in the immediate vicinity of the most important water sources. The desert regions have yielded, however, very many camp sites, and since they have not been disturbed by agriculture, or by the growth of vegetation, or by later human settlements, some of them have been preserved extremely well, and reveal a great deal about early man.

In the Upper Paleolithic open-air sites of the Negev, Sinai, and the Jordanian Plateau, small groups of circles of stones are sometimes found. These outline the ground plan of habitations once built there. These "circles" of rough stones are irregular, oval or round, and usually vary in diameter between twelve and twenty feet. There are not enough stones to suppose that they originally formed walls. It seems rather that they held down the edges of huts or tents made of animal skins or some other perishable material. Probably these huts were supported by wooden poles which were not preserved. These stone circles have been found in isolation, and in small groups of two or three, and in one case five.[8] They suggest how these very early hamlets must have looked: a few small huts or a single one, each unlikely to have sheltered more than a family unit. These sites are frequently found on the surface of the ground, and the circles of stones are generally surrounded by large quantities of flint artifacts. In some instances a few large stones are found standing upright, surrounded by a concentration of flint flakes and other work debris. These upright stones probably served prehistoric artisans as anvils.

These sites are found in places where permanent settlements were never established, and they do not seem to have been disturbed by later nomadic camps, as no later flints or shards occur in the immediate vicinity. They are generally located in small side wadis, near the tops of hills, but in spots well protected from the wind. It is very difficult to estimate how long any of these camp sites were occupied, but they give the impression of having been used for relatively short periods. The toolmakers and hunters who inhabited them appear to have lived in rather small groups, each usually composed of two or three secondary groups of restricted size, and it is not unlikely that each camping unit was some sort of extended family.

The only excavations performed in the Near East at camp sites of this kind are those of two British archaeologists, John d'Arcy Waechter and Veronica M. Seton-Williams, in Wadi

---

[8] See BSPF, Vol. LV, Nos. 3–4 (1958), pp. 209–12.

Dhobai, in eastern Jordan. The stone circles here appear to have been associated with two different industries [9]—once in a late phase of the Upper Paleolithic, probably contemporary with the Kebarian of Mount Carmel, and then in Early Neolithic times.

In 1956, four Paleolithic sites with stone circles were found on the Sinai Peninsula.[1] Three of them yielded Ahmarian tools, while one was associated with a material culture still possessing very strong Mousterian traditions and probably belonging to the Transitional period. At one of the sites four circles were found which varied in size between about twelve and twenty feet in diameter; the fifth was much larger, elongated, its long diameter reaching almost thirty-two feet. Two other sites had three circles each, whereas one had only two. These sites give us a general idea of the numerical size of the human groups which inhabited them. In fact, it is rather unlikely that the normal-sized circles could have sheltered more than two or three adults. Similar camp sites are known in other regions of the Eurasian area of the blade industries. Most of them were found in the southern steppes and tundra of the Soviet Union.

At Gagarino, in the Ukraine, S. N. Zamyatnin found the foundations of a hut measuring some fifteen by eighteen feet. Large stones and mammoth tusks were concentrated near the margins of the floor of the hut.[2] A similar collection of objects was discovered in the locality of Kostenki below the remains of a larger building.[3] A very important site at Malta, in the Siberian province of Irkutsk, has yielded other similar hut floors,[4] and other camp sites of this kind were studied by the archaeologist V. A. Gorodtsov.[5] The form of these huts varies slightly from site to site, but the size remains approximately the same. At Buryet, in

---

[9] Waechter and Seton-Williams: op. cit.
[1] BSPF, Vol. LV, Nos. 3–4 (1958), pp. 209–12.
[2] S. N. Zamyatnin: *La station Aurignacienne de Gagarino* (Moscow; 1934).
[3] P. P. Efimenko: *Pervobytnoe Obshchestu* (Leningrad, 1938), p. 383.
[4] M. M. Gerosimov: *Malta, Paleolithic Camping-Site* (Irkutsk; 1931).
[5] See summary in A. Mongait: *Archaeology in the U.S.S.R.* (Moscow; 1959), Ch. II; see also V. G. Childe: *Antiquity*, No. 93 (1950), pp. 4–11.

the same region as Malta, four such hut floors were found in the same camping ground. There again stones and mammoth bones were piled at the edge of the floor. As suggested by A. P. Okladnikov, it seems that these bones and stones helped to hold down the edges of the roof.

Another kind of Upper Paleolithic building was found in the Soviet Union at Pushkari, Kostenki, Timonovka, and elsewhere. These were long communal houses, extending from forty to sixty feet in length and about thirteen to sixteen feet in width. They generally have a line of postholes in the middle, following the long diameters. At Kostenki (Level IV), two such buildings were found in the vicinity of each other, whereas at Timonovka there is a very complex site containing at least seven such long communal buildings. This new type of habitation, which implies a different kind of social organization, seems to have evolved in the late phases of the Upper Paleolithic and apparently illustrates a local cultural pattern that never reached the Near East.

Very few traces of hut floors have been discovered in Europe so far, but some rare remains in France and Germany indicate that similar habitations existed there in Upper Paleolithic times.[6]

Furthermore, Upper Paleolithic cave paintings in western Europe show a great number of schematic signs, usually called tectiforms, believed to be pictures of huts. Franco-Cantabric art has yielded, up to now, only one naturalistic picture of a hut. It is in the cave of La Mouthe, in France, and shows a small hut, the length of which is only slightly greater than its height. It seems to be an oval hut with a roof supported by two poles.

Throughout the vast spread of the Blade culture, whatever other variations there were, the pattern of settlement, as illustrated by both the caves and the camp sites, seems to have been very similar. In the Near East, both caves and round and oval huts continued to be used as habitations in Mesolithic times. Later in

[6] See *Mannus*, Vol. XIII, p. 76 (Long-Mannersdorf); Archives IPH, Vol. X (1932) (Fourneau du Diable); see also A. Rust: *Hammaburg*, Vol. I (1948), pp. 34–6.

that period the hamlets of huts became larger and evolved into the earliest permanent settlements in the world.

WHAT HAPPENED AT THE END OF THE PALEOLITHIC AGE?—A SUMMARY

We have now surveyed the three periods of the Paleolithic, and we have seen how culture became increasingly complex and sophisticated and how new cultural traits were added to man's heritage in the course of time. "Primitive" men at the end of the Paleolithic were the product of an evolution which had taken 98 per cent of the time mankind has been in existence.

In the Near East, the sequence of material culture started with the Pebble culture, artifacts of which are found throughout large parts of southern Asia and Africa. Two roughly contemporary cultures evolved thereafter, the Bifacial (or Acheulean), found throughout southwestern Asia, Europe, and Africa, and the Tabunian (or Tayacian), which is found mainly in Europe and the Near East. Later, various types of Mousterian culture developed in the Near East, Europe, and Africa. Some secondary patterns seem to have developed separately in various regions, but the preponderance of Mousterian artifacts points to the similarity of traditions in large parts of the Old World. Later still, various kinds of material culture, in themselves uniform and broadly distributed, coexisted with other kinds near by without change.

These cultures retained their distinctive traditions for tens of thousands of years even while adjacent to one another, a fact that suggests extremely poor social relations between human groups. It is hard nowadays to imagine different peoples living in the same area for perhaps several hundred generations without mingling. The social unit must have fiercely resisted external contacts with unaffiliated groups. On the other hand, it seems likely that there were some affiliations and contacts among peoples whose material remains were scattered over considerable distances.

This situation changed during Upper Paleolithic times, when there was a slow regional unification of patterns. In Europe, the abrupt division between Aurignacian and Perigordian cultural patterns would indicate that there the old social customs persisted to some extent, as these two cultures succeeded at least in safeguarding their own autonomy. In the Near East, although there were some slight variations, the Ahmarian culture, which took over the whole area, seems to have been predominant.

Toward the end of the Upper Paleolithic, localization increased. The Atlitian and Kebarian cultures were restricted to small areas. A similar process occurred at the same time in Europe and in other regions. Cultural localization indicates the development of much richer interrelationships within limited areas.

This critical period, which marked the turning point toward regional cultural differentiation, was also a time of internal cultural consolidation. Large regions were more and more subdivided into smaller cultural areas, but within these smaller areas material culture became more homogeneous than before.

Such phenomena as the almost identical tools and the similar quantitative ratios of different types of Mousterian tools found in Europe, in the Near East, and elsewhere, and the extreme representational similarity of the early Upper Paleolithic statuettes of a mother goddess in central Asia, eastern Europe, and western Europe, were no longer to be observed. From the end of the Paleolithic until the present, the world has never seen such widespread cultural unity. The end of Paleolithic times was one of those moments of accelerated cultural change which we call revolutions. This revolution not only resulted in new material cultures, new economic activities, new types of human units, but, most important of all, also produced new methods of interrelation and new kinds of social organization. It made possible the development of larger human groups and the establishment of permanent contacts between different units from the same area, thus opening new horizons for cultural intercourse and eventually changing drastically the rhythm of cultural evolution.

The way of life led by lonely Paleolithic groups through many obscure millennia was ended, and forever. Life had become easier. New technological devices had released men from their daily struggle for nourishment and survival, as well as from many of their superstitions and fears. And, of course, as this happened they discarded many of their ancient traditions related to outmoded activities. It was actually a time of excessive maturity and of overrefinement of a culture, and to this condition men could and did react in different ways.

In Mesolithic times, one of the most important occupations in most regions was fishing. Obviously, fishing was possible only where water was abundant, and this is precisely where the Mesolithic revolution usually started, in both Europe and the Near East. It spread from the shores, but variations in the cultural patterns of different ecological areas became sharper and more defined. Whereas fertile regions offered new economic opportunities, arid zones could provide little but game. Cultural diffusion took place through both migration and acculturation (the grafting of one culture upon another), but in the general process, some groups which maintained the archaic Paleolithic way of life were pushed out to the margins of fertile regions. Hunting and gathering bands penetrated deep into lands which did not at that time attract the makers of Mesolithic culture. In deserts, within large forests, amid chains of mountains, and in other unhospitable regions, bands of hunters formed new small peripheral groups; among them the Paleolithic persisted while elsewhere men were entering a new age.

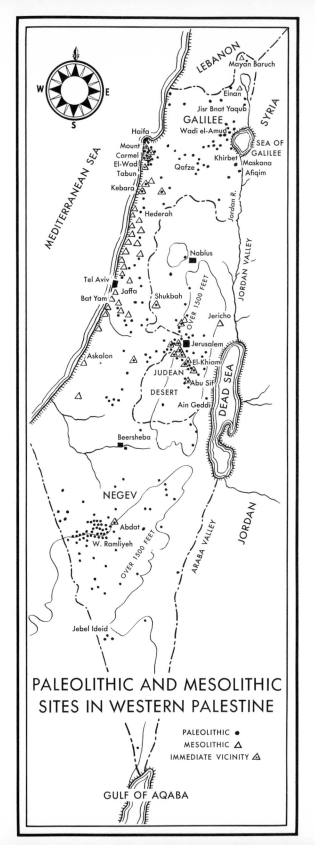

PALEOLITHIC AND MESOLITHIC
SITES IN WESTERN PALESTINE

PALEOLITHIC •
MESOLITHIC △
IMMEDIATE VICINITY △

PART·THREE

THE
TRANSITIONAL
CULTURES

I

The Mesolithic Interlude

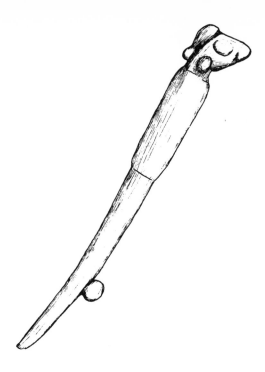

THE NEW AGE

WE DO NOT KNOW the precise causes of the Mesolithic revolution, though we can safely guess that major discoveries in technology and major changes in economics and ideology must have been at the root of it. In every area where it took place, it destroyed the Paleolithic way of life and its material and spiritual expressions. Men started to use new devices to make their traditional occupations easier, and discovered entirely new economic techniques.

At the beginning of the Mesolithic, men were able to reach some offshore islands, an indication that some sort of primitive boats were being made and that seafaring had begun. Islands off the Atlantic coast of France, off Sicily, in Scandinavia, and elsewhere were reached by men for the first time. New human groups came to the British Isles from the Continent, bringing with them their own exotic techniques. Major sea barriers, such as the Straits of Gibraltar, which separate Africa from Europe, and the Red Sea, which separates the Arabian Peninsula from East Africa, no longer put serious limitations on human movements.

Many other fields of technology developed spectacularly and completely changed the life of men. The making of strong and reliable ropes probably enabled people to climb trees and rocks more easily, to make baskets and other objects convenient for transporting materials, to suspend objects and food, to make nets and traps, and probably also to allow early attempts at weaving.

In the Near East, the earliest evidence of basketry is the imprints of baskets left on earth floors at Jericho shortly after the end of the Mesolithic; [1] but by then these occupations were highly developed, and the sophisticated products implied a tradition already old. In other regions, such as Spain, the earliest evidence of basketry is provided by rock pictures of Mesolithic or retarded Paleolithic tradition.[2] Evidence of fish nets is provided chiefly by numerous Mesolithic carvings on pebbles and by rock pictures found all over Eurasia and in North Africa, and by the presence of fish-net sinkers in Mesolithic sites.

The two most important discoveries perfected in Mesolithic times are a new and very powerful weapon, the bow, and a revolutionary device for hunting and fishing, the trap. Both seem to have already existed at the end of the Paleolithic, but new methods of spinning and basket making probably improved them a great deal at the beginning of the Mesolithic.

The bow is the earliest instrument we know of in which mechanical power was used, the mechanical power being that of the taut rope when released. (Upper Paleolithic men had already used a war and hunting machine, the spear thrower. This simply helped the arm in throwing the weapon, but it did not develop true mechanical power of its own.) The advance the bow rep-

---

[1] K. Kenyon: *Digging Up Jericho* (London: Benn; 1957), pp. 114–15, Pls. 12–13.
[2] BSPF, Vol. LVII, Nos. 11–12 (1960), pp. 696–7.

resents, and the superiority it gives its user over the wielder of the archaic Paleolithic spear, are comparable to the superiority of the gun over a medieval crossbow. Whereas only a single spear, or at best a small number, could be carried by a skilled hunter or warrior, a much greater number of arrows could be carried. They were lighter and easier to handle, and had a tremendous effective range compared with that of the heavy hand-thrown spear. The bow and its string were made of organic materials, and traces of them will probably never be found, but Mesolithic sites yield large numbers of small triangular, pointed microliths which seem to have been the earliest arrowheads produced in large quantities. Previously, in North Africa, a Paleolithic culture called Aterian included a certain quantity of tanged implements believed to be the heads of arrows or of light spears. Small numbers of other kinds of tanged points appear in Europe and in the Near East in late Upper Paleolithic levels. In Spain and North Africa, the earliest representations of bows in rock pictures date from the Mesolithic.

The trap, used for fishing and hunting, is the first device we know of that could operate while man was not present. Traps can be set and left alone, and the trapper can come back at his leisure to collect the food his device has caught.

The earliest traps appear to have been of different kinds in the various regions in which they were invented. In the Near East and North Africa, a very early type depicted in the rock pictures is a leg trap used for antelopes, deer, and other game of medium size. Throughout Europe, Mesolithic art portrays various types of fish traps. Both the bow and the trap imply sophisticated and highly refined abstract thought. They are the earliest "machines" men ever created, and they show the extent of cultural development.

This kind of invention must have radically changed man's values. Life was becoming easier. Men were largely relieved of their daily struggle for survival and nourishment, and probably this affected many of their values and beliefs. Most Paleolithic rites and religious practices were quickly abandoned by the sophisticated people of the Mesolithic age, and in the various regions of the Mesolithic revolution, human beings tried to replace them with new ethical and aesthetic values shaped by their own ecological environment, by their experience, and by the different ways in which the separate human groups had evolved. These changes are best illustrated by the evolution of the figurative arts.

The growing importance of fishing as one of the principal economic activities led to the concentration of human communities around lakes and marshes and along rivers and the seashore. Fishing offered men a handy and practically inexhaustible source of food, and induced some groups to settle down in permanent hamlets. This, in turn, fostered more constant communications between regions and the cultural unification of small areas.

The easing of life, the possibility of settling down in one place and ending the continual and tiring pursuit of game, and the abandonment of traditional values and concepts, created a cultural vacuum for mankind which offered many choices, many possible directions; and, indeed, in each small region the Mesolithic evolved in a different way.

In Palestine and along the Mediterranean coast of the Levant, the prevailing Mesolithic culture is named Natufian, after its type-site in Wadi en-Natuf, the cave of Shukbah.[3] The Natufian people developed fishing and began the domestication of animals; they made the earliest attempts at agriculture and trade and sped up greatly the rhythm of evolution in their region. The Natufians developed a new and sophisticated religion, a unique realistic art, and a refined material culture, and they founded the earliest-known permanent settlements in the world.

In Europe, Mesolithic cultures evolved in regional patterns; men usually produced rather degenerate flint artifacts and led for long millennia a less dynamic life than their Palestinian fellows. The intellectual grandeur attained in Europe by Upper Paleolithic men, attested to by their marvelous naturalistic art and its

[3] D. A. E. Garrod: PPS, 1928, pp. 1–20; JRAI, Vol. LXII (1932), pp. 257–69.

ideological and religious implications, was replaced by a "beat" abstract and schematic art. Some European communities specialized in fishing and in collecting shellfish; others mainly concentrated on trapping; still others seem to have made initial attempts at animal husbandry. These specializations further contributed to cultural differentiation.

The Mesolithic is an age of transition between two fundamental types of economic organization. It stands between food-gathering and food-producing economies. In this age men learned how to grow and store food, and the beginning of the following period, the Neolithic, or New Stone Age, saw the earliest farming communities, and animal husbandry, agriculture, and trade had already become a part of daily life.

Most of the new Mesolithic artifacts were made of organic material, such as bone, wood, skin, and fibers, and we learn about them mainly from the figurative art of Mesolithic man. The artifacts found in their camps and caves consist chiefly of the same durable materials common in the Paleolithic—stone, bone, shells, and antler.

The main characteristic which enables us to distinguish Mesolithic cultures wherever they are found is the abundance of very small flint tools, or microliths. Usually these are small blades, pointed or with parallel edges, and various types of small tools forming triangles, trapezoids, rectangles, and so forth, called geometric microliths. Another characteristic object is the microburin, a very small blade truncated on a retouched notch. This truncation makes a sharp angle with the notch, thus producing a small flat point. Some authors, however, believe that the microburin was not a tool, but simply the rejected fragment of a blade after a geometric microlith was made from it.

All these very minute implements were parts of composite tools whose shafts were made of wood, bone, antler, and other materials. In many cases, several of these microliths were used for the same tool. Thus harpoons could be made with many barbs, sickles could be as long and as fine as one wished and easily shaped as desired, knives could have elongated composite blades, and such sophisticated tools as toothed saws could be made for cutting wood and other materials. These tools obviously imply the ability to fit together various materials solidly and firmly. For this purpose bitumen, vegetable resins, plant fibers, wool, and other adhesives and bindings must have come into extensive use.

The fact that some Mesolithic flint implements do not appear as refined as Upper Paleolithic tools does not indicate a technological regression; men had found other and easier ways to give the tools the precise form needed. The small microlithic splinters were relatively easy to fit into a holder, and therefore precision of form frequently became of secondary importance.

The transition between the Paleolithic and Mesolithic ages took place at different times in various parts of the world. In the Near East, it seems to have come about earlier than anywhere else, between 14,000 and 12,000 years ago. In some regions of Europe and North Africa, the transition occurred between 12,000 and 7,000 years ago. In parts of the Near Eastern arid zones, there was a different cultural evolution and Mesolithic artifacts are not found there. Instead, various degenerate patterns of the Paleolithic continued to evolve there in their own way, sometimes into a decadent Paleolithic tradition which archaeologists call "Epi-Paleolithic." Some of these late hunters of the desert were outstanding artists, and the rock pictures they left behind are the most important record of their culture.

The end of the Mesolithic and the transition to the Neolithic also took place at different times in various parts of the world. Parts of the Near East, particularly parts of Palestine, seem to have been the earliest places in the world at which this transition took place. In the Jordan Valley this happened about 9,500 years ago.[4]

---

[4] A radiocarbon dating of Late Natufian, at Jericho, is 7800 ± 210 B.C. A level of evolved Early Neolithic at the same site was dated about 6550 B.C. At Beida, in eastern Jordan, one of the lower levels of a pre-pottery Neolithic village excavated by Diana Kirkbride provided a radiocarbon dating of 6830 ± 200 B.C.

When Palestine entered the new age, the last pluvial was approaching its end. In southwestern Asia the snow lines on the principal mountain chains—the Zagros, the Caucasus, and the Taurus—slowly began to rise, and the ice generally retreated to the highest peaks. The rivers flowing from high mountain ranges were abundantly fed by melting snow and ice. Various smaller pluvial episodes continued to take place. The levels of rivers, lakes, and seas underwent several minor fluctuations, but on the whole the climate was becoming warmer, approaching that of modern times.

In Palestine the Jordan Valley began getting drier, and in the course of time the "Lisan" lake there became narrower and finally only the Dead Sea and the Jordan River remained. We do not know exactly when the present ecological situation was attained in the Jordan Valley, but in Egypt a large lake occupying the Faiyum depression had various late fluctuations and reached its present state only in the course of the third millennium B.C.[5]

The environment in which Mesolithic cultures evolved, both in the Near East and in Europe, was damp, and Mesolithic sites are usually found in the vicinity of rivers, lakes, and marshes. The land was partly covered with tall trees, and good wood was abundantly available for tools and weapons, for fire, and for buildings of various sorts.

The Mesolithic revolution appears to have taken place rather abruptly; strangely enough, its earliest occurrence—in the Near East, Europe, and North Africa—does not seem to have been the fruit of foreign influence, as some local Paleolithic traditions persisted and as each of the innovations was well suited to the local ecology. In most places it appears as the result of a local cultural process. Contemporary Epi-Paleolithic cultures and Epi-Paleolithic art developed in various parts of the Near East, Europe, and North Africa very uniformly and probably quite independently.

[5] G. Caton-Thompson and E. W. Gardner: *The Desert Fayum* (London: Royal Anthropological Institute; 1934), pp. 14 ff.

THE NATUFIAN CULTURE

I have already described the increase of cultural localization in the Paleolithic; by Mesolithic times large cultural areas can no longer be identified. Various patterns of Mesolithic culture were found in the Near East. A microlithic culture, called Zarzian, which was in some ways similar to that found in Palestine, was discovered in northern Iraq, at Shanidar (Zawi-Chemi).[6] Another similar Mesolithic culture was found near the shores of the Caspian Sea, at Belt Cave.[7] In all southwestern Asia, western Palestine is the place where the greatest concentration of Mesolithic sites has been found. They seem to represent various types of microlithic industries; the one yielding the most abundant finds, and the best studied, is the Natufian culture.

The Natufian and the other microlithic cultures of Palestine are concentrated mainly in the central coastal plain and in the Judean Hills. Of about seventy Mesolithic sites found in Palestine, over forty are in the Mediterranean coastal plain, and fifteen in Wadi Kharaitun and other places in the vicinity of Jerusalem. In the Jordan Valley, two very important, but isolated, sites are at Jericho, not far from the shores of the Dead Sea, and at Einan, in the Hula Valley.

North of Palestine, the principal site with a Natufian-like industry is Yabrud, but several other Mesolithic sites have been identified on the Lebanon coast, though very little is known about them.[8] South of Palestine, Natufian-like industries have been found at a few sites on the Mediterranean coastal plain of

[6] R. S. Solecki: "Shanidar Cave, a Palaeolithic Site in Northern Iraq," in Annual Report of the Smithsonian Institution, 1954, pp. 389–425.
[7] Carleton S. Coon: *The Seven Caves* (New York: Alfred A. Knopf; 1957), pp. 128 ff.
[8] H. Fleisch: BSPF, Vol. LI, Nos. 11–12 (1954), pp. 564–8; *Quaternaria*, Vol. III (1956), pp. 101–22.

Sinai.[9] In Egypt, the site of Helouan, in the immediate vicinity of the first broadening of the Nile Valley into the delta, has a microlithic industry very similar to the Natufian of Palestine.[1]

In recent years, several attempts were made to relate the Natufian to other microlithic industries in Europe, Asia, and Africa. Sometimes, in fact, the Natufians made tools almost identical with those of a Mesolithic culture of North Africa called Capsian and with those of the Azilio-Tardenoisian Mesolithic cultures of central and eastern Europe. Despite the similarity of some tools and objects, however, the material cultures as a whole are different, and indicate that all these microlithic industries independently developed local regional patterns, although in some traits they had strong resemblances.

The uniqueness of the Natufians lies in their rapid strides toward food producing and toward the establishment of permanent settlements at a very early date. Most of the other Mesolithic cultures evolved in similar directions, but not always at the same time, or with the same rhythm, or by the same means. And in each case the final results were different.

A very early example of Mesolithic on the southern shores of the Caspian Sea seems not much later than the Natufian of Palestine. However, evidence of the full development of food producing and of permanent settlements has not yet been found there.[2] In North Africa, the Capsian culture seems to have followed an evolution rather similar to that of the Natufian of Palestine, though the process started later and probably persisted longer. It slowly evolved into a Neolithic agricultural pattern, but this stage was reached in North Africa at least three thousand years later than in Palestine.[3]

[9] W. F. Albright: BASOR, No. 109 (1948), pp. 14–15; H. Field: *Contributions to the Anthropology of the Faiyum, Sinai, Sudan, Kenya* (Berkeley, Cal.: University of California Press; 1952), p. 88.
[1] D. A. E. Garrod: *Proceedings of the British Academy*, Vol. XLIII (1957), p. 212.
[2] Coon: op. cit., pp. 128–216.
[3] R. Vaufrey: *La Préhistoire de l'Afrique; I: Le Maghreb* (Tunis; 1955), pp. 368 ff.

The Natufians inhabited caves and open-air sites, and both kinds of habitat seem to have been continuously occupied. Most Natufian sites show thick and uninterrupted levels and persistent secondary differences which point to long occupancy of a living site by a particular group with local traits. However, there obviously was communication between the various Natufian groups. Many aspects of their culture, such as their art, burial customs, body decoration, and settlement patterns, show a general uniformity which transcends variations in secondary local traits. It even seems that some sort of trade or barter was carried on between the various groups. Dentalia and other sea shells used for body decoration, cut and prepared in a style which is found in greatest abundance near the Mediterranean shore at Mount Carmel, have turned up as far inland as Einan and at various sites in Wadi Kharaitun and the Judean Desert. Heavy mortars of a type made at Einan of basalt and other rock from the upper Jordan Valley were found in the caves of El-Wad and Kebara, where they undoubtedly were imported. The distances were not very great, but over a range of about one hundred miles some sort

Natufian skeleton *in situ* in lower Natufian level at El-Wad

of primitive trade must have developed, and Einan, Mount Carmel, Wadi Kharaitun, Jericho, and the other sites of this area must have had some regular intercourse.

Each of these sites had some individual characteristics. Even the ratios of animal bones found in Natufian levels in the coastal plain, the central mountains, and the Jordan Valley show some slight local differences. Gazelles, deer, goats, bears, and wild oxen were everywhere the animals most frequently hunted; however, the preponderance of gazelles and the more frequent presence of animals belonging to the horse family at Mount Carmel, the abundance of goats in the Judean Hills, and the presence of lacustrine fauna near Lake Hula, reflect the different ecological environment of each site.

These ecological differences must have had an effect on the economic conditions in each area. Everywhere hunting, fishing, and gathering played important roles, though hunting seems to have been more important in Judea, and fishing and gathering at Einan, whereas at Mount Carmel shellfishery and other secondary activities were probably added.

At Einan and in smaller quantities at Mount Carmel and in the Judean Desert, grindstones, mortars and pestles, and sickles show that the Natufians had already gone very far along the path from gathering wild grain toward planned agriculture. Whatever was collected and ground and mashed by these tools must have been very plentiful, plentiful enough to justify the abundance of such tools. At the same time, the domestication of animals was attempted, and gradually became a part of the economy (see pages 233 ff.).

The best example of a Natufian settlement found so far was excavated at Einan by the French archaeologist Jean Perrot. There a Mesolithic hamlet of roughly circular huts with stone basements had been established on the ancient shore of Lake Hula. The habitations were between sixteen and thirty feet in diameter, and in several of them were found basins or storage places plastered with mud, fireplaces, mortars, and pestles *in situ*.

Natufian stone circles, once the basements
of huts, at Einan, near Lake Hula

These round houses maintained an ancient tradition described in
previous chapters (see page 127). Later they will be noted in
Early Neolithic levels at Nahal Oren and at Jericho.

The main difference between the earlier round buildings and
those of Einan is that in Einan they had been rebuilt several
times on the same spot. They undoubtedly testify to a certain
degree of sedentary life, and show that the hamlet had a rather
prolonged existence. Persistent settlement is also indicated by the
presence of very heavy objects. Stone basins weighing tens of
pounds obviously were not made by the hands of nomads. As we
shall see, in each of these Mesolithic settlements a large number
of graves have been discovered. These cemeteries indicate persistent traditions and a conventionalized cult, implying the presence of the same group for several generations.

Among over three hundred Natufian skeletons found thus
far, only a very few have been fully studied, but many from Jericho, Einan, Nahal Oren, and other sites are under study at the
present time. Therefore we cannot yet generalize on the few available data or try to describe the traits of a Natufian race. But the
little that we know suggests at least vaguely what the Natufians
looked like.

The skull of a young woman from Erq el-Ahmar, in the

Judean Desert, studied by Professor Henri V. Vallois [4] shows a very marked profile, with a prominent chin, a slight prognathism (forward projection of the teeth), a prominent nose, and a high forehead. The brow ridges are rather massive for a woman, very similar in shape to those of some Upper Paleolithic men. The head is elongated (dolichocephalic).[5]

Sir Arthur Keith described the Natufian men from the caves of Shukbah and Kebara as short in stature; [6] for males the mean was 63 inches and for females 60 inches. The tallest male in the group was only 65 inches. Their hands and feet were small and their long limb bones very slender. These people were long-headed [7] their face was small and elongated, the lower jaw was weak with a slight prognathism and a prominent chin.

Early in the Neolithic there were people in Palestine who apparently were the direct heirs of the gradual development of these Natufians. In the Oren Valley at Mount Carmel, Professor Stekelis found some late Natufian individuals of an apparently transitional type who already possessed some of the traits of Near Eastern Neolithic men and who showed a marked tendency to broadheaded, or brachycephalic, characteristics.[8]

The Natufian is a predominantly microlithic culture in which Upper Paleolithic tools are still present. Since the publication of one of the classics of Palestinian prehistory, *The Stone Age of Mount Carmel*,[9] the cave of El-Wad has become the type-site of this industry. Dorothy Garrod has divided the Natufian levels there into two phases, which were tentatively called Upper and Lower Natufian. Later excavations seem to show that the

[4] L'A, Vol. XLVI (1936), pp. 529 ff.
[5] Cephalic index 72, having a cranial capacity of 1,505 cubic centimeters, which is higher than that of many people living today.
[6] A. Keith: *New Discoveries Relating to the Antiquity of Man* (London: Williams and Norgate; 1931), pp. 202 ff.
[7] Cephalic index between 72 and 78.
[8] See D. Ferenbach: IEJ, Vol. IX, No. 2 (1959), pp. 65 ff.
[9] D. A. E. Garrod and D. M. A. Bate: *The Stone Age of Mount Carmel*, Vol. I (London: Oxford University Press; 1937).

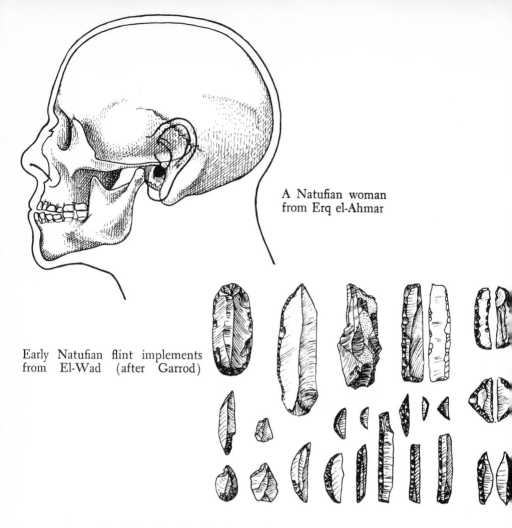

A Natufian woman
from Erq el-Ahmar

Early Natufian flint implements
from El-Wad (after Garrod)

Late Natufian flint implements from Mount Carmel (1–3, 6–11, 13, from El-Wad, after Garrod; 4–5, 12, from Kebara, after Turville-Petre)

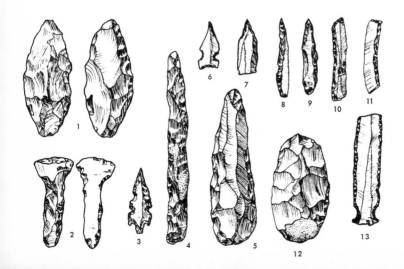

Mugharet el-Wad, where Dorothy Garrod discovered the first extensive Natufian site and cemetery

evolution of material culture was slightly different in various areas, and some of the differences noted by Garrod between her two phases at El-Wad simply represent local developments and individual variations on the part of the group inhabiting that cave. Nevertheless, certain general characteristics revealing the history of the material culture can be discerned. In its early phases, the quantity of tools of the Upper Paleolithic type is always relatively greater than the quantity found in late Natufian phases. In early phases the flint work is usually more accurate, and a higher number of microliths are retouched on both sides, in a fine and sharp retouch which archaeologists refer to as the "Helouan retouch." In later phases, a certain number of "Neolithic" tools appear, among which are new agricultural and hunting implements; these indicate that considerable changes were taking place in the Natufian way of life.

In the two Natufian levels of El-Wad, over two thirds of the artifacts are microliths. The most common implement is the lunate, or crescent-shaped, microlith; but triangles, trapezoids, and curved points are also present, as well as micro-burins and blunt-backed blades. In the later level over three quarters of the lunates have a blunt back, and only about one fourth have a Helouan retouch, whereas in the older phase this retouch is present in well over half of the lunates. The flint implements of medium size include burins, scrapers and blunt-backed blades of the Paleolithic tradition, borers, and sickle blades. Sickle blades are proportionately more numerous in the later phase, as are burins and end-scrapers in the older phase. Among large tools there are picks, steep scrapers, massive scrapers, disks, and other objects.

Other kinds of rock besides flint were employed for toolmaking, mainly basalt and limestone. Pestles and mortars, polishers, and grinders were the principal larger utilitarian stone objects found at El-Wad. The Natufians also made figurines and other artistic objects, but these will be discussed in detail in the following chapter.

Natufian cup marks on the terrace of Mugharet el-Wad

Natufian mortars inside cave of El-Wad

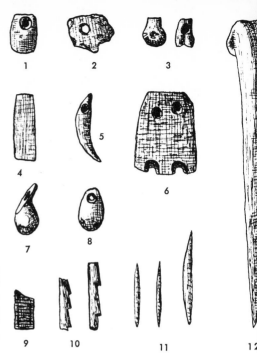

Natufian objects from El-Wad: 1, 7, 8, bone pendants; 2, pierced fragment of shell; 3, pendant made of gazelle phalange; 4, 9, bone tablets; 5, pierced canine of fox; 6, fragment of sickle-blade haft; 10, fragments of bone harpoons; 11, bone gorgets; 12, bone pin (after Garrod)

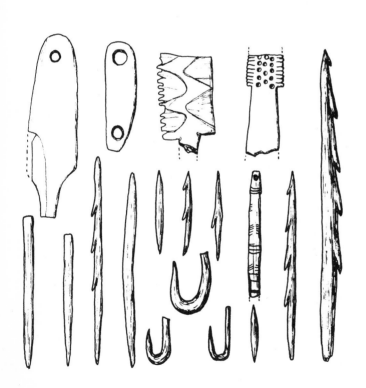

Natufian objects from Kebara (after Turville-Petre)

The stone artifacts were accompanied by a varied group of bone tools. They included points, awls, small bone fragments shaped into points, gorgets (very fine and thin double-pointed tools), lissoirs (flat bone tools presumably used for polishing), barbed harpoons, and sickle hafts. All these objects were finely worked and well polished. The most common bone tool, the point, was usually made of the long bones of the gazelle. One articulation was left in place as a handle and the other end was pointed and polished. Harpoons have small barbs toothed on one side. Better examples of them have been found at Kebara,[1] where beautiful fishhooks also have been discovered as well as two complete sickle hafts.

The hafts were made of long, flat bones with a deep groove running down the edge from the tip to the handle. Flint blades were inserted into this groove. The handle was frequently decorated with carvings of animals or animal heads. The fragments found at El-Wad come from as many as thirteen specimens.

At Einan, Perrot found a material culture differing somewhat from that of El-Wad, Kebara, and Shukbah.[2] The proportion of flint microliths was smaller at Einan, whereas some medium-sized tools were very well shaped and retouched. Besides the usual abundance of lunates of both the blunt-backed and Helouan types, there were small blades (lamelles) truncated on one or both ends, points, and microliths of various geometric forms. Perrot reports on only one micro-burin.

The medium-sized implements included elongated borers with abrupt blunted sides, numerous scrapers, and a great many gravers. The quality of the large tools is poor, and they resemble those of El-Wad. The picks are rough, and some tools made from flakes have a thick cutting edge. Perrot sees in them a sort of prototype of the Neolithic chisel.

[1] F. Turville-Petre: JRAI, Vol. LXII (1932), pp. 271 ff.
[2] J. Perrot: *Antiquity and Survival*, Vol. II (1957), pp. 91–110; IEJ, Vol. X, No. 1 (1960), pp. 14–22.

Mortars and pestles usually are of basalt, and are generally similar to comparable remains at El-Wad and Kebara. However, Einan yielded a far richer and more varied collection of them. Some of these stone tools are simply enormous, weighing over one hundred pounds. Some vessels have an elegant beaker shape, and others are decorated on the outside surface with incised patterns. One bowl has dots pecked between horizontal incised lines. A fragment of a large basin has a triple crenelated motif in relief. Other stone implements include flat pebbles with notches on opposite sides, probably fish-net sinkers, and perforated round, flat pebbles, probably weights for digging sticks.

The bone artifacts are generally similar to the El-Wad and Kebara assemblages, and include awls, points, needles, fishhooks, and bone hafts for sickles.

In the Judean Desert, the sequence of Natufian material was studied at several sites. The early artifacts resembled those of the coastal plain, whereas late Natufian seems to have developed quite differently, finally turning into a type of Early Neolithic culture which is more common in the mountains and the Negev than on the coastal plain, and which is characterized by a great abundance of arrowheads. These late phases are known mainly from the site of El-Khiam,[3] where the stratigraphy seems to have been disturbed, so that the various steps of this evolution cannot be followed in detail at present.

A slightly different evolution occurred at Nahal Oren and at Jericho, where late Natufian developed into variant local patterns of Early Neolithic. Winged arrowheads appear at both sites, though in smaller quantities than in the Judean Desert, but they are accompanied by other variant factors. The quantitative index of microliths sharply decreases. The main innovations were various sorts of large flint tools in the form of axes, adzes, and picks for agricultural use. Some substantial changes in art and religion show that some important psychological changes accompanied the progress in technology.

[3] J. Perrot in R. Neuville: Archives IPH, Vol. XXIV (1951), pp. 134 ff.

THE ART OF THE NATUFIANS

A widespread cultural trait links most of the Mesolithic assemblages found throughout Europe, central Asia, and North Africa. This is typified by schematic designs incised and painted in geometric and abstract patterns, and by highly schematic figures of animals and human beings carved and painted on bones, pebbles, antlers, and the walls of caves. The Natufian is an exception to this trend, and its art is very different from that of the other Mesolithic cultures. In place of the usual schematic designs, the Natufians created a unique naturalistic plastic art. This consists mainly of small sculptures of animal and human figures.

Most of the sculpture decorates tools, often sickle hafts, and it is likely that there was some relation between the carved figures and the work done with the tools on which they appear. A number of archaeologists today agree that this decoration of utilitarian tools had magical purposes intended to increase the effectiveness of the tool and ensure an abundant harvest.[4] In Paleolithic times animal figures were associated with hunting magic, and there are several later examples of people transforming such traditional beliefs and adjusting them to their new economic activities.[5] Some of the Natufian art is probably an example of this.

At present we have no indication of whether the animals depicted by the Natufians were wild or domesticated. Most of them seem to be very young ruminants, and their posture suggests that the artists observed them from very short distances in such acts as sucking milk. From Neolithic times on, a similar kind of animal art was connected with a fertility cult or with fertility magic. Usually domestic animals were portrayed, but the question of whether this was also true of Natufian art is still unsolved.

[4] M. Stekelis: *Eretz Israel*, Vol. VI (1960), p. 21.
[5] See E. Anati: *Camonica Valley* (New York: Alfred A. Knopf; 1961), p. 173.

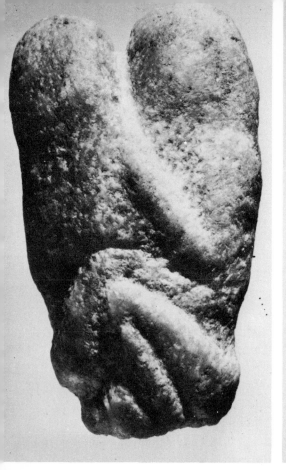 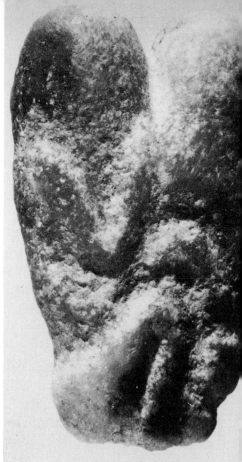

Two sides of the erotic figurine
from Ain Sakhri

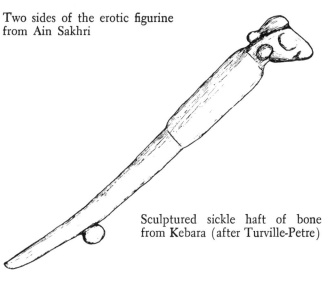

Sculptured sickle haft of bone
from Kebara (after Turville-Petre)

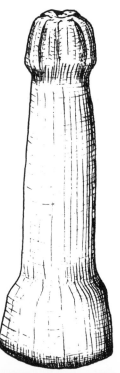

Basalt pestle with phallic handle from Ain Sakhri

Other utilitarian tools decorated in such a way as to suggest fertility magic are stone pestles shaped as phallic symbols, presumably used for grinding or mixing food. But the most interesting figurine associated with fertility rites is an erotic statuette in calcite discovered in the cave of Ain Sakhri, in the Judean Desert.[6] This was found in the same level as a phallic pestle, and shows a human couple copulating in a strange sitting posture. This art emphasizes two elements which are closely associated in our minds and also, apparently, in the Natufians': one is fertility, and the other is the organs and the act of reproduction.

We shall find that in later periods animal figurines are frequently connected with rites invoking both the abundance of the earth and the fertility of women. In Neolithic times and thereafter both kinds of fertility are frequently interrelated, and this conceptual association between the mother-of-man and the mother-earth has been the basis for many mythologies. (As we shall see, figurines of a fertility goddess and of animals were found near each other in a building believed to be a temple in Prepottery Jericho.) A cult connected with a mother goddess or pregnancy goddess is known to have existed in the Upper Paleolithic. The riddle of pregnancy and birth had troubled man long before Mesolithic times, but it seems that Natufian art is the first clear evidence that cause and effect were related by man. Natufian art also shows that the concept of fertility had become very broad and complex, and had been extended from woman to the earth.

Besides the possible magical or religious motives of this art, there may have been aesthetic motives. As in the case of the vast quantities of necklaces, pendants, headdresses, and other body decorations, the Natufians, with a unique sense of beauty and harmony, also embellished their tools and other utilitarian objects. From the aesthetic point of view, the Natufian artist had

[6] See R. Neuville: L'A, Vol. XLIII (1933), pp. 558 ff.; Archives IPH, Vol. XXIV (1951), pp. 132 ff.

a unique plastic, three-dimensional sense that finds no contemporary parallels.

The artistic complex of the Natufian of Palestine indicates a great difference in the psychological background of its makers from that of other Mesolithic groups. Whereas the Mesolithic in most regions marked the Middle Ages of prehistory, so to speak, a period of abandoning the old values and of searching at random for new ones, in Palestine a true artistic renaissance was born, accompanied by a new rhythm of life and a gradual evolution toward new economic horizons. The art of the Natufians is one of their important characteristics, and it reveals a cultural vitality, a sense of harmony, and an ideology which seem to spring from values partially inherited from the Upper Paleolithic, but which reveal a vigor with no parallels in other Mesolithic cultures. Little more can be said at present about the origins of Natufian art. As soon as it appeared it exhibited outstanding artistic skill, and this certainly demonstrates the persistence of evolved artistic traditions already old at the time.

The whole collection of bone and stone objects uniformly exhibits signs that they must have been used mainly for working wood. Tiny flint scrapers and burins, as well as flint blades, were used to carve these art objects. The original models for some of these representations, especially for the sickle hafts, seem to have been made of long wooden branches, the natural form of which must have inspired the artist. Therefore, what remains of Natufian art in stone and bone is probably only a small fraction of the artistic creation, the bulk of which is lost forever.

This fact also suggests why it is not yet possible to trace the origins of Natufian art. From the very beginning of the Mesolithic, it had highly evolved and sophisticated traditions, and there can be little doubt that these traditions were inherited from Upper Paleolithic times. However, the Near East has not yet yielded art objects definitely identifiable as Paleolithic, and we may guess that the prototypes of Natufian art were made of wood and other perishable materials, and were not preserved.

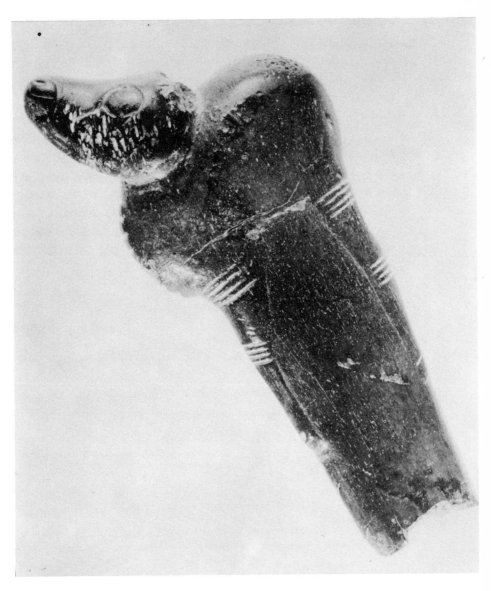

Ruminant sculptured on handle of sickle haft from El-Wad

In the Near East, the flourishing of this Natufian naturalistic art seems to form a bridge between the art of the hunters and that of the farmers. In Palestine an unbroken continuity in the persistence of the artistic trait can be traced in various Neolithic industries.

All the Natufian art objects discovered so far have been found in only three regions: at Mount Carmel, in Wadi Kharaitun, and at Einan. In all they number about thirty objects, and less than half of them can be considered naturalistic; the others are decorated with geometric and other non-figurative patterns.

At Mount Carmel, art objects were found in the caves of El-Wad, Kebara, and Nahal Oren. Those from the first two sites seem to be early Natufian, but some from Nahal Oren are late Natufian.

Statuette of a ruminant from Umm ez-Zuetina

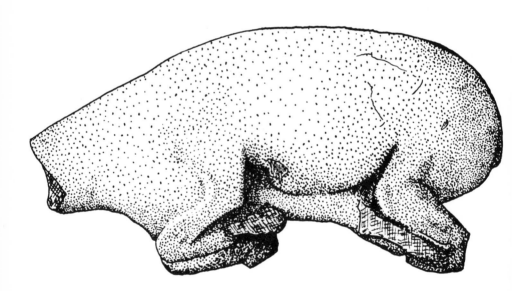

At El-Wad, Dorothy Garrod found two objects of outstanding interest, both fragmentary. One is a carving of a young deer on the handle of a bone sickle haft, the other a small human head in calcite.

The deer was fashioned by using the natural protuberances of the bone articulation, a particular trait of Natufian art. Its head is raised, and Garrod suggests that it might represent the posture of nursing. Details such as the large eyes, the ears, the mouth, and the legs are carved with a very high sense of harmony and with fine observation. The legs of the young deer are decorated with two groups of four parallel lines each, engraved with a flint. There is also a series of parallel notches along the breast. This carving was highly polished, probably by means of sand and leather, and its surface has a high glaze on which no signs of tooling can be recognized.

The human head is much cruder and looks very much as if it was not finished. It was shaped and carved with a pointed tool, probably a flint burin. A band in high relief around the head probably represents a headdress similar to those found on Natufian skeletons. Garrod points out that the general form was determined by the natural shape of the stone. This carving was found in the immediate vicinity of the skeleton of a child.[7]

Other minor finds that may be considered artistic expressions include various decorated basalt pestles, three polished stones having vaguely phallic shapes, a few pieces of bone decorated with engraved lines, and a long animal bone perforated at the upper articulation, similar to some found in the Upper Paleolithic of Europe.[8]

At Kebara, a bare ten miles from El-Wad, Turville-Petre found four decorated sickle hafts.[9] On one, the handle is sculptured as the face of a ruminant, probably a goat. On the second

[7] Garrod and Bate: op. cit., p. 38.
[8] Garrod: *Man*, 1930, pp. 77–8.
[9] F. Turville-Petre: JRAI, Vol. LXII (1932), pp. 271 ff.

there is the face of another ruminant similar to that on the figurine of a young animal at El-Wad. The very large and prominent
eyes are a characteristic trait of this animal art. The two others
were fragmentary and again show ruminant faces. This Kebara
group is extremely homogeneous, and its individuality is particularly interesting considering its proximity to Nahal Oren, at which
more art objects have been discovered by Moshe Stekelis.

The excavation at Nahal Oren is still going on at the moment and all of the material found in it has not yet been published.[1] It is to be hoped that a thorough examination of the
stratigraphy here will establish a better chronology for Natufian
art. Here the works of art seem to show a degeneration from the
artistic standards of El-Wad and Kebara and from those we shall
find in the Judean Desert.

Each of the three objects described by Stekelis in his preliminary report had some individual characteristics, and as a group
they do not seem to show a uniform artistic approach. One of
them, engraved on a small horn, has a sculptured figure at each
end. The figure on the thicker end has a schematic face in which
the nose is emphasized and the eyes are in prominent relief. It
has a carved outline on the forehead, and on the whole it bears
some resemblance to the limestone human face from El-Wad,
though it is much more schematic.[2] The other end has a well-
polished face of a ruminant, with typically protruding eyes and
upraised muzzle. This object, though less realistic than the
other finds from Mount Carmel, can be safely classed in the same
artistic group, for it has the Natufian characteristics noted elsewhere.

The second object is very different. It is a piece of limestone
on one side of which is a figurine vaguely representing a head, but
it is impossible to tell whether the head is human or animal.[3] The

[1] See M. Stekelis: *Eretz Israel*, Vol. VI (1960), pp. 21–3.
[2] Stekelis believes it to be the muzzle of an animal, but I am more inclined to
see in it a human face.
[3] I am reluctant to accept Stekelis's interpretation of this object as a "bird
figurine."

natural shape of the stone must have inspired the artist. A very important difference between this figurine and the other art objects in the group lies in the eyes, which are carved only as rough and very light circles lacking the usual Natufian emphasis. The opposite side has a very deep groove which might have served as a grip for a cord. This object has no similarities with the art objects of Mount Carmel or Judea. (Its general design may be related to finds at Einan, but only future discoveries can verify this.)

The third object is an anthropomorphic figurine on a pebble. The only clear engraving is a vertical line indicating the legs or the sex.[4] No comparable objects have as yet turned up in Natufian art. Further discoveries might lead Stekelis to modify his original Natufian dating for the third object; the last season of excavation at Nahal Oren has rewarded Stekelis with two addi-

[4] See Stekelis: op. cit., p. 21.

One of the double-sculptured horns from Nahal Oren. Top, a human face; bottom, face of a ruminant.

tional pebble figurines which belong to the Early Neolithic level.[5]

In the Judean Hills, two extremely interesting objects were discovered by René Neuville and attributed by him to early Natufian.[6] One is the erotic couple I have already described, the other is the figurine of a deerlike animal, probably a gazelle, from the cave of Umm ez-Zuetina. The head is missing, but the body shows a greater perfection and balance of proportions than any other Natufian object. Remains of red-ocher paintings were found on it. The animal is shown sitting, a posture quite unusual in the art of hunters. The object was worked with a flint burin, traces of which were found all over it.

Various decorations on tools and objects found at Einan [7] as well as a human figurine from the same site [8] stand outside the classical Natufian tradition. Here the decorations of meanders, lines, dots, and crenelations seem to be the precursors of patterns which became more common and widespread in Early Neolithic times. From the economic point of view, Einan represents a transitional period, and it is extremely impressive to find confirmation of this in its decorative art.

In the next section we shall see how the Natufians used to decorate the bodies of their dead. They held ornaments in high esteem and had a very marked aesthetic sensibility. Their art reveals some of their beliefs and some interesting details of their psychological background. But most important of all, it reveals a refinement which did not exist among other Mesolithic groups and which gave to the Natufian of Palestine one of its unique traits.

---

[5] Communication by Stekelis at the annual convention of the Israel Exploration Society, October 1960.
[6] Neuville: 1951, op. cit., Pls. 14–15.
[7] J. Perrot: IEJ, Vol. X, No. 1 (1960), p. 19.
[8] J. Perrot: IEJ, Vol. VII, No. 2 (1957), p. 127.

Schematic human figure from Einan

THE NATUFIAN BURIALS

Over three hundred Natufian skeletons have been discovered in Palestine, and this is truly an enormous number when we consider that the Natufian period probably lasted only between four and five thousand years, and that there have been found in this region less than one tenth this number of skeletons belonging to the previous half million years. This is probably a result of the Natufian habit of always burying their dead in their own settlements and caves; and skeletal remains have been found in practically every excavated Natufian site. These burials reveal many customs and rituals, and taken together probably comprise one of the richest and most significant paleoethnologic documents of prehistoric Palestine.

Some attempts have been made to distinguish between Upper and Lower Natufian funerary customs, but the dead were buried in pits below the habitation level and this somewhat obscures the connection between the burials and the levels. In fact, two major Natufian burial types are recognized, but it is not yet clear how they evolved during this period. One type is the burial of the entire body in a bent, contracted position. The second type is the burial of skulls, without the rest of the body. Both kinds of burial can be traced back to the Paleolithic, and both continued thereafter, in Neolithic times. The main innovation introduced by the Mesolithic people is the first wide use of collective, or group, burials; in the Paleolithic, usually only a single body was buried or a single skull worshipped at one time.

In these collective tombs, several of which are sometimes found in the same settlement, a number of bodies had to share the same "home" after death. In most of these burials, each body appears to have been entombed at a different time.

In most Natufian burials the corpse was placed on its side in a contracted position, in pits excavated for the purpose. Many skeletons, especially those of women, bore decoration of shell, bone, and stone pendants, necklaces, headdresses, and anklets, as

Natufian burial at Mugharet el-Wad. The skeleton is in contracted position, with a head decoration of dentalia.

well as red body paint. Traces of red ocher are frequently found around the skeleton as well as on the skull and the limb bones. The best-known burial site is the cave of El-Wad. Dorothy Garrod, who found skeletons both inside the cave and in front of it, claimed that both groups represent burial. The skeletons inside the cave, however, do not show any of the characteristics of Natufian burials, and none of the skulls was decorated, as they usually were in ritual burials of the time.

In the terrace of El-Wad, Garrod discovered fifty individuals and distinguished two main types of burial posture.[9] In both,

[9] Garrod and Bate: op. cit., p. 14.

the skeleton was placed on its side; but one type shows a highly flexed position with the knees, in many cases, drawn up to the chin. The second exhibits a loosely flexed position. This difference of posture probably depended on the space available for the body in the burial pit. Garrod assigned the first type to Lower Natufian and the second to a later phase of the same period. Only one skeleton in the terrace was in neither of these postures; this belonged to an adult woman named by the excavators Homo-13. It seems that this individual actually was a part of the complex found inside the cave, which will be described later.

Most of the other skeletons were buried in small pits and were packed in with stones placed both on the sides and on top. Several of them were decorated with shell, bone, and other ornaments, mainly headdresses; but necklaces and breast ornaments were also found, as well as bracelets and strings of shells decorating the legs.

The lightly flexed skeletons were found in three collective burials, two of five individuals each and one of seven. A fourth group had three individuals, a child and two adults. In one burial there were two. The other skeletons were single burials.

Another collective pit burial was discovered at Erq el-Ahmar by René Neuville.[1] Here seven skeletons were buried together, four of which belonged to adults. Neuville noted the highly interesting fact that only one adult had his whole skeleton buried there, whereas the others were represented by their skull alone. Horse molars, dentalium shells, and pendants of gazelle phalanges constituted the usual body decorations. The pit, 21½ inches deep, had been covered with some flat stones which formed a roughly rectangular table almost 3 by 6 feet in size.

At Einan over sixty skeletons have been discovered by Jean Perrot.[2] The most extraordinary of these burials can perhaps be considered the earliest-known megalithic funerary monument in the world. It is a very large circular pit, about 16 feet in diameter,

[1] Neuville: 1951, op. cit., p. 109.
[2] J. Perrot: IEJ, Vol. VII, No. 2 (1957), p. 126; Vol. X, No. 1 (1960), p. 18.

with plastered walls, surrounded by a stone circle about 21 feet in diameter. In the center two complete skeletons and other fragmentary bones were found. No estimate of the number of individuals is given. They had been covered with a large table of flat stones. On it, there was an approximately square fireplace, still containing ashes, surrounded with stones. Near by a human skull was found, accompanied by the upper two cervical vertebrae. The second bore signs of mechanical cutting. Even without this detail, the presence of the two vertebrae clearly indicates that this head was removed from the body and interred while flesh was still attached to it. Another table of flat stone covered all this, and on the very top three large stones and some smaller ones completed the monument. From the posture of the three stones on top it seems that they held something between them, perhaps a wooden pole or standing object.

The two buried skeletons were fully adult and probably belonged to a male and a female, and in this case they seem to have been buried at the same time. The female had a dentalium shell headdress similar to those known from El-Wad.

This pit burial, surrounded by a stone circle and covered by large stone slabs, is the earliest-known monument in the world to reveal a kind of burial method that was to become widespread in Neolithic times. It is interesting to note that "dolmen"-like megalithic monuments from later times are abundant in the immediate vicinity of Einan.

Obviously, a whole series of rituals and conventional practices is behind this very strange funerary monument of Einan. Until other similar monuments are found and studied, it is difficult to reconstruct exactly its ritual significance, but it seems that the tomb was built to bury the people found in the lowest level. When they were interred a fire was lit on a stone table, and a human being was then sacrificed. The head of the sacrificed man was buried on the level of the fireplace, and the whole was covered with stones. If this interpretation is correct, this tomb is of tremendous importance, for it reveals a complex combina-

Natufian skeleton from Einan. The skull is pressed between two stones; others were piled on the body.

tion of ritualistic practices and ideological concepts of a people who lived over ten thousand years ago.

Another collective pit burial at Einan contained five skulls and a few fragmentary bones. The pit had a diameter of a little over three feet. A third pit had nine skulls. Each of these skull pits contained pieces of red ocher, and one skull had clear traces of red paint. Various burials contained three, two, or single skeletons. In most of these smaller burials, the skeletons lay on their sides in the usual flexed position and the usual shell and bone body decorations were found.

A fourth important Natufian cemetery with over twenty burials was discovered at Nahal Oren by Moshe Stekelis.[3] Here most of the burials were single. In two pits, however, two bodies were found together. Usually a stone bedding was placed under the skull (several examples of the same custom have been re-

[3] M. Stekelis: IEJ, Vol. X, No. 2 (1960), p. 119.

ported at Einan and El-Wad). The pits were sometimes covered with stones, mostly small flat ones. Most skeletons were in the contracted position. The usual decorations of shell, bone, and stone were common in most pits. In the center of the burial area there was a large fireplace containing ashes, encircled by flat stones. Probably this is another indication of the use of ritual fire in connection with the cult of the dead.

An interesting phenomenon seen both at Erq el-Ahmar and at Einan is the filling of pits with skulls that had been detached from the body. Cranium collecting is a custom well known both from prehistoric times and among primitive groups of modern times.[4] The search for an ethnological significance in this practice has given rise to many theories. Some authors are convinced that it indicates an ancestral cult, others that the head-hunters were "cannibals who piously buried the heads of their victims," still others that these skull pits were little treasure troves of war trophies.[5] Actually we simply do not know the motive behind the custom; it is quite possible that different peoples had different motives for the same practice.

In Mesolithic times this custom was widespread throughout the Old World,[6] but probably the closest parallels to the Palestinian practice are found in central Europe. In at least three sites in Germany collections of skulls were found buried in pits. The best-known is the cave of Ofnet, near Nördlingen, in Bavaria, where W. Scheidt as early as 1908 found two such burial pits related to an Azilio-Tardenoisian Mesolithic culture.[7] One of them contained twenty-seven skulls, and the other, only about three feet away, had six of them. Most of these skulls were accompanied by cervical vertebrae, and some of them clearly

---

[4] P. Wernert: L'A, Vol. XLVI (1936), p. 33.

[5] J. Maringer: *L'Homme préhistorique et ses dieux* (Paris: Arthaud; 1958), p. 202.

[6] R. Lacam, A. Kliederlender, and H. V. Vallois: Archives IPH, Vol. XXI (1945), p. 53.

[7] W. Scheidt: *Die eiszeitlichen Schadelfunde aus der Grossen Ofnet-Höhle und von Kaufertsberg bei Nördlingen* (Munich; 1923).

showed signs of mechanical cutting. Many of the skulls were decorated with shells, bone ornaments, and deer teeth, particularly those belonging to women. They were surrounded by pieces of red ocher, and some of them had indications of red paint. Several disclosed fractures that had been produced by sharp blows. The anthropologist Theodor Mollison believed that these were produced by axes or celts, which are not found in the material culture associated with the skulls,[8] and this supposition has prompted many subsequent speculations on the possible causes of death of the Ofnet people.

In the vicinity of Ofnet, at Kaufertsberg, another such pit was found, containing a single skull, and at the entrance of Hohlenstein cave, in Württemberg, the cranial pit yielded three skulls surrounded by red ocher. They had belonged to two adults, a man and a woman, and to a child.

Several other similarities between the Azilio-Tardenoisian of central Europe and the Natufian can be stressed. The flint industries have common traits, and in past years it was suggested, on the basis of certain physical-anthropological considerations, that the prototype of the European assemblage might have originated in the Near East.[9] Both the Natufian skulls and those found at Ofnet frequently show the practice of evulsion (extraction) of the incisor teeth.[1] However, the relationship is not so plain, for there are many cultural differences between these groups, and many traits of the Natufian have not yet been found in central Europe. Another factor to be taken into consideration is that in its general chronology the Azilio-Tardenoisian is certainly later than the Natufian, and that late Natufian might be contemporary with an early phase of that complex.

Coming back to Palestine, mention was previously made

[8] T. Mollison: *Anthropologischer Anzeiger*, Vol. XIII (Stuttgart; 1936), pp. 79–88.

[9] See Carleton S. Coon: *The Races of Europe* (New York: Macmillan; 1939), p. 68.

[10] This detail seems to be present also in the Capsian of North Africa. See Archives IPH, Vol. XIII (1934); and R. Vaufrey: op. cit., pp. 221, 234.

that the skeletal material inside the cave of El-Wad was not consistent with the general practice. It should be mentioned that
the facts described above refer only to the skeletons discovered
in the terrace. Inside the cave were found a total of twelve skeletons, and Garrod describes them brilliantly and clearly. I am sure
that the reader will be able to reconstruct for himself the events
behind the archaeological evidence summarized here.[2] "Inside
the entrance of the cave there was an important change in the
position of the skeletons," Garrod writes. "Whereas all burials in
the terrace showed some variety of flexed position, in the cave-
mouth and inside, they lay on their back in extended position.
This difference is not easy to explain, as there is no evidence
that the two groups are not roughly contemporary."

Two of the skeletons lay near the mouth of the cave. One
(Homo-59) was that of a child, the other (Homo-60), that of an
adult. A large fragment of limestone lay close to the adult's right
side. On the thorax was a broken limestone mortar. In the center
of the chamber was a heap of ten bodies. Homo-1, an adult male,
was missing a leg. At one arm's length from Homo-1 was an
infant (Homo-8). These two were at the top of the heap, with
the eight other skeletons beneath them. Homo-2 and Homo-3
were an adult male and an adult female. The right arm of Homo-
2 was missing, and the right arm of Homo-3 was badly crushed.
A young adult, Homo-4, lay fully extended at right angles to
Homo-2 and Homo-3. The mandible was slightly displaced. The
legs of Homo-2, Homo-3, and Homo-4 all sloped slightly upward
from the level of the skulls (obviously they followed the natural
slope of the soil at that point). Close to the left side of Homo-4
were the remains of two infants (Homo-6 and Homo-7) and a
young child (Homo-5). Immediately beneath the cervical vertebrae of Homo-5 was a piece of a basalt pestle. Both legs were
broken at the middle of the femora. Beneath them was found
another skeleton of a young child (Homo-10), whose legs were
stretched underneath the thorax of Homo-2. Close to Homo-10

[2] See Garrod and Bate: op. cit., pp. 14–19.

(near his hand?) was found the small carving of a human head in calcite.

What would Agatha Christie think of this situation? Whatever one may think of it, it is hard indeed to believe that this was a burial. The ten bodies must have been piled in a heap intentionally, but it is extremely improbable that the inhabitants of a cave would have done that in the middle of their own shelter. It seems more likely that it was done by people who did not inhabit the cave. Here a question arises: Were the various broken pestles, mortars, and stones really grave goods deposited in the supposed tomb? Or are they evidence of some less peaceful purposes? The mutilation of the skeletons is not systematic: one body lacks a leg, another an arm. Whether this is the result of a fight or of brutal mutilation after death we do not know, but it does not seem to be a ritual mutilation.

Of these twelve individuals five were adults. Two were male, one female; the sex of two is not stated.[3] The seven others included one young adult, three children, and three infants. They were probably the offspring of two or three women. Does this represent a household group? The people of the cave at a given moment? I shall let the reader put two and two together for himself and imagine a moment in the existence of these cave dwellers.

[3] It is probable that one of the skeletons found in the terrace (Homo-13) must be classified with the cave group. This was an adult female, and her position is not that of the usual deliberate burial. Her stratigraphic position fits this guess well.

The village of Liftah, a suburb of Jerusalem in the Judean Hills

II

The Artists

of the Desert[1]

[1] This chapter is comprised mainly of the results of a research project in which the author was helped by the Israel Department of Antiquities and the Wenner-Gren Foundation for Anthropological Research.

THE MARGINAL BANDS

WE HAVE TRACED the increasingly strong differentiation of cultures in Upper Paleolithic times and then the localization of regional cultures in the Mesolithic. We shall soon watch the peoples living in fertile lands slowly move toward a food-producing economy and toward village life and subsequent urbanization. But first we must describe the human bands living in areas where agriculture was rendered impossible by the environment and where a totally different kind of evolution took place.

The gradual expansion of the stronger human groups, their seizure of increasingly large strips of fertile land, and the expulsion of more primitive or weaker human groups to the arid periphery can be traced through practically every prehistoric period; but it became more important as incipient food-producing societies placed a progressively higher value on fertile land. The highly inventive culture of incipient farming was strongly influenced by the natural environment and had to adapt itself to local natural resources. In fertile regions, it became increasingly localized and fragmented, and cultural traits were frequently restricted to narrow geographical areas such as a single river valley, a plain, or a hilly region. In arid areas, lack of water forced the human bands who lived there to be continually on the move, and the uniformity of natural resources allowed them to develop a much more homogeneous culture. Even up to our own time, fertile areas have tended to be divided into small provinces, each of which has its own type of settlement, its own human type, its own language and culture; but deserts still frequently contain extremely large cultural areas where economic activities and social organization are quite uniform.

One of the common traits of marginal groups is the retarded rhythm of their evolution and the persistence of tradition. Thus, an occupation such as hunting, which in fertile regions ceased to be the main economic activity at the beginning of Neolithic times, persisted much longer in the desert. Agriculture was not possible in the desert, but other occupations, such as herding, trading, and mining, were useful to nomads. Not unnaturally, therefore, some desert peoples came to specialize in such activities.

The material culture of marginal nomadic groups is conditioned by their way of life, and thus it usually does not include heavy objects, which are hard to transport. Furthermore, breakable materials such as pottery are usually replaced with other, less fragile ones, such as dried calabashes, skin jars, ostrich eggshells with a perforation at one end, wooden vessels, baskets of vegetable fiber, and woven sacks. Thus, it is a reasonable guess that most of their artifacts were made of perishable materials and were destroyed by time. Sometimes nomadic peoples continued until a late date to make stone artifacts in a decadent Paleolithic tradition. This culture, as has been noted, is called Epi-Paleolithic, and it is not uncommon in the deserts of the

Rock carvings, central Negev

Near East. Most of these bands lived in tents or in natural caves, and remains of their habitations are extremely scanty. Whereas caves and other sites in well-watered regions could be settled practically uninterruptedly for ages, the wandering bands of the desert had to move constantly from one water source to another, never remaining more than a short time in one place.

In later times, some pastoral nomads left behind stone circles which probably were animal pens; but the early hunters hardly ever left much more than the remains of a fireplace, a few stone circles which probably trace the outlines of their huts or tents, and a few flint implements spread over the surface.

The desert yields very few artifacts dating from after the end of Paleolithic times, and only for a few very short periods is there better archaeological evidence. But this evidence usually was left by sedentary or semi-sedentary peoples who invaded the marginal areas of the desert in times of special political stress or climatic change, and do not represent the traditional way of life of the marginal bands.

Practically nothing would be known of these bands had they not developed the habit of making rock pictures in the desert. This is a widespread custom which has been practiced at one time or another almost everywhere in the world. Strangely enough, often it was practiced by peoples who must be considered marginal, or backward, in relation to the culture of surrounding areas and surrounding populations.

Whereas flint implements, pottery, and the other remains of material culture are technological expressions of a culture, rock pictures are intellectual expressions disclosing the interests, beliefs, and aesthetic sense of their makers. The remains of a material culture and associated rock pictures are found together only very rarely. There are several instances in European Paleolithic cave art. In the Atlas Mountains, Raymond Vaufrey found a certain constancy in the relation of rock pictures to the material culture found at the foot of the rocks on which they were depicted.[2] Other, but less successful, attempts at a correlation of this kind were made by Henri Lhote in the Tassili Mountains, by J. H. Dunbar in Nubia, and by Hans Rhotert at Kilwa in Jordan, but definite conclusions could not be reached, and for the time being, little can be said about the material possessions of the desert artists of these regions.

Occasionally, near or even on top of rock pictures the tools used to make the engravings have been found—large rough flint burins which bear no resemblance whatsoever to any tool known

[2] R. Vaufrey: Archives IPH, Vol. XX (1939).

Finely engraved horned animal of
Style I at Kilwa (after Rhotert)

Coarse flint tool *in situ* on rock carving, central Negev

from a recognized culture of the fertile regions. Frequently groups of rock pictures are found near or actually within a prehistoric site, but who can tell whether or not they were made by the same people who left flint implements and stone circles there? However, rock pictures reveal the economic activities of their makers, and their style reveals the psychological background, the influence of contacts with other groups, and the general cultural pattern, so that this desert art is useful in reconstructing the way of life of the artists.

In the Near and Middle East, rock pictures have been discovered in Transcaucasia, in southern and eastern Anatolia, and in southern Arabia; and each area has its own local stylistic differences. The rock pictures discovered in the Israeli Negev belong to an area of rather uniform culture which includes Sinai, the Jordanian Plateau, the Syrian Desert, northern Arabia, and the Hejaz—in other words, the marginal regions at the southern borders of the Fertile Crescent. The search for rock pictures in this area has a long history. As early as 1856 the French theologian Caignart de Saulcy published a report on some of them, and in subsequent years more discoveries were announced by the British explorer E. H. Palmer, by Dussaud and Macler, by the French fathers Vincent, Jaussen, and Savignac, and by other scholars. However, the first important concentration of rock pictures was discovered by Georges Horsfield and Nelson Glueck at Kilwa in the early thirties,[3] and was subsequently studied by the German archaeologist Hans Rhotert.[4] In recent years, a second important concentration was discovered in the Israeli Negev and in Sinai,[5] and other scattered examples were found elsewhere in the area.[6]

[3] AJA, Vol. XXXVII (1933), pp. 381 ff.; ILN, June 3, 1933, p. 802.
[4] H. Rhotert: Transjordanien, vorgeschichtliche Forschungen (Stuttgart; 1938).
[5] E. Anati: PEQ, 1955, pp. 49 ff.; PEQ, 1956, pp. 5 ff.; Archaeology, Vol. VIII, No. 1 (1955), pp. 31 ff.; BSPF, Vol. LII (1955), Nos. 11–12, pp. 722 ff.; BSPF, Vol. LV (1958), Nos. 3–4, pp. 209 ff.; etc.
[6] B. Howe: JNES, Vol. IX, No. 1 (1950), pp. 8 ff.; E. Pittard: ASAG, Vol. VIII, No. 2 (1939), pp. 187 ff.; etc.

Some of these rock pictures were found in association with Nabataean, Thamudic, Safaitic, and other late inscriptions; and until the discovery at Kilwa it was believed that all belonged to a single period dating from Hellenistic and Roman times. At Kilwa, it was clearly determined for the first time that only a small portion of this art belonged to literate times and that another part belonged to much older periods. Rhotert was able to distinguish three main phases, the older of which was attributed to the Stone Age, the second to the Early Bronze Age, and the third to Nabatean-Thamudic times.

Further work in the Negev distinguished seven styles ranging from the Stone Age to recent times. Some Bedouins of the area even today engrave rock pictures. The earliest pictures have a range of subject matter and a style of representation that discloses the economy and mentality of hunters. Then domesticated animals begin to appear, first the dog, then various goats and oxen. Obviously herding slowly was becoming an important occupation for the marginal groups. But this appears to have happened rather late, when agriculture, animal husbandry, and urban social organization were already well developed in the fertile regions.

One of the criteria by which the primitive artist chose the rock on which to engrave his picture was the shade of patination. The patina is a thin crust of dark color which becomes darker and deeper with age. The incision exposes the lighter interior part of the stone and creates a contrast with the darker surface. The process of patination continues, and the engraved surface becomes progressively darker with age, until it reaches the same shade as the original surface. The rapidity of coloration depends very much upon the various natural influences, such as rain and sun, and it is impossible therefore to use patina as an element of absolute chronology. However, shades of patination can supply information on the relative dates of various layers of engravings found on the same surface or in the immediate vicinity of one another. If these layers show stylistic differences, and if the same

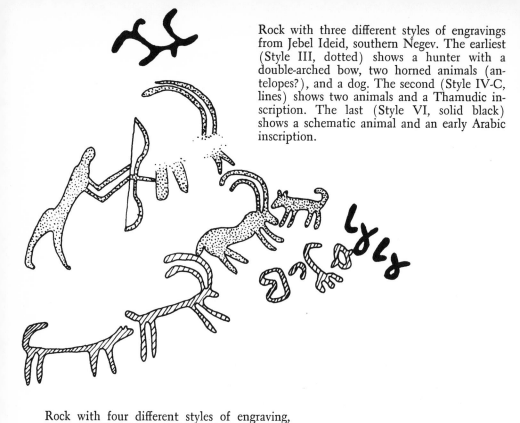

Rock with three different styles of engravings from Jebel Ideid, southern Negev. The earliest (Style III, dotted) shows a hunter with a double-arched bow, two horned animals (antelopes?), and a dog. The second (Style IV-C, lines) shows two animals and a Thamudic inscription. The last (Style VI, solid black) shows a schematic animal and an early Arabic inscription.

Rock with four different styles of engraving, from Ain Kudeirat, northern Sinai. The earliest (Style III, dotted) shows an ox with legs missing. The second (style unknown, diagonal lines) shows a two-wheeled chariot with two animals (horses?). The third (Style V, crosshatching) shows a horned animal, and the fourth (Style VI, solid black) a schematic animal.

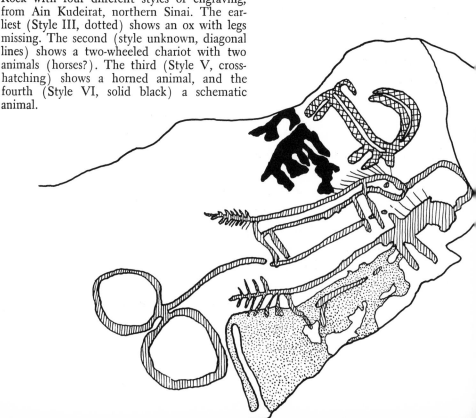

sequence of styles is determined in several different spots through patination shading, the method will have been an important element in establishing the general sequence of styles and art groups.

Some other general rules can be used. Engravings with a very dark patina can hardly be recent, whereas it is unlikely that engravings with a light patina are very old. In the Negev, the seven styles of rock pictures have been given numbers according to their relative age, Style I being the oldest. In this region we know of no engraved surface from Style IV-B (Iron Age) to Style VII (recent) with a patination identical with that of the original rock surface. This seems to mean that in this area it took a minimum of 2,500 years to reach an "O" shade, the natural color of patina on the surface of the rock. However, there are examples of lighter engraved surfaces in all styles, with the exception of Style I. Dark-brown patina is mainly found in Styles II, III, IV-A, and IV-B. Styles IV-C and V usually have a light-brown color, Style VI has a yellowish-brown color, and Style VII is very frequently yellow or light yellow, thus approaching the natural color of the inner rock.

Style IV-C is the one associated with Thamudic and Nabataean inscriptions, and it can be safely dated from Hellenistic and Roman times, that is, from the end of the first millennium B.C. and the beginning of the present era. Style IV-B appears to belong to the Iron Age, roughly to the first half of the first millennium B.C.; while Styles I to IV-A are earlier. We shall be concerned mainly with these last.

They show that the deserts across the southern borders of the Fertile Crescent have continuously been inhabited, usually by marginal groups which were less developed, from the technological point of view, than the inhabitants of the fertile regions, but still evolving their own patterns of culture in their own way.

Since the end of the Paleolithic, the major ecological areas of the Near East, the "green land" and the "yellow land," have always been two distinct cultural areas, dominated by different kinds of society, economic organization, settlements, and technological assemblages. But cultural intercourse has always existed between the two regions, and each has contributed something to the other.

This intercourse has been much more important than one would believe at first. Most of the Near Eastern sedentary populations in historic times have had legends of a desert origin or at least of an ancestral relationship with people of the desert. It will suffice to recall the origin of the descendants of Israel and Ishmael as described in the Bible.[7] Among all recent desert nomads there are legends about their supposed origins in lands of "milk and honey" or in Eden-like regions where fruit grew abundantly by itself.

In the fertile lands, the archaeological sequence provides only part of the evidence. Frequently provinces in the vicinity of the desert, and even large regions, were suddenly invaded by foreigners and the previous settlers killed or pushed out. The cultural sequence then undergoes a sharp change, and in many cases it is impossible to find, in the fertile regions themselves, evidence of the origins of the newcomers. Some of them first turn up as peoples without sedentary traditions who probably came from the desert. The origin of most of these groups must be looked for in the peripheral areas which have no remains of tells, or city mounds, and other long-settled sites and thus have been left blank on archaeological maps.

On the other hand, desert archaeology shows that groups of sophisticated inhabitants of the fertile areas have several times occupied vast regions on the border of the desert and established there, for short periods, small semi-sedentary settlements.

As we shall see, in several instances the art of the nomads shows patterns that occur also in the art of settlers who lived in the vicinity of the desert. Some of these styles are strictly limited

[7] Genesis 16-25.

to small areas; others are spread widely throughout the southern borders of the Fertile Crescent and over to Egypt.

I shall not yet attempt to draw far-reaching conclusions, but I must emphasize the role played by the nomads in the transmission of traits from one cultural center to the other by way of the periphery.

We must keep in mind that these peoples were extremely mobile, incessantly moving from one corner of the desert to the other. Cultural transmission is not necessarily always the result of well-conceived and planned political and ethnic movements. Ideas and things may also be transported and spread through random wanderings, sometimes even indirectly through the agency of marginal bands.

THE NATURALISTIC HUNTERS

The art of the early hunters is best represented at Kilwa.[8] In the Negev it is found chiefly in a cave at Wadi Ramliyeh, near Abdat, where a horned animal and a stylized human figure are depicted.[9]

Similar rock pictures were found in a rock shelter near the village of Adi Yaman, in southern Anatolia.[1] Their style is characterized by deeply incised, sharp and sure outline drawings. The drawings are predominantly of animals, the most common of which by far is the ibex. Oxen, felines, and a doubtful rhinoceros also appear. Human figures are rare, occurring mainly in connection with hunting. At Kilwa a unique copulating scene was also found. Domestic animals are totally absent, and even the dog, which appears in all the later styles of hunting rock carvings, is absent here.

The rock pictures have very large dimensions, usually show-

[8] Rhotert: op. cit.
[9] E. Anati: *Archaeology*, Vol. VIII, No. 1 (1955), pp. 4 ff.
[1] Pittard: op. cit.

Wounded animal with arrow in his
body, from Kilwa (after Rhotert)

Horned animal, spitting blood(?), from Kilwa

Human couple, from Kilwa (after Rhotert)

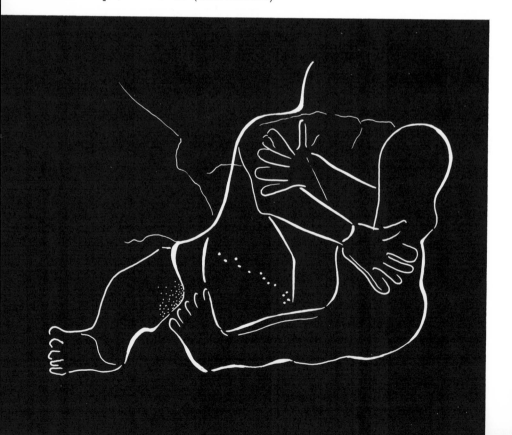

ing their subjects in natural size. The largest picture, that of a
wild ox, is about ten feet long. Deliberate composition of scenes
is extremely rare. In later styles there are very complex scenes,
but here, in order to suggest successful hunting, it sufficed to
depict a wounded animal. A human figure in the act of throwing
his weapon was not a necessary addition. Hunting is the only economic activity illustrated, and it appears to have been the main
concern of the artists. The most frequent weapon shown is the
spear. No bows are depicted, but there is a weapon that seems
to be made of rope, although it is very difficult to determine
whether this represents a lasso, a bolador,[2] or some other device.
The spears are usually rather small and light, and bring to mind
the hunting spears of some Bushmen tribes of South Africa.

The bodies of the animals are sometimes covered with dots
and peck marks, probably representing wounds or blood. Some
animals have one or two lines drawn from their mouths; these
have been interpreted as representing the spitting of blood.
These details are very common also in the Paleolithic art of
France and Spain; moreover, the general style of drawing, the
size of the animals, and the emphasis on animals to the neglect
of human figures are traits which occur in the Franco-Cantabric
Paleolithic art of Europe. However, the monotonous repetition
of the same subjects again and again cannot be compared with
the richness of subjects, signs, and symbols of the Franco-
Cantabric art; and the representational artistry here is far in-
ferior to the perfect proportions and form of the European
Paleolithic hunters.

There is also some resemblance to several naturalistic engravings from the Libyan Desert,[3] but the technique of execu-
tion and the size of the subjects are different there, and the only
sure conclusions one can draw from these comparisons is that

[2] A bolador is a missile consisting of two or more balls connected by a rope; it
was thrown at game and enemies.
[3] See P. Graziosi: *L'Arte rupestre della Libia* (Naples; 1948), Vol. II, Pls. 111–31.

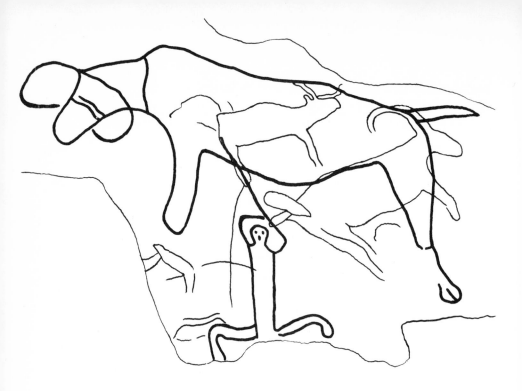

Rock carvings, Style I, from Kilwa. The large ox and the human figure are more deeply engraved than the three other animals, and seem to have been superimposed later.

they point to some similarities in the way of life, the figurative conceptions, and the psychological background of these various groups of hunting artists.

The problem of dating has been attacked by various scholars, but no agreement has been reached yet. The two discoverers of Kilwa, Horsfield and Glueck, relying upon the expert opinion of the Abbé Breuil and other authorities, attributed this group to "Paleolithic and Neolithic times"; but Rhotert, who made the principal study of them, proposed a dating of "Natufian, Tahunian and Chalcolithic times." The comparison with Natufian art is based on the two objects found by Neuville in the Judean Hills, the limestone figurine of a ruminant from Umm ez-Zuttiyeh, and the erotic statuette in calcite from the cave of Ain Sakhri. However, no engravings have been discovered yet in Natufian caves,[4] and no Natufian flint implements have ever been found at Kilwa, at Wadi Ramliyeh, or at Adi Yaman, in the vicinity of the engravings.[5] Other scholars had tentatively proposed to date this art group from Neolithic times, but more careful analysis has shown that the "Neolithic" way of life is not illustrated by the pictures. The main error made by all the various students of this art in their efforts to identify it and to date it was their use of a terminology created for the prehistoric sequence of the fertile regions, one thoroughly unsuitable for studying a culture never found in the fertile regions of the Near East.

The Kilwa artifacts include flint implements of various kinds—Bifacial hand axes, blade-tools of a tradition quite different from that of the Upper Paleolithic known from Palestinian caves, Epi-Paleolithic implements, a local pattern of Early Neolithic Tahunian, and a few flints of Late Neolithic or Chalcolithic type found there without the pottery that usually accompanies them. It is not certain, but the early style of rock

[4] A supposed discovery of cave paintings, by Neuville, was subsequently refuted. See R. Neuville: ILN, Nov. 2, 1932, pp. 730–8.

[5] The only flint tools common to these three sites belong to an evolved and probably late blade industry.

Horned animal wounded by arrows or spears, from Kilwa (after Rhotert)

pictures might belong to the people of one of these cultures. Which one, we do not know.

For the absolute dating of this style there are just two tenuous hints. The first is that in a few cases the subsequent Style II was found superimposed on it, and Style II probably belongs to the fourth millennium B.C. The second is the portrayal of such animals as wild oxen, which could not possibly live in the present climate of Kilwa. If these animals were ever hunted there, as they probably were, the region must have been much wetter at that time. Evidence from Faiyum, Kharga Oasis, and the Nile Valley suggests that smaller pluvial episodes took place rather late in Egypt and the Near East; thus the pictures of wild oxen at Kilwa and elsewhere can hardly be used as evidence for a great antiquity.

Therefore all we can say is that Style I reflects a way of life of small bands of hunters who wandered in what was probably grassland in their time, and that this happened before the fourth millennium B.C. But it might be much more ancient than that.

A puzzling question raised by this style concerns its origins. As with Natufian art, these desert rock pictures, from the very earliest ones, were executed with a sure technique which marks an old tradition. (Style I to some extent even has an air of decadence, which suggests the end rather than the beginning of an art cycle.) Thus, whatever may be the absolute age of these works of art, we can be sure that they are not the earliest ones made by the people of this culture.

As it is known that both the Natufians and the desert artists inherited their artistic talents from previous generations, the failure as yet to discover in this region traces of the art from which both these artistic traditions descended is extremely frustrating for Near Eastern archaeologists.

Within Style I there are several variants, each one having its own character and technique. Some at Kilwa have been found superimposed on one another, so that it is possible to establish their relative chronology. The earliest distinguishable variants

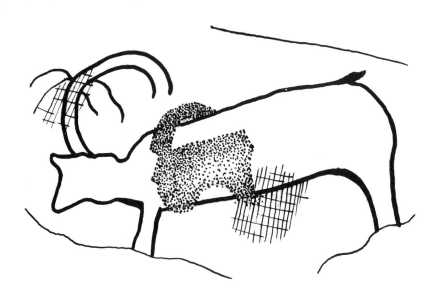

Style II (dotted) superimposed on late Style I at Kilwa

have delicate and fine naturalistic drawing and good proportion, with details such as rounded horns on the ibexes and eyes frequently represented. The second variant is much more deeply incised. The drawing is rough and less regular but still well proportioned and naturalistic. The third variant has a marked tendency to elongate the bodies of the animals; the design is less naturalistic and harmonious than in the two previous groups. This variant is the only one to show the use of leg traps for hunting big game. Similar traps are well known from prehistoric rock pictures of Upper Egypt, left by a people called Autochthonous Mountain Dwellers.[6] The pictures found at Adi Yaman are very similar to those of this variant at Kilwa, which also resembles some rock pictures of the central Sahara.[7]

The latest variant of Style I is much more schematic, its design is of very poor quality, and an imaginative approach defi-

[6] H. A. Winkler: *Rock-Drawings of Southern Upper Egypt*, Vol. I (London: Oxford University Press; 1938), Pls. 18 and 19.
[7] See L. Frobenius and H. Obermaier: *Hadschara Maktuba* (1925), Fig. 10; Graziosi: op. cit., Vol. II, Pl. 122, etc.

nitely replaces naturalism. Nothing remains here of the naturalistic beauty of the earlier variants.

As I have mentioned, Style I seems to represent the late phases of an art cycle. What follows is totally different in spirit and provides information about different human groups. Site 19 at Kilwa, where the naturalistic hunters have left most of their art, is a low stony hill dominating the plateau. The valley around it, which is today flat, broad, dry, and loess-covered, must have been green and well watered when wild cattle roamed in it. The hill was a landmark visible from all around, and from it the movements of wild game in the valley could easily be watched.

REALISM, STYLIZATION, AND THE SPREAD OF PASTORALISM

The second style of rock pictures from the marginal areas of Palestine is totally different. It is characterized by figures entirely dotted. Linear design and outlined figures do not appear at all. Dotting is frequently very light and delicate, and surfaces were patiently covered with tiny regular dots made with small pointed instruments. Occasionally there were several tones of shading on the figures, produced by intentionally varying the density and depth of dotting. Sometimes parts of the bodies of animals were left unchiseled, apparently to indicate actual patches of color.

The design puts a definite emphasis on spatial values and markedly tends toward rounded forms. A few animals have all four legs shown as pairs of spindly lines, but in most cases they have bellies shaped like a "lazy C" whose arched form is continued downward in elongated wedges. These wedges represent the front and hind legs.

Subject matter is still mostly restricted to animal figures. These seem to be wild game, and here again the ibex is the principal subject. A few wild felines are also present. In the Negev no sure figures of dogs have been found as yet. However, Hans Rhotert has published at least four figures from Jordan representing this animal, belonging to Style II.

Photograph and drawing of a carved rock from the central Negev. Three animals of Style IV (outlined) have been superimposed on animals of Style II (dotted).

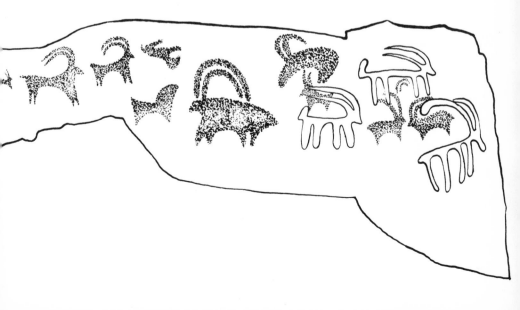

Rock carvings, Style II, dogs chasing
horned animals, from Kilwa (after Rhotert)

Human figure in short skirt and triangular hat, Style II, central Negev

In the Hejaz, among rock pictures of similar style is a herd of domestic oxen.[8] Such animals are totally absent in the Negev and Jordan in the art of that time.

At present, we know of only four human figures belonging to Style II, one in Jordan, one in the Negev, and two in the Hejaz. Three of them appear with sticks in their hands, in a posture well known from the pastoral rock pictures of the Sahara and which usually indicates a shepherd. Two of these figures have pointed hats or headdresses, a detail which occurs also in human figures on pottery of the late part of the fourth millennium B.C. (the proto-literate period) in southern Mesopotamia. These men wore short skirts and were hunters and herders.

In Style II nothing is left of the naturalistic art of the early hunters: the idealization of lines and space,[9] the sense of composition, and the attempt at depicting scenes are the work of a sophisticated people who must have had a more complex economy, ideology, and way of life, and who probably had some contacts with more evolved civilizations.

The relative chronology of Style II is quite well established. Several superimpositions prove that this style is later than that of the early hunters. It has never been found in association with Style III, but its patina is usually darker. Both Style II and Style III have been found in several cases under superimpositions of Style IV, and from the difference in patination one can only say that a long period of time must have elapsed between Style II and Style IV, and that Style III probably came between them.

When the Abbé Breuil saw copies of the rock pictures of Style II, his first reaction was to point out the stylistic similarity between them and the drawings on Mesopotamian pottery of the early Susa style in the proto-literate period (about 3500–3000 B.C.). This comparison is very tempting indeed and might well

[8] See Howe: op. cit.
[9] Great care is taken in order to achieve harmonious shapes. This is usually done by exaggerating curves and by clearly preferring curves to angles.

Two horned animals, Style II, central Negev

turn out to be a good lead for the dating of Style II. The most striking resemblance occurs in some animal figures with the same "lazy C"-shaped body forms and the same idealized rounded and exaggerated horns found on pottery from Susa.

It is interesting to note that Susa was located at that time on the edge of the sedentary area and that this style of pottery decoration appeared there rather suddenly. The rock pictures lack the perfection and the sophistication of the work of the artists who settled down in Sumer and Elam, but some resemblance exists between the art of the marginal peoples and that of these founders of a civilization.

Whereas the stratified debris of sedentary settlements shows precisely the duration of a culture in the fertile regions, in the desert things are not so easy and we have no hints whatsoever concerning the duration of an art style.

As we shall see, various other peoples living in Palestine at roughly the same time as that to which Style II must belong, developed various styles of art. From the symbolic and highly imaginative frescoes of Tuleilat Ghassul to the realistic ivory and bone figurines of the Beersheba culture and the cave engravings of cattle-herding people at Megiddo and Gezer, there is evidence of an extremely rich variety of very different artistic expressions in this period. This artistic variety coincides with cultural and settlement patterns which divide the sedentary regions into very small, restricted cultural areas. Conversely, the desert appears at that time to have had a broad uniformity of customs and culture throughout very large areas. While the agriculturalists were becoming increasingly specialized in their activities and even more attached to their fields and to local natural resources, the marginal bands were keeping to a nomadic way of life and were slowly developing new economic activities such as herding to supplement traditional hunting.

In settlements, the top of one layer and the bottom of a new one clearly mark a succession of two cultures. In the desert, the superimposition of one style of art on another on the same rock does not necessarily indicate that the first style had come to an end and that the second had replaced it in the whole region.

In the central Negev, a drawing in Style IV-C was found underlying a man on horseback in Style V, which, in turn, underlay another animal figure in Style IV-C. This example comes from a much later period than that dealt with here, but it shows what might have happened at all times. Bands of nomads with different cultures may easily coexist in the desert, and unless we find several superimpositions in the same order of succession, it is extremely hard to decide whether or not two art styles of the same general era were partially contemporary. This is why we cannot tell whether Style III, the creation of realistic hunters, partially overlapped Style II or came distinctly later. There is little doubt that Style III continued into much later periods than Style II, but other evidence suggests that in some regions it must have been roughly contemporary with Style II.

The realism of Style III produced well-proportioned, harmonious forms. Most figures were dynamic and full of action: animals are depicted running; human figures occur abundantly now for the first time, and are shown hunting with bows and arrows. The designs are homogeneously dotted, and details such as the eyes are frequently emphasized. The four legs of the animals are almost always drawn separately.

In no other style of Near Eastern rock pictures does composition reach such a perfection and harmony; nor are scenes ever so well conceived. Several interesting traits can be detected in the compositions. In order to show that an arrow shot by a hunter was aimed at a certain animal, the arrow was sometimes depicted several times, first when leaving the bow, then several times in flight, to show its trajectory, and finally wounding the game. Dogs chasing wild game frequently have magnified mouths, and lines are drawn to connect the mouths with the leg of the animal the dogs are chasing. For the sake of a greater unity of composition, figures often touch one another.

In Style III there also seems to be a primitive concept of perspective. A difference in the size of each figure gives a rough, realistic image of a three-dimensional scene in which each subject stands at a different distance from the eye of the observer. This is quite exceptional and impressive when we consider the way of life and the cultural level illustrated by this style.

Beautiful hunting scenes are the central subject. These generally cover entire rocks and are naturally framed by the irregular edge of the smooth surface on which they were engraved. The most frequent animal is still the ibex, and the range of animals is not much wider than in the two previous styles. Felines and mountain goats are part of the wild fauna. There are at least two, and probably three, figures of domesticated oxen, and two horned animals seem to represent domesticated goats. The most important domestic animal is the dog, depicted in every hunting scene. Several dogs were used by each hunter, who appears surrounded by these animals. In this style there is also a richer variety of human figures. Some are represented in long skirts; others in shorter garments around the hips.

Despite the considerable differences between Styles II and III, both illustrate a way of life based on hunting and incipient animal husbandry. The second of these occupations is better represented in Style II than in Style III. Bows and arrows make their first appearance in Style III. The spear is not present in this style, but it will come back into use in the course of Style IV. The bow suddenly appears as an already well-developed weapon. Two kinds of bow are shown in this style. One is small and single-arched; the other, larger and double-arched. In one case, a human figure bears in his hand a mace with a spherical head. Style III occurs in Jordan, the Hejaz, and Sinai, but for the time being is best and most abundantly represented in the Israeli Negev. An almost identical group of rock pictures occurs in Upper Egypt, Nubia, and the eastern Sahara, where both the representational techniques and the subject matter are extremely similar to those of the Near Eastern group.[1] At their closest point these two groups are no more than three hundred miles apart and there might well be some relation between them.

In Upper Egypt, Style III was found not far from Luxor, and nothing seems to indicate any connection with the cultures of the Nile Valley. It appears there, as in the Near East, as the art of a people who relied mainly upon hunting. The Pre-Dynastic age proposed as a date by Winkler seems very probable for these Egyptian pictures. In the Negev, Style III was found less than thirty miles away from Beersheba, and the question arises: Up to what date could bands of hunters have lived there?

It is impossible at present to answer this question. Both the way of life and the weapons used are in the traditions of the Late Stone Age, but in terms of absolute dating it is difficult today to establish how long these traditions lasted in the desert. During the second millennium B.C. the decoration on pottery in some settlements on the edge of the desert seems to have been influenced by the art of the realistic hunters, and this might well be an indication that Style III persisted as late as the second millennium B.C.[2] If this was so, then the realistic hunters of

---

[1] H. A. Winkler: op. cit.; H. Rhotert: *Libysch Felsbilder* (1952), Pls. 12 and 27.
[2] See E. Anati: *Bible et Terre Sainte*, No. 22, July 1959.

Rock carving from Wadi Hamra, Upper Egypt (after Rhotert)

Photograph of the actual carving redrawn on facing page

Hunting scene, Style IV-A, from Jebel Ideid

Drawing of carving showing hunting scene, Style III, Jebel Ideid

Style III coexisted in the desert with very different groups of people: the makers of early Style IV.

The earliest evidence for the appearance of human bands which relied mainly on herding is provided by Style IV. Until recently, this style was considered to be very late,[3] but a reanalysis of this material in 1960 provided proof that at least three different phases can be recognized in it, each one probably the work of different peoples. One of these phases, IV-A, seems to fall within the time limits of this book.

Stylistically, it shows mixed characteristics of Style III and late Style IV, but in subject matter it differs from both. Style IV-A centers on the figures of goats, isolated and in herds. Larger animals such as oxen, camels, and horses, are totally absent.[4] Weapons are very rare and hunting practically disappears. Design becomes less realistic; dynamics gradually disappears. Scenes and compositions are given much less care and details are forgotten. Obviously a very marked change was taking place in the psychological background of the artists.

An extremely interesting picture describes a scene of dancing and music. This scene is divided into two parts; the lower one depicts five human figures, four of them apparently performing a dance, while the fifth is sitting on something resem-

[3] See E. Anati: PEQ, 1955, pp. 49 ff.; PEQ, 1956, pp. 5 ff.
[4] The horse appears for the first time in Style IV-B, and the camel not until Style IV-C. Oxen have not yet been detected after Style III.

Hunting scene, Style IV-A, from Jebel Ideid

bling a chair, seemingly playing on a round drum.[5] The three central figures seem to have a dagger or another tool or weapon at their belts, each one keeping a hand on the pommel. The fourth standing figure carries an object in his hand, and, considering the subject of the scene, it is probably a musical instrument. The upper part shows two human figures playing a stringed instrument and dancing in front of an animal. The instrument is an asymmetrical lyre mounted on a boxlike base (known to archaeologists as a lyre-on-case) similar to those shown in numerous Mesopotamian pictures and to actual instruments excavated at Ur and various other sites. Pictures showing such striking similarities with Mesopotamian and northern Syrian musical instruments had never been found before in Palestine. However, it is well known that the lyre was used here since very ancient times. In the Tell of Megiddo, a Chalcolithic engraving shows a lyre, and at Beni Hassan, in Egypt, a nineteenth-century-B.C. fresco depicting a procession of Asians includes a musician with a haircut very similar to those of the people of our Style IV-A scene, and with a slightly different lyre-on-case.

The problematic instruments of the lower part of the rock picture find their best comparison in a high-relief orthostat found by the German archaeologist Max von Oppenheimer at Tell Halaf, in northern Mesopotamia, now in Berlin and called "the animal Orchestra." [6]

Although the lyres most nearly resemble those from Mesopotamian and northern Syrian sites, in the course of the second millennium B.C. asymmetric lyres mounted on a case also appeared in Egypt, where they are best known from actual instruments and from frescoes at Thebes. Their inspiration is probably Mesopotamian, but they are much smaller and have more elaborated lines.[7]

[5] See E. Anati: *Rivista di Scienze Preistoriche*, Vol. X (1955), pp. 70 ff.
[6] Orthostat No. 57-C.
[7] A lyre of Theban inspiration is also depicted on a Megiddo ivory probably dating from the very end of the Late Urban Age. See G. Loud: *Megiddo Ivories* (Chicago: University of Chicago Press; 1939), Pl. 4, etc.

Upper part of rock carving portraying dancing scene, central Negev. The two human beings are dancing in front of an animal and are playing musical instruments (asymmetric lyres of Mesopotamian type).

Drawing of dancing scene shown above

Lower part of dancing scene, central Negev

Drawing of dancing scene shown above

The figures from this scene look as if they were an inter-mediate type between the Mesopotamian and the Egyptian. In this very broad cultural context these rock pictures of the Negev are particularly significant. The same question arises again and again: What was the role of the desert nomads in the transmission and spread of cultural traits?

That nomadic pastoral and trading bands wandered from Mesopotamia to Egypt during the Urban Age is well known. A great many ethnic movements took place along the periphery of the Fertile Crescent at the time of the early dynasties of Ur. Additional information on the movements of these or slightly later times is provided by the stories of the Patriarchs in the Bible. In Genesis (12:5) we read: "And Abraham took Sarai his wife, and Lot his brother's son, and all their substance that they had gathered, and the souls that they had gotten in Haran, and they went forth to go into the land of Canaan . . ." And a few lines further on (12:10): "And there was famine in the land: and Abraham went down into Egypt to sojourn there . . ."

The dancing scene was found less than twenty miles from Wadi Kudeirat, probably the Biblical place of Kadesh Barnea, but it is doubtful whether it will ever be possible to identify its artists or to determine its precise date. Whatever the date, Style IV-A must belong to the period called the Urban Age (or the Bronze Age) in the fertile regions, and the scene was inspired by a way of life very similar to that of the pastoral Hebrew Patriarchs. Their artists must have moved about along the southern edges of the Fertile Crescent, coming in contact from time to time with various sedentary populations, and probably wandering over very large areas from southern Mesopotamia to Sinai and Egypt.

The Patriarchs appear to have also wandered within the boundaries of settled areas, a point to be dealt with in more detail later, but the Patriarchs were only one of the many nomadic and semi-nomadic bands which circulated around the settlements of the Urban Age.

THE SEVEN ART STYLES OF
THE ROCK PICTURES FROM THE NEGEV
AND SURROUNDING REGIONS

STYLE	Major activities depicted in order of importance	Significant weapons and tools in order of importance	Domestic stock in order of importance	Connections and chronological estimates
I	hunting	spear, lasso (?), bolador (?)		
II	hunting, herding	spear, stick	dog, ox, goat	
III	hunting, herding	bow, round macehead	dog, goat, ox	Connections with Pre- and Proto-Dynastic Egypt (?)
IV A	herding, hunting, dancing, religious ceremonies	bow, musical instruments	dog, goat	Mesopotamian connections, 2d millennium B.C.
B	herding, hunting	bow, stick, spear	dog, goat, horse	
C	herding, trade	bow, stick, spear, shield	dog, goat, horse, camel	Thamudic and Nabataean inscriptions, ca. 300 B.C.– A.D. 200
V	herding, trade, warfare	spear, shield, bow	horse, camel, dog, goat	Greek and Nabataean inscriptions, Roman-Byzantine connections, ca. A.D. 200–600
VI	herding, hunting	spear, shield, bow	camel, goat, dog, horse	Kufic inscriptions, Medieval
VII	herding	bow, spear	camel, goat, dog, horse	Post-Medieval

Most probably only certain groups had the habit of making rock pictures, and these pictures therefore shed light on the daily life of only these particular groups. Many other nomads must have existed in the desert who did not carve pictures on rocks, and of these little is known at present. Some of the stone circles and the other rough remains in the desert might be traces of these groups. There were also nomads who built megalithic monuments in the desert. These are different and most likely considerably later than other megalithic monuments I shall speak of, but they help to show that many different groups with different traditions lived in the peripheral regions while the fertile areas were slowly evolving into farming and subsequent urban societies.

From the times of the Patriarchs onward, the Bible and a great many Mesopotamian, Syrian, Hittite, and Egyptian documents provide rich sources of information on the nomads of the desert. By then they had become part of the general political, economic, and cultural nexus of the Near East, and by degrees they moved into the historical framework. In the last part of this book we shall see how important the marginal populations became in the political development of the Near East. But first we shall go back to the fertile regions and see what was going on there at the time of incipient farming.

PART·FOUR

THE AGE OF EARLY FARMING

I

The Beginning of
Food-Producing
Activities

THE NEW AGE

T HE AGE OF Early Farming began when food-producing economies acquired a certain local importance, and ended when those same economies were developed enough to support the growth of urban societies.[1] In this age, agriculture and stock raising became the principal means of subsistence in large parts of the Near East, and various human groups gradually evolved from a way of life based mainly on hunting and fishing to that of village farmers.

In this age man acquired a new physiognomy, one more familiar to us, and a mentality and a behavior which we can understand better because they are nearer to our own. Man was becoming an industrious and productive being, able to affect

[1] The corresponding period in Iraq has been called by Robert J. Braidwood "the era of the primary village farming communities." See R. J. Braidwood and B. Howe: *Prehistoric Investigations in Iraqi Kurdistan* (Chicago: University of Chicago Press; 1960), p. 170.

his environment substantially by his daily activities. He was learning to settle himself in one spot, to devote his time to developing it, and to exploit whatever nature offered that he was able to use. In this period, the population of the Near East grew considerably, social units became larger and more densely concentrated, and some units felt the need to assure their rights to certain favorable spots which could provide them with their economic needs.

Settlement did not result, in all cases, in an easier life. Sedentary activities gave man busy days: stock raising demanded continuous care of the livestock; the grazing and watering had to be supervised; they had to be guarded from straying, or from being stolen, or from being preyed upon. Agriculture demanded a knowledge of the yearly cycle of seasons and a planned schedule of activities throughout the year. Other activities such as trade demanded planned travel and planned encounters with other human groups.

The new way of life was conditioned by planning to a great extent. Life acquired a rhythm which we are able to follow and to understand, and which differs enormously from that of hunters and gatherers, for whom luck played such an important part and for whom life was, frequently, a series of unrelated and accidental adventures.

Envisioning the daily life of one of the excavated hamlets or villages of the incipient-farming period, we can imagine how it was filled from morning to night with various activities in which all the people, regardless of age, participated. The work of the fields and herding occupied some of the people; others were probably busy building or repairing the huts or houses, the silos, the fireplaces, the floors, the storage spaces, and the tools and weapons of which so many traces are found in each settlement. The fireplaces, grindstones, mortars, and pestles found in every court and every house afford hints of a busy domestic life. Food was becoming more varied and more elaborate, and more time was needed to prepare it. Social and religious institutions

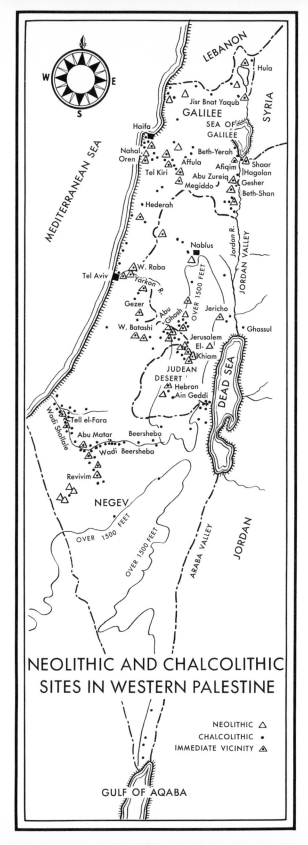

NEOLITHIC AND CHALCOLITHIC
SITES IN WESTERN PALESTINE

NEOLITHIC △
CHALCOLITHIC ·
IMMEDIATE VICINITY ⧩

are indirectly revealed by public buildings, non-utilitarian art, and other cult objects.

In the Age of Early Farming, people who settled in permanent villages and devoted themselves to new occupations were continuously obliged to plan far ahead and to perform a series of complex actions in order to achieve distant goals, such as the harvesting, the planting of orchards, and the raising of livestock. These people were able to think very much the way we do, and to some extent we see in them our own earliest likeness.

The Age of Early Farming was a very inventive age, as I have said. Not only new economic pursuits and the variety of settlements indicate this, but also all the secondary expressions of material and spiritual culture. Life became increasingly sophisticated, society increasingly complex, cultural patterns increasingly varied. Men developed new methods in technology and discovered new materials for their tools, weapons, and other objects of daily use. In this period they first learned how to make pottery, then how to produce metal and work it. They developed new forms of ideology and religious beliefs, and new aesthetic values.

Men were mentally ready to engage in new agricultural and pastoral activities, but each group developed them very much in its own way. Some populations appear to have engaged in both activities; others for various reasons gave more emphasis to the one than to the other. Obviously, in regions where the environment made it impossible to carry on agriculture, only stock raising could be developed; whereas in some fertile regions where crops turned out to be more profitable than pastures, and where animals could seriously damage the crops, it is likely that more importance was given to agriculture. But from the first efforts at stock raising and agriculture to the time when they became major occupations, thousands of years had to pass. The earliest attempts at each go back to Mesolithic times. They developed in very slow and uneven steps, in which every group used its own experiences, adapted new inventions to the resources offered by nature, and gradually systemized casual experiments and unexpected results.

In previous sections we have seen how fishing developed in Mesolithic times, and sometimes remained an important source of food thereafter. Hunting game and collecting wild roots, fruits, and herbs also were practices that persisted long after the Stone Age was over.

Another activity that evolved in the Neolithic was trade. Through it various materials became available in regions where they were not found or produced, people could become specialists in activities other than those directly connected with food gathering and producing, and cultural traits could be transmitted and spread more regularly.

After the localization and diversification of cultures at the end of the Paleolithic, the Transitional cultures, which relied primarily on food gathering but began to produce some food, lasted much longer in the arid regions than in the fertile regions. The desert fostered economies and ways of life adapted to the scarce and uneven distribution of water and to the environmental impossibility of fishing and agriculture. There the major food resource was the livestock which eventually became partially domesticated.

In fertile Palestine, on the other hand, the widespread Natufian culture gave way to three main patterns, one along the coast, the second in the mountains, and the third in the Jordan Valley. This localization further increased in the course of the Age of Early Farming. Some intercourse existed with various nearby regions, as has been disclosed by the discovery of exotic goods in archaeological sites—goods which were imported from elsewhere and which imply some sort of exchange. These exchanges furthered the diffusion of cultural traits but apparently were not powerful enough to submerge local traditions or stop their development. The balance between novelty and tradition changed when trade became important enough to permit the accumulation of substantial surpluses, and when large political units with centralized leadership felt the need for expansion. This happened with the growth of urban societies. Before that the opposite attitude was dominant. Man concentrated his attention on his fields, on his water resources, and on all possible devices for making his land become more productive. These were local preoccupations, and they intensified the localization of cultural patterns.

The Near East is still covered today with small villages and farming communities of which the earliest examples we know date from some eight thousand years ago. In the intervening years civilizations and empires rose and disappeared, and some towns grew to vast size while some small villages and hamlets simply persisted. The major patterns of settlement existing today were established in the Near East in the Age of Early Farming; the fertile regions were differentiated into special, varied, mosaic-like habitat patterns.

The Age of Early Farming is divided by archaeologists into two periods, the Neolithic, or New Stone Age, and the Chalcolithic, or the period of transition between the Stone and the metal ages. The Neolithic started in Palestine in the eighth millennium B.C. The Chalcolithic started at the end of the fifth, or at the very beginning of the fourth millennium, and ended with the spread of urban society, late in the fourth millennium B.C.

In the Near East, and particularly in Palestine, there is no sharp cultural change between the Mesolithic and the Neolithic. Late Mesolithic shows some elements of material culture which are typically Neolithic, while early Neolithic has large quantities of microliths and other Mesolithic elements. In various parts of Palestine, mainly at Nahal Oren, on Mount Carmel, at Wadi Kharaitun, in the Judean Desert, and at Jericho, in the lower Jordan Valley, Natufian gradually evolved into local patterns of

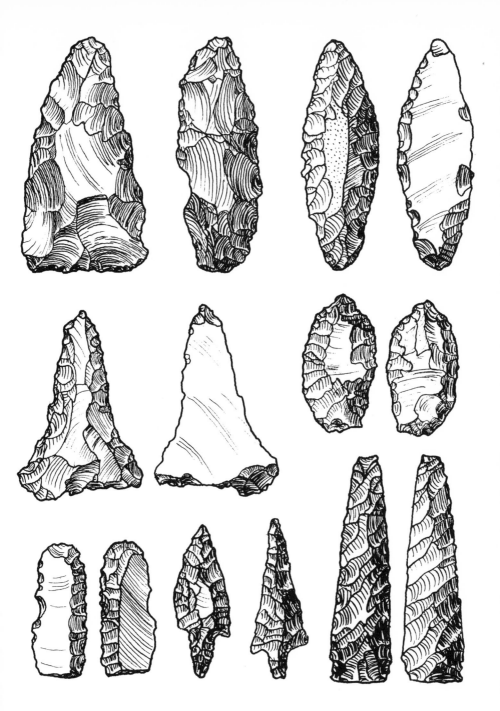

Tahunian flint implements from Kilwa (after Rhotert)

early Neolithic.[2] The term "Neolithic," in Palestine, and indeed all over the Near East, creates several serious problems, as it includes a large number of cultures which are much more diverse than those of Neolithic Europe. Some were the way of life of small bands which still relied mainly on hunting or fishing; some were the way of life of agricultural communities; others were the cultures of semi-nomadic shepherds; and still others were the cultures of highly stratified societies settled in fortified towns and relying on complex economies. These very different ways of life went on in the Near East side by side at the same time, and all are considered Neolithic cultures.

The clearest common denominators in the artifacts of all these different cultures are to be seen in three typical flint objects: the pick, which presumably was an agricultural tool; the ax, presumably a tool for cutting wood; and the winged arrowhead, a new weapon which reached the peak of its popularity in early Neolithic times. All three had first appeared in the course of the Mesolithic, but only in Neolithic times did they become relatively numerous.

Pottery came into use in the Near East in the course of the Neolithic, although in some other parts of the world it appeared in Mesolithic and Upper Paleolithic times. It was a discovery of great importance, as it afforded an easy way of cooking food and a cheap means of transporting and preserving liquids. One significant aspect of pottery is that it was manufactured from the first substance made by man. It was a tremendous step for prehistoric man to find out that when clay and water were worked and baked, a new substance was produced. Pottery is found wherever it was made or used, as its fragments are practically indestructible; like flint tools in the Stone Age, in later periods pottery became a very important means of archaeological identification, for each culture had its own way of making and dec-

---

[2] K. Kenyon: *Digging Up Jericho* (London: Benn; 1957); K. Kenyon: PEQ, 1960; M. Stekelis: IEJ, Vol. X, No. 2 (1960), pp. 118-19.

orating it. The nature of the archaeological layers changed considerably with the appearance of pottery, because pottery is easily breakable and potsherds began to mix with, and to cover, the floors of habitations. Therefore archaeologists have divided the Neolithic into two major phases: Pre-pottery Neolithic and Full Neolithic, or Neolithic-with-pottery.

Until recently, Pre-pottery Neolithic was considered a uniform culture throughout Palestine, but the excavations at Nahal Oren and Jericho, and recent explorations in the Negev, have shown that various patterns of this culture existed and developed side by side. Contrary to what was believed only two or three years ago, Pre-pottery Neolithic and Full Neolithic appear to have partially coexisted in Palestine, and while in the northern coastal region and the Jordan Valley some peoples already made extensive use of pottery, in the Judean Hills, in the region of Wadi Shallale, near Gaza, and in other parts of Palestine, Pre-pottery cultures continued to exist.

Full Neolithic cultures assumed various patterns in Palestine. While in the north the most widespread culture was related to those of other regions of the Levantine coast, another pattern developed on the shores of the Yarmuk River and in the middle Jordan Valley, and still another evolved at Jericho and in other localities in the south. These various patterns appear to be partially contemporary with one another, and each one was influenced by different foreign connections and by different traditions. In this period we also have the earliest evidence in Palestine that men had discovered the principle of the wheel. This is attested indirectly by the fact that some pottery was made with the help of a turntable.

The Chalcolithic people lived in agricultural settlements and raised large herds of domestic livestock. They had highly developed handicrafts. Their basketry, pottery making, and decorative art were very rich and varied. These are the products of the intellectual gifts of men whose culture was conditioned by a stable and unique environment. One of their major technological achievements was the initiation of working metal, the raw material upon which most of the technology of the future was to rely.[3] Culture became even more localized in small areas, but at the same time interchanges between localities increased greatly. Behind the appearance of provincialism, culture was progressing toward homogeneity in its major traits.[4]

Main Subdivisions
of the Age of Early Farming in Palestine

PERIODS	APPROX. DATE OF START (B.C.)
Pre-pottery Neolithic	shortly before 7000
Full Neolithic (with pottery)	5500
Chalcolithic	4000
Proto-Urban	3350

THE BEGINNING OF AGRICULTURE

On the face of it, there is only a slight difference between choosing a camp site because some edible plant grows there and actively doing something to make that plant grow better or multiply. But the two acts are categorically different because they spring from completely different psychological motives and because they are the basic acts of two different types of economy and modes of life. It is not a matter of the slight difference between the one and the other; the second is the result of a very slow conceptual and technological development.

Date palms, olive trees, fig trees, wild apples, wild grapes,

[3] Palestine was one of the few regions where metalworking evolved before 3000 B.C. Other centers of early metalworking were Iran, Iraq, and Anatolia.
[4] Cultural transmission and parallel development of previous common characteristics were both undoubtedly present in small provinces which evolved in the Chalcolithic period, but a problem that still demands a satisfactory solution is the extent of the influence of each one of these two processes.

berries, and several other species of fruit trees and shrubs still grow naturally in several parts of the Near East and North Africa. Probably man slowly noticed that trees grow better along a river or near a water source than in arid places, and that a tree yields better fruit when it is pruned. Some men probably also cut root suckers from fruit trees and occasionally perhaps tried to transplant some of these. Thereafter it probably took several thousand years to develop the first systematic plantation.

The systematic cultivation of cereals must have been the result of an extremely long development. Wild barley grows throughout the hilly regions of Palestine, Syria, Anatolia, Transcaucasia, Turkestan, Iran, and Afghanistan.[5] In Syria-Palestine and in other areas of the Near East, wild emmer and other kinds of wild wheats have also been found. Today they occur mixed with other plants on hillsides and in uncultivated fields in the immediate vicinity of the Natufian caves of El-Wad and Kebara and on the hills surrounding the Mesolithic site of Einan.

Unfortunately, paleobotany, the study of ancient vegetables and plants, was much neglected in the Near East until a short while ago, so that the information we possess on the early stages of the domestication of food plants is very fragmentary. At Jarmo, in northeastern Iraq, a farming community in Pre-pottery Neolithic times already knew how to plant wheat and barley, and these grains had already acquired some incipient characteristics of domesticated seeds as early as the seventh millennium B.C.[6] There is no certain knowledge that any grains or vegetables were domesticated and cultivated in Palestine before Full Neolithic times, so that, for the time being, we have to rely on indirect evidence in tracing the development of incipient agriculture.

In Palestine, the Mesolithic Natufians have left quantities of stone mortars and pestles, some of them very large and heavy. These obviously served for grinding something, and the quan-

---

[5] Harold J. E. Peake: JRAI, Vol. LVII (1929), pp. 22 ff.; Peake: *Antiquity*, Vol. VII (1933), pp. 73 ff. See H. Holback in Braidwood and Howe: op. cit. pp. 119 ff.
[6] H. Holback in Braidwood and Howe: op. cit., pp. 119 ff.

tity and the size of these tools clearly imply two facts: Making these tools demanded a great deal of time and energy, and because of their weight they could not be transported. Thus their makers must have led a rather sedentary life; and whatever was ground by them, was ground in quite large quantities and quite regularly. They were part of the everyday equipment of the household. For the time being no evidence tells us what was ground, but most probably it was some sort of cereal. These large, heavy stone tools were found in each site and on each hut floor of the Natufians. The food prepared with them obviously occupied a prominent place in the diet of these Mesolithic people.

The sickle is one of the typical tools of the Natufians. Flint sickle blades have been found in large quantities. Sickle hafts and handles were carefully made and artistically decorated. As we have seen, this decoration of tools was probably connected with fertility magic and implies a ritualistic behavior toward the object and its product. The harvesting of cereals must have been very important. The problem still unsolved is to what extent the harvest was domestic. In other words, what did the Natufians do in the course of the four seasons to increase the abundance of the harvest? Did they simply collect wild cereals, or did they deliberately cultivate them in some way?

A full answer cannot be given yet, but considering the importance of grain in the food supply, it seems probable that the Natufians relied on this resource, stored and preserved it, knew in advance the season of the year in which it became available, and presumably somehow fostered its growth. It is not unlikely that some of the collected seeds were scattered in the fields at the right time of the year, and that the Natufians carried seeds with them to sow in new fields whenever they moved from one place to another. If this is so, they can be considered the earliest incipient agriculturalists.

From modern "primitive" examples we learn that several

different methods are used by incipient agriculturalists. These vary according to the plants and cereals available, the kind of soil and natural environment, the amount of rain, and the experience of the people. Narrow valleys and broad plains offer different opportunities, as do regions with different kinds of natural vegetation. The same was true for the incipient agriculturalists of the Near East.

Palestine and, indeed, all the other countries of the Old World have never had a homogeneous economy since the beginning of food producing. While some groups were already busy with agriculture, others continued to rely on hunting; others specialized in fishing, in stock raising, and in other economic activities; still others had a mixed economy. In Palestine and in other Near Eastern countries some Bedouins and other nomadic and semi-nomadic populations still ignore agriculture in our day.

A Neolithic survey of the northern Jordan Valley[7] has shown that several Neolithic settlements were located in a geographical position which hardly took defense into consideration. These were very small settlements, usually not over 100 by 150 feet, and apparently the main factors in the choice of the site were the presence of a perennial spring and the availability of a strip of good agricultural land within a narrow side valley.

Such narrow valleys are frequently chosen today in Syria and Palestine by Bedouin incipient agriculturalists or by herding Arabs in transition to a sedentary life. The reason for such a choice is a simple one. There is no need for manuring in these narrow valleys, as winter rains drain down from the side slopes enough virgin soil to renew the fertility of the plot. Even today, people using neither fertilizers nor crop rotation are unable to settle down in larger, flat valleys for more than a few years. In the narrow valleys the strip of land cultivated by the incipient agriculturalists was rather small, usually not over a couple of acres. The size of some of these settlements makes it very doubt-

[7] M. Prausnitz: IEJ, Vol. IX, No. 3 (1959), pp. 166–74.

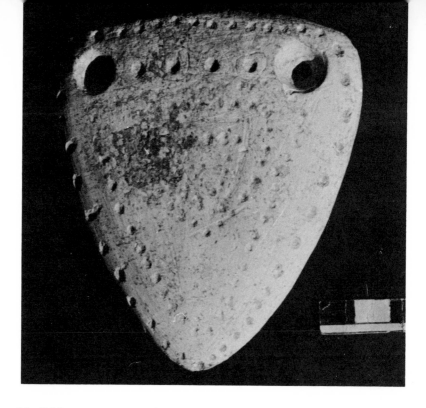

Neolithic stone pendant from Tell Eli (excavated by Prausnitz)

ful whether they were inhabited by more than one large household.

Some of these settlements seem to have had a rather short existence. The material culture is quite homogeneous in each, and in most of them there is no evidence of more than one habitation layer. However, there are some exceptions. Tell Eli, at the confluence of Wadi Fejjas and the Jordan River, had an ecological situation rather different from most sites. Agricultural land around it was much more extensive, and the settlement was larger.

Each one of these small areas of incipient agriculture developed in its own way. Some died out after a time, while others throve and expanded and sometimes became small villages.

There is evidence of a parallel but somewhat different development on the northwestern edge of Mount Carmel, at the

southwestern end of the Esdraelon Valley (between Tell Yokneam and Megiddo, extending for some twelve miles). Several
Neolithic sites were found along the strip of land at the foot
of the hills, near the entrances of the wadies.

The pattern of these settlements is extremely interesting.
Most of them were composed of a single house, ranging in size
from 65 by 25 feet to 30 by 15 feet. These obviously are sites
of single households; these settlements cover the whole cultivable area between the rocky hills and the marshy plain. Unlike the
sites in the side wadies of the Jordan Valley, these sites can be
seen from very far away, and even seem to mark the line of a
main highway along the Esdraelon Valley from west to east,
from the Mediterranean to the Jordan Valley. Also unlike the
incipient settlements of the side wadies, this strip of land was
very thickly inhabited in Neolithic times, and the density of
population must have been then one of the greatest in Palestine.
Frequently the distance from one settled spot to another is no
more than a thousand feet.

Water has always been plentiful in this region, and almost
every one of these sites had its own spring. Small perennial rivers
still flow from the opening of the wadies toward the valley, and
along some of these rivers there are slight accumulations of
human debris. These must be leavings from Neolithic times,
for, toward the end of this period and in the Chalcolithic, some
of these accumulations form the basis of tells which later on
were fortified by a ring of walls.

However, the single-household type of agricultural settlement did not disappear, and several of them containing Chalcolithic and even Early Urban Age pottery have been discovered
in the vicinity of Yokneam, Hazorea, Tell Kiri, Abu Zureiq, and
Megiddo. From aerial photographs the pattern of settlement
throughout this strip of land shows up very clearly. The foundations of many of these settlements are clearly visible wherever
the land has been freshly plowed. The better land was more

Tell Abu Zureiq, with the Plain of Esdraelon in the background

thickly inhabited, and at its center slowly grew the tell, the future town.

A type of incipient agriculture carried on by relatively limited groups, and still found in primitive societies today, is what African ethnologists call garden culture. Small plots are tilled with hoes—usually by women—and the grain is sown there. Fertilizers are not used, and when after a few years the soil is exhausted, the small settlement is transferred to a spot near a new strip of virgin land, which is cleared and tilled in its turn. This constant removal must involve temporary habitations which last only a few years and are thereafter abandoned. The same site may be resettled only after a period of time long enough to let the soil renew its fertility.

Such a pattern is found in Palestine only in Chalcolithic times, and mainly along the major wadies, such as Wadi Shallale and Wadi Beersheba, in the semi-arid loess zone of southern Palestine. Here a people was settling down and slowly evolving a local pattern. Its agricultural methods and its material culture were in general different from that of the earliest agriculturalists of northern Palestine, who by that time probably already knew how to manure the soil and let fields lie fallow, and how to preserve fertility through other sophisticated agricultural devices. Again and again different patterns of settlement grew up in the vicinity of one another. While Jericho already had a thousand-year-old urban tradition, the Yarmukians lived in camp sites in the same valley.

During Neolithic times agricultural settlements slowly concentrated along perennial rivers, each one finding the best spot for its particular way of life, each one developing its economy according to the natural resources at its disposal. Thus were settled the plains of Nahal Sorek, the plains of the Yarkon River, the plains of the Kishon River, and of course the plains of the largest Palestinian river, the Jordan. But at the same time other people focused more on fishing, on stock raising, and on other occupations, while on the arid Jordanian Plateau and in the Negev, as well as in the central hills of Palestine, other people still relied mainly on hunting and gathering.

THE BEGINNING OF THE DOMESTICATION OF ANIMALS

In previous sections we have seen how the development of new hunting devices, such as the trap, allowed Mesolithic men to catch animals alive. When food was abundant, there was no need to kill the captured animal immediately and it could be kept until its meat was needed. This might have been one of the various ways through which the idea of animal husbandry came to human minds. Other animals might have been found while young and kept as pets. Sometimes men and animals had to share the same water sources, and this probably gave animals and men opportunities of coming into contact with each other. Some animals turned out to be unfit to be kept in captivity for long periods; others, on the contrary, were able to adapt themselves quite well to their symbiotic life with men. The idea of stock raising, or of letting animals reproduce in captivity, probably developed in the course of time; and after capturing and breeding had become successful and customary, men probably began to use animal by-products such as milk and wool.

The two main ways of detecting the presence of domestic animals in an ancient culture are through rock pictures and other kinds of representational art and through the study of animal bones in archaeological levels. The first of these methods has been used systematically only recently, but obviously it is of no help in the case of people who left no figurative animal art. The second presents its own difficulties, as it is not always easy to distinguish the bones of a domestic animal from those of its wild cousin.

Where herding was the general practice, animals were usually killed at an optimal age, and thus a statistical study of the age of the skeletons at the time of slaughter theoretically could help to distinguish domestic from wild animals. But in the earliest examples of domestication only very few animal skeletons were found in each archaeological site, so that paleontologists thus far have had to rely on what they could learn from isolated bones.

Animals and men alike undergo physical changes with a changing diet and a changing way of life, and these changes are revealed by fossil bones. In domestication, organs which animals did not use any longer, such as the horns, sometimes atrophied and decreased in size. The whole skeleton of domesticated animals in the course of generations usually became more delicate, and frequently also smaller in general size; but often these differences are very difficult to detect.

Fully domesticated animals, in the modern sense of the phrase, do not seem to appear until the Neolithic age, but their stage of evolution implies a long process of adjustment to captivity. We do not know how long such a process took, but it was certainly many generations. On his side, man underwent a long period of trial and error before he was able to raise livestock successfully in captivity, so that it is likely that the earliest attempts at domestication were made before Neolithic times. Despite the rich finds of animal bones in Mesolithic layers, it is doubtful whether the fauna killed in captivity was ever more than a small percentage of the total killed for food. The percentage increased considerably during Neolithic times, between the seventh and the fifth millennium b.c.,[8] but it became predominant only with Chalcolithic times, in the fourth millennium b.c. For this period the site of Horvat Beter, near Beersheba, has produced faunal remains 84.4 per cent of which belonged to domestic animals.[9] In other Chalcolithic sites in the same region, domestic animals constituted 95 per cent of the fauna.[1]

In regard to stock raising in incipient-farming communities, we must make distinctions between three stages: early attempts at taming, stock raising as a secondary economic occupation, and herding as the main means of subsistence. In the fertile regions of Palestine, taming seems to have been tried by the Natufians, between the thirteenth and the eighth millennium b.c. Secondary stock raising was practiced constantly from Neolithic times on; while the third stage probably occurred only during Chalcolithic times. This last was probably a time of great ethnic movements by bands relying on herding, and we find considerable traces of them in peripheral areas.

The domestic animals of the Age of Early Farming in the Near East included dogs, goats, sheep, cattle, pigs, various kinds of donkeys and half-asses (*Hemionus*), and probably also cats. Each one of these animals appears to have had a different history of domestication and a different use. Goats, sheep, cattle, and pigs were, from the beginning, animals raised for meat, whereas it is doubtful whether the others ever served the same purpose. It is not unlikely that donkeys, asses, and the other animals of the

---

[8] It is interesting to note the similarity between the late Neolithic faunal assemblage of Palestine and that found in Egypt from about the same time. See G. Caton-Thompson and E. W. Gardner: *The Desert Fayum* (London: Royal Anthropological Institute; 1934).

[9] S. Angress: Atiqot, Vol. II (1959), pp. 53–71.

[1] T. Josien: IEJ, Vol. V, No. 4 (1955), pp. 246–56.

horse family were used for transportation from very early times. The dog probably had the same major tasks it has today, and helped men in hunting, herding, and guarding. If, as it seems, cats were also domesticated so early, it is not clear how they were used.

The earliest animal to have been domesticated is believed to be the dog. Dog bones are commonly found in Mesolithic levels outside the Near East as well. The makers of the Maglemosian Mesolithic culture of northern Europe had the dog as their companion. In the Near East, bones of dogs have been found in the Palestinian caves of El-Wad and Shukbah.[2] In northern Iran, at Belt Cave, dog bones were found in a Mesolithic level dated by radiocarbon at about 11,500 years ago.[3]

Like all other animals in an incipient phase of domestication, these dogs still preserved many of the features of their wild ancestors. Various breeds of wild canines became familiar to men in Mesolithic times. Whereas most scholars believe that the dogs of the fishermen and hunters of northern Europe were the off-spring of wolves, in the Near East the two main breeds of dogs associated with man up to the end of the Age of Early Farming appear to derive from the jackal and from an extinct species of dingo. The jackal-dog seems to have been domesticated also, perhaps independently, by the Capsian culture in Algeria.[4] In the fourth millennium B.C. this dog was depicted in the rock pictures of Upper Egypt.[5]

In the course of the Neolithic, the dog became common in

[2] D. A. E. Garrod and D. M. A. Bate: *The Stone Age of Mount Carmel*, Vol. I (London: Oxford University Press; 1937); D. M. A. Bate: PPS, Vol. VIII (1942), pp. 15–20.

[3] Carleton S. Coon: *Cave Explorations in Iran, 1949* (Philadelphia: University of Pennsylvania; 1951); E. K. Ralph: *Science*, Vol. CXXI (1955), pp. 149–51 (Carbon 14: 11,480 ± 550 B.P.).

[4] R. Vaufrey: *La Préhistoire de l'Afrique*; I: *Le Maghreb* (Tunis; 1955).

[5] See H. A. Winkler: *Rock-Drawings of Southern Upper Egypt*, Vol. I (London: Oxford University Press; 1938), Pl. 16-2. In Pre-Dynastic Egypt, both the jackal-dogs and the wolf-dogs seem to have been domesticated. See M. Hilzleimer: *Antiquity*, Vol. VI (1932), pp. 411–19; Y. S. Moustafa: *Bulletin de l'Institut d'Egypte*, Vol. XXXVI (1944), pp. 105–9.

all the fertile regions of the Near East, and in the fourth millennium B.C. it was also kept by the peripheral hunting-and-pastoral bands of the desert (see page 198).

Although dogs were probably domesticated independently in various parts of the Near East and in North Africa, meat animals were first domesticated in the Near East, and this custom presumably reached other regions later as a consequence of diffusion.

The wild ancestors of goats and sheep came originally from the Near East. While in captivity, these animals underwent some mutations in their horns and in their skeletons, and the presence of these changes indicates a long prior period of domestication. Domesticated goats have been found in Pre-pottery Neolithic levels at Jericho dating back to the seventh millennium B.C.,[6] and to shortly thereafter at Jarmo, in northeastern Iraq.[7] These are the earliest goats on whose domestication paleontologists unanimously agree. However, various scattered evidence seems to indicate that the domestication of this animal began earlier. Bones of a small goat believed to have died in captivity were discovered in the rock shelter of El-Khiam, in the Judean Desert, in a Mesolithic level.[8] Fragmentary bones of a goat believed to be domestic were found in a late Mesolithic level in northern Iran at Belt Cave.[9] Also, in North Africa domestic goats seem to have first appeared with makers of a Mesolithic culture.[1]

After the seventh millennium B.C., the breeding of this animal quickly became a significant activity. By the early part of the sixth millennium B.C. the domestic goat had already spread widely over the Near East, and was found at Jericho in Palestine, at Amouq in Cilicia, at Hassuna in northern Mesopotamia, and at Sialk on the Iranian Plateau. In the course of the same millennium it was to be seen also in Lower Egypt, where it is present in the earliest levels of Faiyum.

[6] F. E. Zeuner: PEQ, 1955, pp. 70–86.
[7] C. A. Reed: *Science*, Vol. CXXX (1959), pp. 1629–39.
[8] R. Vaufrey in R. Neuville: Archives IPH, Vol. XXIV (1951), pp. 215–17.
[9] Coon: op. cit.
[1] R. Vaufrey: L'A, Vol. XLIII (1933), p. 476.

The domestic sheep, which was to become such an important food animal in later times, does not seem to have been favored in Palestine before the fourth millennium B.C. This animal is first in evidence at Belt Cave in the Early Neolithic, in the sixth millennium B.C. Shortly thereafter it appeared also at Sialk (Level I) and at Amouq (Amouq B). By the fifth millennium B.C. it had already spread very widely and was common from Mesopotamia to North Africa. In northern Egypt, it seems to be present in the earliest levels of Faiyum, and shortly thereafter it appeared in southern Egypt (in the Badarian and the Amratian civilizations). Early in the fourth millennium it was introduced as far south in the Nile Valley as the Sudan (Shabeinab).

In the Atlas Mountains in Morocco and Algeria rock pictures connected with Neolithic industries of Capsian tradition have produced several figures of goats which seem to be domestic, as well as some undoubtedly domestic sheep.[2] The interesting fact is that no wild sheep existed in Africa, and that the sheep of the Neolithic Atlas Mountains were undoubtedly introduced from western Asia, which is their land of origin, by men. In a similar fashion domestic sheep were introduced to central Europe, where they are first found in the course of the third millennium B.C.

Domesticated cattle are the descendants of *Bos primigenius*, the long-horned ox hunted by Paleolithic man throughout Europe, Asia, and North Africa. Its presence in a domesticated form in the sixth millennium B.C. has been traced in various parts of the Middle East, mainly at Hacilar, in Anatolia, in the lowest level of Amouq, at Sialk (Level I), and at Belt Cave.

The only place in the world where it is claimed that cattle existed before the sixth millennium B.C. is Palestine. The mandible of a small ox from Natufian levels at El-Khiam is regarded by Raymond Vaufrey as that of a domestic animal.[3] Other bones of small oxen were recently found at Einan.[4] These oxen are at

---

[2] R. Vaufrey: Archives IPH, Vol. XX (1939).
[3] R. Vaufrey in Neuville: op. cit., p. 215.
[4] J. Perrot: *Antiquity and Survival*, Vol. II (1957), pp. 91–110.

least three thousand years older than any other domesticated oxen ever found, and scientists are still very much undecided as to whether they were domestic.

After the sixth millennium B.C. cattle breeding became widespread. In Africa the earliest evidence of the domestication of oxen is provided by rock pictures in the Moroccan Atlas Mountains associated with a Neolithic culture of Capsian tradition and presumably dating back to the fifth millennium B.C.[5]

The rock pictures of Upper Egypt show how a population of hunters who lived in the vicinity of the Nile Valley in Pre-Dynastic times, and who were called by Hans Winkler "Eastern Invaders," used lassos to capture wild cattle alive. Such pictures are repeated rather often, and it seems likely that the oxen were captured alive and kept in custody in order to preserve the meat they provided. We do not know how far the "Eastern Invaders" went with the domestication of cattle. There is no evidence that they owned large herds, but hunting with lassos presumably could have led to the domestication of the penned cattle.[6] These rock pictures seem to represent the earliest-known attempts at domestication of cattle in Egypt, and probably go back to the fifth millennium B.C. Rock pictures from about the same time in southern Arabia, in the area of Dahthami, and elsewhere, portray very large oxen with huge horns. In the same pictures other oxen, smaller and humped, are shown. They seem to be of a central Asian breed which was brought to Arabia most probably by man. In later times some of these herds of cattle apparently crossed the Red Sea and reached the African continent.[7]

The domestication of the pig seems to have been fully accomplished in the Middle East by the fifth millennium B.C., when this animal was present at Sialk (Level II), in the lowest level of Warka, in Mesopotamia, and elsewhere. For the sixth

[5] R. Vaufrey: 1939, op. cit., Pl. 45, etc.
[6] Winkler: op. cit., p. 26.
[7] This material is being studied at present, and it is hoped that an extensive report will be published in the near future.

millennium B.C., the only place where the domestic pig has been found so far is Amouq. At Jericho the pigs from early Neolithic levels are believed to have been wild, and only Natufian sites in Palestine have yielded remains of pigs claimed to have been domesticated earlier than that.[8] The pig was found in all the major Natufian sites, at El-Khiam, at Einan, and at El-Wad, Kebara, and Nahal Oren. All the adult specimens still had the chief characteristics of the wild pig.[9] However, a very interesting fact could be noted. A high percentage of the pigs found in Natufian sites were extremely young, and it is quite possible that they had been captured alive and kept in the camp for some time. Capturing young animals and penning them up alive for days or even for months is a technique well known among several hunting populations of today. Quite possibly this technique led to taming and eventually to breeding the adults, and may have been one of the many ways in which domestication was achieved.

Two other animals were domesticated in the course of the Age of Early Farming, but of these we know very little. At Jericho, it seems that the cat became a house animal in the seventh millennium B.C.[1] We know as yet of no other place where this animal became friendly with men before the third millennium B.C. At Sialk, the horse seems to have been domesticated for the first time in the fifth millennium B.C., while in Sumer, the half-ass had become a captive in the fourth millennium B.C. At the same time donkeys were domesticated in North Africa. Both in the Moroccan Atlas Mountains and in Egypt this animal which was already serving man is depicted in rock pictures. In the Atlas Mountains the pictures date from Neolithic times, probably from the fifth or fourth millennium B.C., whereas in Upper Egypt they were drawn by a people called by Winkler "Early Nile Valley dwellers," who were contemporary with the Amratian culture (middle of the fourth millennium B.C.).

[8] R. Vaufrey in Neuville: op. cit., p. 215.
[9] Despite the claim of Raymond Vaufrey that the domestic pig was present at El-Khiam.
[1] Zeuner: op. cit.

From all this evidence one can gather that the earliest attempts at domestication took place in Mesolithic times, probably somewhere between the thirteenth and the eighth millennium B.C., but the turning point of organized domestication came only when the Neolithic was already advanced, in the fifth millennium B.C. Then stock raising began to be an important economic occupation, and even more so in the fourth millennium B.C.

An accurate study of the fauna from the fourth millennium B.C. at Beersheba, in southern Palestine, gives an interesting picture of stock raising at that time. The French paleontologist Thérèse Josien found there remains indicating a ratio of 60.2 per cent sheep, 16.7 per cent goats, and 12.8 per cent oxen. The bones of only three dogs and one horse were found. The horse was an aged specimen of small stature. If Josien is right in considering it domesticated, this is the oldest domesticated horse found in Palestine. No domesticated horses from later periods left traces in our area until the time of the Hyksos, who seem to have reintroduced them early in the second millennium B.C.

This short survey of early domestication shows how it developed as the result of many coincidences, as a slow process of random trial and unexpected discoveries, and sometimes also as the result of cultural communication. There was an interplay of many different methods, and they were used by hunters, gatherers, agriculturalists, and populations with mixed economies. Some societies specialized in them and became professional stock raisers. This seems to have occurred mainly among nomads. For permanent settlements stock raising became only one of the various activities of a complex economy.

THE ECONOMIC BASIS OF THE EARLIEST TOWN
IN THE WORLD

Tell es-Sultan, the site of ancient Jericho, in the sloping valley to the north of the Dead Sea, is at present the only place in the world where a town is known to date back nine thousand years.[2] This walled city, four thousand years older than any other urban settlement known at present, is one of the biggest puzzles of Near Eastern archaeology. Various attempts have been made to find a logical explanation for this very early urban flourishing in a depression about 1,000 feet below sea level, which is one of the hottest places in the world. It is also a very dry spot, averaging only about 4 inches of rainfall a year.[3]

Jericho does not fit into the general picture of Near Eastern settlements. Small farming communities usually spread over Mesopotamia, Anatolia, Syria, and Palestine in the sixth millennium B.C.,[4] and other than Jericho, there is no trace at present of a fortified town before the late part of the fourth millennium B.C.

Today Tell es-Sultan is about six miles away from the shore of the Dead Sea. We do not know exactly what its situation was nine thousand years ago, but probably the Dead Sea was much larger then than it is today. At that time a large lake existed at

---

[2] Radiocarbon tests of Urban Jericho have provided the dates ca. 6850, 6770, 6250, and 5850 B.C.

[3] Jerusalem has about 24 inches a year; Mount Carmel about 30 inches a year; and Upper Galilee over 40 inches a year.

[4] With only a few earlier exceptions, Robert J. Braidwood (in Braidwood and Howe: op. cit., p. 159) believes that at Jarmo a farming village was established in the seventh millennium B.C. At Hacilar, in Anatolia, James Mellaart has recently discovered a farming village believed to have existed in the seventh millennium B.C. (see J. Mellaart: "Excavations at Hacilar." Fourth Preliminary Report, *Anatolian Studies*, Vol. XI, 1961, pp. 39–75; see also J. Mellaart: ILN, April 5, 1961, pp. 588–90, and *The New York Times*, July 23, 1961). Diana Kirkbride is presently excavating the site of Beida, in Jordan, where she found an extremely interesting pre-pottery site which yielded a radiocarbon dating of 6830 ± 200 B.C. (British Museum). With the exception of Urban Jericho, these three seem to be, so far, the earliest farming villages of the Middle East. At Mersin, in Cilicia, the Carbon-14 dating of 5990 ± 250 B.C. (W. 617, U. S. Geological Survey) seems astonishingly early. A slightly later cultural assemblage with a similar material culture has been dated at Byblos "A" ca. 4600 B.C. (W. 627, U. S. Geological Survey), and a probable date of late in the sixth millennium B.C. can be safely accepted for the earliest Byblos. In Egypt, village life did not start until the middle of the fifth millennium B.C. The lowest levels at Faiyum are dated by Carbon 14 ca. 4437 and 4145 B.C. (Libby, University of Chicago radiocarbon datings, 1950, Nos. 457, 550, 551).

Faiyum, in Egypt,[5] and the Persian Gulf covered most of the Basra region in southern Mesopotamia. The expansion of the land seaward in the Persian Gulf was probably caused by two major factors: the drainage of debris by the two Mesopotamian rivers and a decrease in their water and current. The last pluvial age was just over, and very likely climate was wetter than today: most of the Near Eastern rivers had a greater flow of water then. It is therefore quite likely that Jericho was then much nearer to the shore of the lake than now.

Kathleen Kenyon, the British archaeologist who directed the excavations at Jericho during the last few years and who discovered the Pre-pottery town, estimates that Jericho had over two thousand inhabitants at the time of that culture, and in comparison to the small hamlets and isolated huts of this period discovered elsewhere, this is an enormous figure.

This town enjoyed an abundant spring of fresh water; probably a line of green trees and bushes followed the brook from its source to the point at which it evaporated in the middle of the yellowish "Lisan" chalky floor of the valley, or at which it reached the once larger lake.

The Pre-pottery town was surrounded by an enormous defensive wall built of massive stones, some of them weighing several tons. Behind the wall lived a very wealthy community in a monumental city which, in that epoch, was certainly considered one of the marvels of the world. The fortifications included one, and perhaps more, massive round towers, which are a model of sophisticated architecture. While most of the people of Palestine and the rest of the world still lived in tents and huts, the inhabitants of Jericho had succeeded in building a tower many feet high, with an internal passage through which guards could climb a solid-stone staircase and reach the top. At the foot of the surrounding wall, Kenyon discovered an even more astonishing detail: the town and the wall were encircled by an artificial moat.

[5] Caton-Thompson and Gardner: op. cit.

The people of Urban Jericho did not yet know how to make pottery, and their material culture was of a kind similar to that of other descendants of the Natufians, who were incipient agriculturalists still largely dependent on hunting and gathering. Considering that the other known contemporary groups were much less numerous than the people of Jericho, the gigantic military structures of Jericho are very puzzling, and their significance escapes us at first.

To spend all that energy in building these military works, the people of Jericho must have feared an attack by outsiders. And for such an attack to be conceivable in the political, social, and economic situation of nine thousand years ago, a considerable amount of wealth must have been hidden inside the town. If the people of Jericho were just incipient farmers, what could they possess to make such a system of defense worth while?

The fortifications were not the only public works uncovered at Jericho. Kenyon also found large storage or water reservoirs and large public buildings, at least one of which (belonging to the "Pre-pottery B" levels) appears to have served for ceremonial purposes. This had a strange ground plan; its central rectangular room had rounded annexes at the four corners. A basinlike depression in the middle of the room appears to have served as a container for fires.[6] In this room were several objects having probably a ritualistic purpose, among which were two little feminine figurines and some animal figurines. As we have seen in a previous section, both kinds of statuette are usually related to fertility cults.

In order to conceive and execute such sophisticated public works, the inhabitants of Jericho must have had powerful leadership and a co-ordination of labor which are not known from any previous time and which were not to become cultural traits of other Near Eastern societies until over three thousand years later. The town must have had at its disposal such a quantity of workers

[6] Kenyon: *Digging Up Jericho*, p. 59.

The round tower of Pre-pottery Jericho. The two men
are looking into entrances to the interior staircase.

not needed in other activities as was rather unlikely to be available without some sort of slavery system, or at least some kind of highly centralized leadership which could plan these works and dispose freely of manpower.

Most of the huge stones were carried from the foot of the Judean Hills a mile and more away, and the circuit of the defense wall was over a half mile. It was rebuilt and repaired several times, but its original height was probably over 23 feet. The moat was about 23 feet wide and 10 feet deep. We do not know what mechanical methods, if any, were used to transport the stones. Obviously ropes were used, and the tools employed to cut, extract, and transport the stones and to build them into the wall were of flint, wood, and bone. The wall was constantly repaired, and labor was constantly required for the task. Jericho's fortifications are indeed more amazing than the pyramids of Egypt, executed by armies of slaves in Pharaonic Egypt four thousand years later.

In order to be able to feed all the laborers engaged in public works, Jericho must have had a very large economic surplus, and this implies a wealth that is elsewhere unknown in a community of incipient farmers.

It is probable that some date palms and other fruit trees grew naturally in the vicinity of Jericho, and most archaeologists agree today that its inhabitants had already mastered the incipient cultivation of cereals. This led Kenyon to attribute the early settlement of Jericho to the flourishing of agriculture. She rightly claimed that two thousand people, at a site such as the arid lower Jordan Valley, "could not have been supported on supplies of wild grain and wild animals obtainable within the reach of the settlement." Kenyon fell back upon the old theory according to which "the need for irrigation had called into being the social organization of which defences are evidence." [7]

However, some doubted whether the enormous surplus at

[7] K. Kenyon: *Archaeology in the Holy Land* (London: Benn; 1960), p. 45.

Jericho was simply the result of incipient farming. The eminent American archaeologist Robert J. Braidwood rightly remarked [8] that climate and natural vegetation, almost 1,000 feet below sea level in the arid plain of Jericho, were certainly not better adapted to agriculture than the hilly regions, where farming hamlets like Jarmo were much less developed at an even later period. The material culture of Pre-pottery Jericho points to some sort of incipient farming: stone mortars, pestles, and grindstones indicate the use of cereals. But these tools were already used in much smaller settlements and in caves in Palestine in Natufian times. At Mount Carmel, at Einan, and elsewhere, earlier or less developed sites have produced an abundance of sickle blades and sickle hafts which has not yet been reported from Jericho. From all this, it seems likely that agriculture was not the main reason for or the basis of the unparalleled growth of this town. For reasons we do not know, in Chalcolithic times, during the fourth millennium B.C., while farming villages were flourishing all over Palestine, Jericho was suddenly abandoned, and remained deserted for almost a thousand years. If this spot was such a good place for agriculture, logically this should not have happened.[9]

The other main occupation of Pre-pottery Neolithic groups was hunting, and it is even more unlikely that an urban center like Jericho could rely on an occupation so itinerant, usually requiring a nomadic or semi-nomadic way of life. Arrowheads and other flint implements seem to show that hunting was another current occupation, but it is unlikely that the enormous surplus suggested by the gigantic public structures of Jericho could be accumulated through hunting.

If the lake was, as is believed, much nearer Jericho, and the river much broader than it is today, and if the lake was less salty than today, fishing might have been another occupation; but

---

[8] R. J. Braidwood: *Antiquity*, Vol. XXXI (1957), p. 73.
[9] Kathleen Kenyon suggests in a private communication: "This hiatus might have been caused also by the annihilation of Jericho's inhabitants by such natural phenomena as an earthquake, malaria or some pestilence."

again it is unlikely that Jericho was the product of a fishing economy.

The urban nexus of Pre-pottery Jericho, its defense system, its public buildings and storage structures, and the implied political and social organization bespeak another and very important occupation—the occupation which in all times to come was to be the major means by which a human group could accumulate a surplus. Only trade could have been the main source of wealth and power at Jericho.

We find at Jericho tools made of obsidian probably obtained from Anatolia, lumps of turquoise matrix from Sinai, various coloring materials from the Jordanian Plateau, and cowrie shells imported from the shores of the Mediterranean Sea. These materials point to some external trade but do not explain the wealth of Jericho. Jericho must have had something which could have purchased food and very cheap labor. So we have to look around and see what nature might have offered on the spot. Jericho is located near the Dead Sea, a source of various raw materials highly praised in antiquity. The three major ones among them are salt, bitumen, and sulfur.

Hunting societies make little use of salt. When flesh is consumed raw or roasted, its salts are not lost and it is not necessary to add sodium chloride. On the other hand, a cereal or vegetable diet calls for a supplement of salt and so does boiled meat; thus salt has always been a necessity in all food-producing societies. In the Near East, it was becoming an indispensable substance at exactly the time when farming activities started to develop and Jericho was becoming a town.

In historic times the Dead Sea has always been the principal source of salt for the surrounding regions.[1] Remains of ancient salt mines on the shores of the Dead Sea are very common, and these salt mines are frequently mentioned in the Bible.[2] Salt was highly praised by the ancient inhabitants of Palestine for season-

[1] See Genesis 14: 3; Numbers 34: 3; etc.
[2] Zephaniah 2: 9; see also I Maccabees 11: 36.

ing food. This is probably best expressed by Job in the question: "Can that which is unsavory be eaten without salt?" [3] Salt appears also as an essential part of sacrifices,[4] a custom which undoubtedly went back to prehistoric times. Salt is frequently mentioned in the Bible also as an antiseptic or a medicine. Newborn babies were bathed in and sprinkled with salt,[5] and the prophet Elisha is said to have "healed" the waters of Jericho by casting a cruse of salt into the spring.[6]

The inhabitants of Palestine today prefer the finer and purer salt of the Mediterranean to that of the Dead Sea, but until a few years ago, Bedouins used to build artificial evaporation lagoons on the shores of what the Bible calls the "Salt Sea." From there they carried salt to markets in Jerusalem, Hebron, Beersheba, and Gaza.[7]

In the Near East, some of the oldest trade routes were created for traffic in salt; salt and incense, the chief economic and religious necessities of the ancient world, play a paramount role in all that we know of the ancient highways of commerce. If the people of Jericho succeeded in developing the salt trade, they are probably the earliest people in the world to have done so, and this could have provided them with the greater part of the surplus indicated by the archaeological excavations.

Bitumen too might have been an important article of trade. It is found in lumps which float on the surface of the water or drift to the shore, and the Dead Sea has been such an important source of it as to deserve the name Lake of Asphalt, as various Roman authors called it. In the Bible, the tradition of using bitumen goes back as far as Noah's time, when it served to build the ark.[8] Later, Moses' mother is said to have daubed with bitumen

---

[3] Job 6: 6.
[4] Leviticus 2: 13; Ezra 7: 22; Ezekiel 43: 24; Numbers 18: 19.
[5] Ezekiel 16: 4.
[6] II Kings 2: 20 ff.
[7] See L. Picard: "History of Mineral Research in Israel," *Economic Forum*, 1954.
[8] Genesis 6: 14.

the ark of bulrushes in which Moses was set afloat on the Nile and in which he was found by the daughter of the Pharaoh.[9] From archaeological evidence we know that bitumen was used as early as Mesolithic times to cement sickle blades and other composite flint tools into their hafts.

Bitumen became a necessary raw material, and the Dead Sea was a very important source of it. Flint implements with bitumen still adhering to them were actually found in Pre-pottery Jericho.

Another possible source of wealth was the sulfur which is gathered on the surface of the plain of Jericho even now, and is still used by Bedouins for preparing medicine, for lighting fires, and for various ritualistic and magical purposes. Lumps of sulfur were actually found in the prehistoric levels of Jericho.

Jericho was indeed located in an ideal spot for prehistoric trade. In view of the availability of raw materials there, all other occupations, such as farming, hunting, and fishing, must have been relegated to secondary importance by trade. Perhaps other towns arose in spots as favorably situated, for Jericho is proof that a fortified town could be built nine thousand years ago, but we know of no others.

Meanwhile in nearby hills primitive bands of hunters continued a semi-nomadic way of life, while incipient farmers lived in small hamlets and led a much humbler existence. It took these agricultural peoples over three thousand more years of trial and error to evolve into urban societies.

---

[9] Exodus 2: 3–4. A very similar account occurs in Mesopotamian mythology, regarding the ark in which Sargon of Akkad was put afloat on the Euphrates.

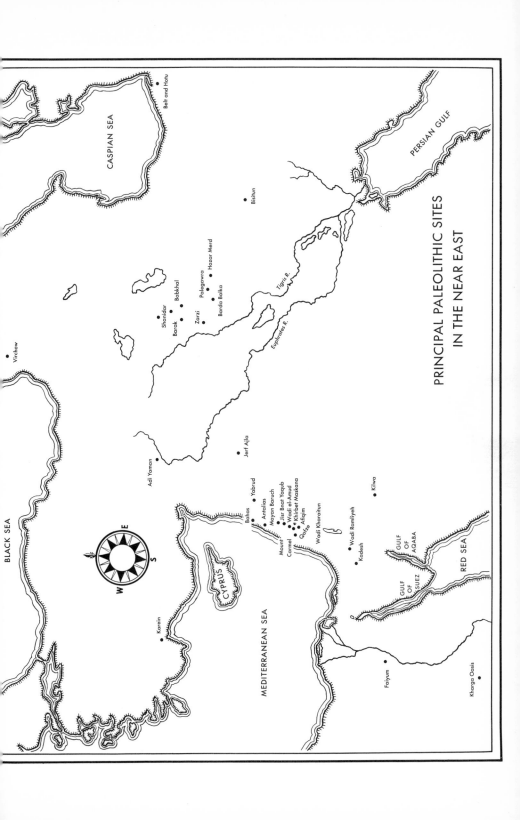

CASPIAN SEA

Belt and Hotu

PERSIAN GULF

Bisitun

Hazar Merd

Palegawra

Babkhal

Shanidar

Barda Balka

Barak

Zarzi

Tigris R.

Euphrates R.

Virchow

Jerf Ajla

Adi Yaman

BLACK SEA

Karein

CYPRUS

MEDITERRANEAN SEA

Bahas

Yabrud

Antalias

Mount Carmel

Mayan Baruch

Jisr Bnat Yaqub

Wadi el-Amud

Khiribet Maskana

Afiqim

Qafze

Wadi Kharaitun

Wadi Ramliyeh

Kadesh

Kilwa

GULF OF AQABA

GULF OF SUEZ

RED SEA

Faiyum

Kharga Oasis

N
W — E
S

PRINCIPAL PALEOLITHIC SITES
IN THE NEAR EAST

I I

The Neolithic
Cultures

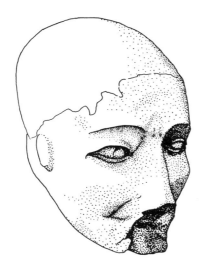

THE PRE-POTTERY NEOLITHIC CULTURES

THE NATUFIAN had gradually evolved into Pre-pottery Neolithic. The new culture maintained many of the Mesolithic traditions and at the same time acquired new traits. Though various cultural patterns evolved side by side, the general trend was toward an increase in the importance of food-producing activities, toward settlement in fixed localities, toward more populous groups, and toward complexity and sophistication in the material culture.

We have seen how special ecological conditions allowed Jericho to evolve very early into a town, while at Nahal Oren, at Mount Carmel, a small hamlet was thriving on the terrace in front of a cave, and while other people in the Judean Hills still persisted in living in caves.

Pre-pottery Neolithic lasted a long time at Jericho, and the excavators distinguished two major types of it, which they labeled "A" and "B." Pre-pottery A was at first an open settlement of habitations with curvilinear foundations of the same kind as those at Einan and Nahal Oren. Some of these habitations appear to be half-sunken houses with steps inside the entrance. At Jericho the Mesolithic level is dated by radiocarbon at around 7800 B.C. The earliest Neolithic developed shortly thereafter. The first defense wall was built after the settlement had reached a considerable size. This probably happened around the year 7000 B.C., as a later level that succeeds a long series of rebuildings after the fortifications was dated by two radiocarbon tests at around 6850 and 6770 B.C.

In one place, twenty-six levels of Pre-pottery B were found, and the ninth from the bottom provided the radiocarbon date of approximately 5850 B.C. Another date for a similar level was 6250 ±200 B.C. Pre-pottery Neolithic probably lasted at Jericho until late in the sixth millennium B.C.[1] The people of both type A and type B buried their dead beneath the floor of their houses. This seems to be a tradition transmitted from the Natufians. The custom suddenly stopped with the end of the Pre-pottery levels, and is not found when a new culture, the Jericho Pottery Neolithic, made its appearance.

One of the most outstanding discoveries at Jericho was that of several plastered skulls. Kathleen Kenyon's vivid description reads as follows: "The lower part of these skulls had been covered with clay plaster, moulded into the likeness of individual human features. The eyes are inset in shells. Six had bivalve shells, with a vertical slit between two sections giving the appearance of the pupil. The seventh had cowry-shells, and the horizontal opening of the shell gives a strange realistic effect."[2]

About forty individuals were found buried beneath another house. From some the skull had been removed, with the lower

---

[1] K. Kenyon: *Archaeology in the Holy Land* (London: Benn; 1960), pp. 44–5.
[2] Ibid., p. 50.

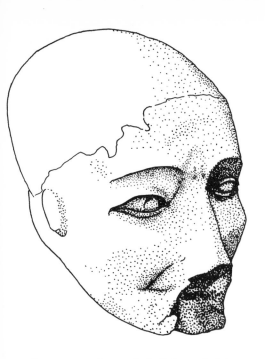

Pre-pottery plastered skull from Jericho

Painted head of clay statue from Jericho (excavated by Garstang)

A plastered skull from Jericho with shells as eyes and bands of color painted on the head

jaw left behind. Most of the plastered skulls lack jaws, and there may be some relation between the two phenomena.

Collecting skulls, as we have seen, was a habit of the Natufians, and in Jericho the archaic habit probably was continued. Plastering, however, is a new factor. Plastering skulls and putting cowrie shells in the place of eyes is still today a widespread custom among primitive tribes, especially in Melanesia. Jericho provides the earliest-known example of this practice.

Pre-pottery Jericho has revealed another kind of extremely interesting art, first discovered in a public building, probably a temple, during John Garstang's excavations in the early thirties.[3] He found three almost life-sized plaster figures portraying a trinity of anthropomorphic beings: a bearded male, a female, and a child. Here again shells were used for the eyes. The figures were decorated with red (ocher?) paint, and must have stood so as to be seen only from the front, as they were flat, almost two-dimensional statues and only the front was modeled and decorated in detail. Fragmentary parts of other similar but more stylized statues were more recently discovered in another building. In their general features these statues are strangely reminiscent of some Neolithic and Bronze Age menhir statues of southwestern Europe.

These large sculptures seem to come mainly from late Pre-pottery levels. We have seen that an earlier temple contained small feminine figurines as well as figurines of domestic animals, and was probably connected with a fertility cult (see page 244). The large human statues suggest a more complex and sophisticated mythology. The three divine anthropomorphic figures found by Garstang are the earliest-known example of a holy triad composed of the Father, the Son, and the Mother Goddess side by side in a place of worship. Such a triad will turn up again in the fourth millennium B.C. in the Sumerian civilization, and thereafter it was widely worshipped in the Orient.

Pre-pottery Neolithic culture at Nahal Oren developed dif-

[3] J. Garstang: AAA, Vol. XXII, p. 71.

ferently. The settlement was started in Mesolithic times, when several terrace walls were built on the slope in front of the cave. Probably this terracing supported structures of perishable materials. Circular and oval huts were constructed thereafter in early Pre-pottery times, and the latest Pre-pottery level yielded the remains of square buildings with rather massive stone basements. However, this settlement never became more than a small hamlet. It contained an unusual quantity of imported objects, including small polished axes, used probably for ritual purposes, made of nephrite and other hard stones not found in Palestine, and some tools made of Anatolian obsidian.[4] At Nahal Oren religious art consisted of small and rather schematic feminine figurines carved on pebbles, strangely resembling objects from the Yarmukian Late Neolithic.[5]

Excavations are now under way at Beida, in eastern Jordan, where Diana Kirkbride has discovered another Pre-pottery Neolithic village, which was at least partially contemporary with the Pre-pottery A town at Jericho.[6] Today this site has no water for nine months a year, but when the village was flourishing there, climatic conditions probably were different.

Four series of buildings were discovered at this small, elongated tell; several of them have square rooms, regularly built, facing each other along central corridors, and some are believed to have been used not as dwelling places but as storage areas, a fact that would seem to be evidence of extensive trade. The buildings were laid out around a central rectangular plaza according to a well-conceived plan.

Beida is located about five miles north of Petra, the site that later became the famous caravan city of the Nabataeans. The Pre-pottery settlement was established near the junction of two caravan routes that were heavily trafficked in later times: one was the

[4] M. Stekelis: IEJ, Vol. VII, No. 2 (1957), p. 125.
[5] M. Stekelis: IEJ, Vol. X, No. 2 (1960), p. 119.
[6] A radiocarbon test made at the British Museum has provided the date of 6830 ± 200 B.C.

so-called "King's way," which led from Arabia and the Gulf of Aqaba along the edge of the Edom and Moab mountains to Syria and the North; the other came from the Negev and the Araba Valley up to Petra and led through Ma'an and Wadi Sirhan to central Arabia and the Persian Gulf.

Before we can come to any definite conclusions, however, we must wait until Diana Kirkbride finishes her work and writes up her final report. We know that coloring materials are still made today from the stones of this region. Red and yellow sandstones, green and bluish malachite, and other copper minerals are still gathered in large quantities. Turquoise is found not far away, and so are various other types of semi-precious stones. But if Beida was a trading colony, the excavations have not yet revealed what the major trading goods were.

Until a few years ago, all the various types of Pre-pottery Neolithic were called Tahunian, after Wadi Tahun, in central Palestine, where a similar industry was first studied.[7] All Pre-pottery Neolithic industries in Palestine have some resemblances. But the local differences are rather marked, and they cannot all be lumped together as a single culture. The industry of Nahal Oren is nearer to the typical Tahunian than the two Pre-pottery industries of Jericho, but both sites are quite different from the

[7] R. Neuville: RB, Vol. XLIII (1934), p. 255.

Neolithic flint celt with polished edge from Ain Murra, central Negev

Tahunian industries of the Judean Hills and of the Negev, for which this term is now reserved.

The flint industry of the Tahunians still included some of the geometric microliths of the Natufians, but most artifacts had new forms. Flint celts were sharpened by a transverse blow with a tranchet (a chisel-shaped flint tool), and generally resemble some late Mesolithic tools of western Europe. Winged arrowheads, which were rare in Upper Natufian, now appeared in large quantities. Sickle blades became larger than in Natufian times, while large tools—picks, gravers, large rabots, and elongated blades—greatly increased in quantity.[8]

In the Judean Hills, evolved phases of the Tahunian culture produced pottery similar in texture to that found at Jericho in the earliest Pottery level, as well as new types of stone objects. Polished tools greatly increased in number, and axes, celts, and picks increased in number and in variety of shapes.

Abu Ghosh is a typical Tahunian site; there Jean Perrot also found the remains of a square building.[9] A few miles away, at Motza, a similar site yielded a rich flint industry which best represents this culture.[1] Probably part of the mixed material at El-Khiam belongs to the same culture.[2]

Several flint knives or daggers, highly retouched, found at Jisr Bnat Yaqub in Upper Galilee, at Umm Qal'a in the Judean Desert, and in various spots in the vicinity of Revivim in the western Negev, are probably to be attributed to this culture.[3]

In the western Negev, Tahunian seems to have endured longer, and in Wadi Shallale, near Gaza, several late Neolithic

---

[8] See R. Neuville: RB, Vol. XLIII (1934), p. 255; J. Perrot: IEJ, Vol. II, No. 1 (1952), p. 74; M. Stekelis: IEJ, Vol. X, No. 2 (1960), p. 119; Kenyon: op. cit., pp. 44-5.

[9] J. Perrot: *Syria*, Vol. XXIX (1952), pp. 119 ff.

[1] A. Vigodzky de Philippis: *Archivio per l'Antropologia e l'Etnologia*, Vol. LXV (1935), pp. 124 ff. Additional material was collected there by the present writer (unpublished).

[2] J. Perrot in R. Neuville: Archives IPH, Vol. XXIV (1951), pp. 134 ff.

[3] The best examples, from the Negev, were found by P. L. O. Guy and are in the Rockefeller Museum, Jerusalem, Jordan.

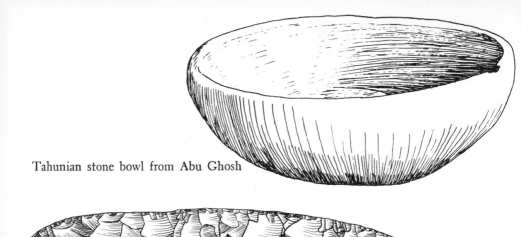

Tahunian stone bowl from Abu Ghosh

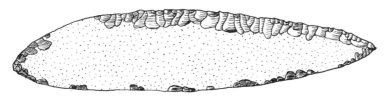

Flint blade of dagger from Umm Qal'a

Flint adzes from Wadi Shallale

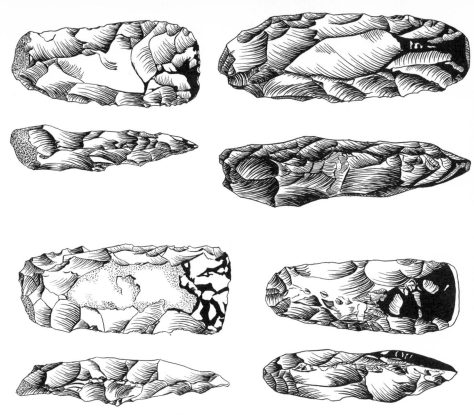

Flint implements from Wadi Shallale

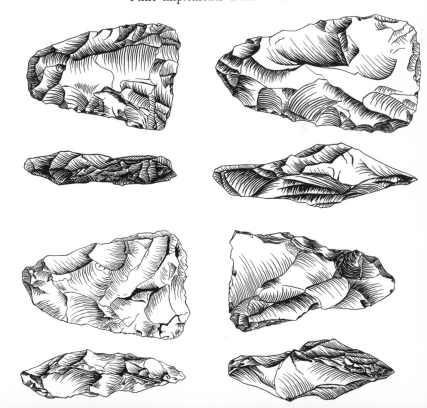

sites containing pottery have a flint industry of undoubted Tahunian derivation.

This late Tahunian is the first culture which seems to have supplied regular channels of communication between the prehistoric populations of southern Palestine and those of Egypt. The Negev has yielded at least two tools made of Egyptian flint. Late Tahunian also shows strong similarities with the Tasian flint industry of Egypt.

Late Tahunian spread widely over the deserts on the southwestern periphery of the Fertile Crescent. It has been reported at Wadi Dhobai, at Kilwa, and in Sinai. In these areas the high ratio of arrowheads points to the peculiar peripheral character acquired by this culture in the desert areas.

Early Neolithic goes back to the eighth millennium B.C. The latest date for Pre-pottery Neolithic at Jericho (obtained by Carbon-14 tests) is around 5850 B.C.; the late Tahunian influences on the Tasian culture of Egypt seem to go back only as far as the fifth millennium B.C. and even the beginning of the fourth. By this time new ethnic and cultural factors had already entered Palestine.

Such contacts with Egypt were to occur off and on throughout Pre-Dynastic times. Probably nomadic bands from the Negev and Sinai occasionally reached the Nile Valley in just the same way as some Bedouins still do today.

There is testimony to Pre-Dynastic contacts between Egypt and southern Palestine also in the rock pictures of the Negev and other surrounding areas, which show the same artistic approach, the same weapons, and the same hunting methods as those of the peripheral hunting bands who lived at the margins of the Nile Valley during Pre-Dynastic times (see pages 198 ff.).

While the Tahunians were penetrating deep into the desert and spreading out from their homeland, new peoples were entering Palestine from the north and the east. Some of them already possessed an evolved pottery, and their material culture was exotic. They were the first people in Palestine to establish a widespread system of permanent hamlets whose economy was based primarily on farming, fishing, and hunting.

THE YARMUKIAN CULTURE

While some late Tabunians were on the way to a mingling with the marginal populations of southern Palestine, and others were slowly moving deeper into the desert in their search for game, three new Neolithic cultures made their appearance in Palestine —the Yarmukian, the Coastal, and the Jericho Pottery Neolithic.

Until a few years ago, archaeologists believed that the evolution of the Neolithic cultures of Palestine was a continuous process, and that Palestine was a single, unified cultural area. Lately, however, archaeological evidence seems to show that things were not so simple and that various cultures within the small area of Palestine were contemporary with one another. There were some centers in which they were rather isolated, and others in which one culture shared some aspects of its neighbor. But the dynamics of cultural evolution in this period cannot yet be traced in detail.

Even within this scientific limitation, the Yarmukian culture remains one of the big riddles of prehistoric Palestine. In its integral form it has been found up to now only in one spot, at Shaar Hagolan. This site is located at the very end of the cul-de-sac formed by the Yarmuk Valley at its junction with the Jordan River. It is a triangle of alluvial land bounded by the Sea of Galilee, the Golan-Bashan Mountains, the Yarmuk River, and the Jordan; it is well defended and isolated by these natural barriers and is the natural delta of the narrow Yarmuk Valley.

Although remains of buildings have not yet been reported, this site must have been a rather permanent settlement for several generations. The Yarmuk has been throughout historic times part of a very important caravan route connecting the Jordan Valley with the Syrian-Jordanian plateau. At Al-Hassim, northeast of Amman, this highway divides in two. One branch enters Wadi Houran, and follows the direction of the modern highway from

Amman to Baghdad; the other enters Wadi Sirhan and is still today the main caravan route joining Jordan with the Persian Gulf. We do not know where the Yarmukians came from, but it is not unlikely that their origin must be looked for to the east. A certain number of tools and objects from Shaar Hagolan were made of chalcedony, quartzite, and other raw materials collected either in the Syrian Desert or on the Jordanian Plateau.

The Yarmukian culture appears to have occupied a rather limited area. Besides Shaar Hagolan, it has so far been found at a few minor sites in the Beth-Shan Valley.[4] In the Esdraelon Valley there are several places near Tell Kiri and Yokneam in which Yarmukian material culture is mixed with the Coastal culture, which we shall describe shortly. A few Yarmukian artifacts traveled greater distances, to southern Palestine and to Syria.

The Yarmukian is a typical mixed-economy culture. The major activities were fishing, farming, and hunting, and the location of its type-site was ideal for the first two of these occupations. The Yarmuk delta is surrounded by waters teeming with fish, and it is covered with very fertile alluvial soil.

The outstanding characteristic of the Yarmukian culture is its art. About a hundred art objects have been discovered so far at Shaar Hagolan, and they include engraved and incised pebbles and small stone and clay figurines. Many of the pebbles were given phallic forms; others had schematic human heads incised on them. Some of them seem to combine phallic forms with the shape of heads.

The art of the Yarmukians chiefly portrays human figures, particularly those of women. Other art objects, more schematic, seem to represent the sexual organs of both sexes. This art was highly stylized and symbolic, and its significance escapes archaeologists for the time being. However, it has been suggested that the marked emphasis on the female breast and sex and on phallic symbolism indicates that this art was connected with fertility magic or a fertility cult.

[4] M. Stekelis: IEJ, Vol. I, No. 1 (1950); N. Tzori: PEQ, 1958, pp. 44 ff.

Decorated pebble from Shaar Hagolan

Anthropomorphic phallic stone
figurine from Shaar Hagolan

Neolithic human figurine on pebble from Shaar Hagolan

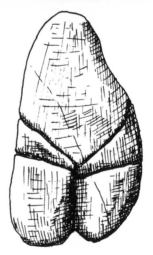

Another Neolithic pebble figurine from Shaar Hagolan (after Stekelis)

Neolithic clay figurine with stylized face, raised head, and elongated eyes, from Shaar Hagolan

One of the statuettes has been variously interpreted as a "female bust," a "steatopygic figurine," and a "bisexual symbolic object," and no agreement on it has been reached. Another small limestone figurine, about three inches high, represents a human figure apparently dressed in a piece of cloth around the hips.

The most beautiful Yarmukian figurine represents a highly stylized human head with a high hat or an upraised headdress. It was made by modeling small rolls of clay onto the basic design to form the eyes, ears, and mouth. This figurine and some fragments of other similar clay figurines from Shaar Hagolan are unique, and bear no similarities whatsoever to other known art objects.

Pebble figurines similar to those of Shaar Hagolan were found at the nearby site of Gesher and at other places in the immediate vicinity of the Yarmuk; at Byblos, a very important harbor on the Mediterranean coast of Lebanon, they were present in the context of the Neolithic Coastal culture.

The flint industry of Yarmuk is characterized by toothed saw blades, well-retouched and pointed awls, axes, celts, and hoes with a partially polished cutting edge, arrowheads and spearheads, sometimes with an elegant partial pressure-retouch, and some scrapers, burins, and microliths of older traditions. The flint complex is totally different from the Tahunian. It shares some characteristics with the Jerichoan culture, which we shall describe in a following section, though it is much richer and better formed, and is the product of a culture in which flint occupied a more important place and in which archaic traditions were more marked.

The abundance of axes suggests that there were trees in the vicinity of the Yarmuk and that these people were accustomed to using timber intensively. And the abundance of arrowheads and spearheads suggests that hunting must have occupied a rather prominent place in the economy. Also agricultural tools such as picks and weights for digging sticks were abundant, as were fishnet sinkers.

In the stone industry, spindle whorls (perforated, disk-

Neolithic decorated stone objects
from Shaar Hagolan

Neolithic pottery with herringbone
decoration from Shaar Hagolan

Yarmukian pottery from Shaar Hagolan

shaped weights for manipulating the thread, also found in clay)
and stone mortars, pestles, grinders, bowls, and cups turn up.
Stone pendants and beads join bone, shell, and pottery as body
decorations. Bone artifacts are not abundant, but those that have
been found include awls, points, and borers.

The pottery of Shaar Hagolan shows that its makers already
had a long tradition of pottery making; it is well fired and has a
rich variety of sophisticated forms. So far we know nothing of
what might have been its origins. We know only that when the
Yarmukians arrived at Shaar Hagolan, their material culture was
already fully formed and that it is unlikely that any earlier development took place in Palestine. Many vessels had flat bases on
which they could stand firmly. They had all sorts of knobs and
handles (both loop handles and ledge handles) which helped in
carrying them and by which they could be suspended. They took
the form of jars, vases with rounded necks, basins, deep bowls,
small open bowls, and open hole-mouth vessels (vessels with
round rimless openings).

A large portion of this pottery was decorated with simple
geometric patterns. Both incised decoration made before baking
and color were used by the potter. The most typical decoration is
the incised herringbone pattern, arranged in triangular zigzag
lines. Lines of red paint are sometimes burnished, and they frequently occur next to herringbone decoration. In general, this
incised ware is totally different from painted Jerichoan pottery,
and has only some distant resemblance to the Coastal pottery.

THE COASTAL CULTURE

While the Yarmukians were developing their culture at Shaar
Hagolan, and while the late Tahunians were living in the Judean
Hills and the Negev, a new culture made its appearance in
northern Palestine and along the Mediterranean coast. It was
of northern origin, and seems to have first developed in Cilicia, in
southern Anatolia. From there it gradually moved down along

the coast and reached Palestine. In the course of time it sub-divided into three main provinces whose material culture developed minor local variants.

In Palestine, the two southernmost sites known to be related to this culture were excavated by Jacob Kaplan in the southern coastal valleys, one at Tuleilat Batashi, in the Sorek Valley, the other at Wadi Raba, near Petah Tikva, on the Plain of Sharon.[5] Several sites of this culture with more northern affinities have recently been discovered in the Esdraelon Valley, mainly concentrated along the hilly slopes at the southwestern end of the valley, between Tell Yokneam and Megiddo. In Israel the site of this culture most distant from the coast, as far as we now know, is Tell Eli, in the upper Jordan Valley, south of the Sea of Galilee. It is being excavated by Moshe Prausnitz.

The material culture found in the Antioch region at the bottom of Tell al-Judaidah [6] and at Tabbat al-Hammam is closely related to that of Mersin.[7] Little has been published so far from the lowest level of Ugarit (Level V), a very important ancient harbor of Syria, but it seems that the material culture along the Syrian coast is more like that of the Palestinian sites.[8] On the Plain of Antioch and at Ugarit the incised ware of Mersin is accompanied by pottery vessels which were burnished to a high luster and were colored the reddish brown and smoky brown of amber.

In Lebanon the material culture resembles that of the Palestinian sites more than that found farther north, and at Byblos the flint industry is also very similar to the Palestinian. In the lowest level of Byblos the French excavations directed by Professor M. Dunand uncovered a material culture which is an outstanding clue for correlating the Syro-Cicilian and the Pales-

[5] J. Kaplan: *Eretz Israel*, Vol. V (1958), pp. 9 ff. (for Tuleilat Batashi); J. Kaplan: IEJ, Vol. VIII, No. 3 (1958), pp. 149 ff. (for Wadi Raba).
[6] R. J. and L. S. Braidwood: *Excavations in the Plains of Antioch*, Vol. I (Chicago: University of Chicago Press; 1959).
[7] F. Hole: *Syria*, Vol. XXXVI, Nos. 3–4 (1959), pp. 149 ff.
[8] See C. Schaeffer: *Ugaritica*, Vol. I (1939), pp. 8 ff.

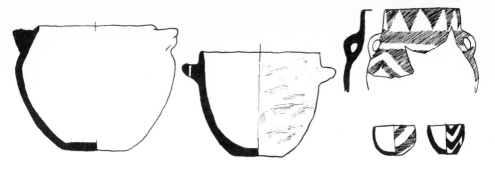

Neolithic pottery from Jericho (after Ben Dor and Kenyon)

tinian complexes.[9] The incised patterns on ceramic ware are identical with those found at Tell Abu Zureiq, Tell Kiri, and Hazorea, in the Esdraelon Valley, and the decoration of impressed cord patterns is the same as that of the Plain of Antioch and Mersin. The toothed saw blades, the sickle blades, the arrowheads, the celts, axes, adzes, and picks, are identical with those found in Palestine.

What mainly characterizes the pottery of this culture is the abundance of incised ware. Various patterns occur, but the most common is one of indentations which are sometimes distributed in lines, at other times in bands or geometrical designs, frequently covering the entire surface. Within many pots the interior also has these indented designs, which must have been executed with a pointed bone or stick before firing the pot. The so-called "nail-impression," probably made with the edge of a shell, is also common, as are various other designs. Bands of "comb impressions," or fine parallel lines, are both straight and

[9] M. Dunand: BMB, Vol. IX (1949), Vol. XII (1955), and Vol. XIII (1956).

Neolithic basalt mortars and pestle from Mayan Baruch

wavy, but some pots have simpler patterns of parallel scratches. The cord pattern is rare in Palestine. The herringbone pattern appears everywhere in small quantities, but nowhere is it so prevalent as in the Yarmukian. Along with these rich varieties of incised ware, color slip and burnished decoration are common. The color varies from intense red-orange to amber to dark brown and to almost black. Shapes include low-necked jars, open hole-mouth vessels, bowls of various kinds, and fat, oval bodies. Both round and flat bases are found. Small and heavy ledge handles, knobs, and small loop handles are common.

The flint industry is not as rich as at Shaar Hagolan, but the same basic forms appear in both assemblages. At Tell Abu Zureiq there is an unusual quantity of stone balls and biconic stone projectiles. The bone tools include awls, points, and borers.

Coastal Palestine was a marginal region for this culture, which arrived there rather late in its history, at a time when people of other cultures probably had already put an end to it in its major places of development, at Mersin and on the Plain of Antioch.

The makers of this culture probably followed the basic

Various types of coastal Neolithic impressed ware from Tell Abu Zureiq

Stone implements from Tell Abu Zureiq: bola stones, biconic projectiles, weights for digging sticks, and flint tools

occupations of the Yarmukians, though their material industry seems to suggest that agriculture occupied a more prominent place, and hunting a minor one.

THE POTTERY NEOLITHIC CULTURES OF JERICHO

After the flourishing urban development of Pre-pottery times, the settlement at Jericho came to a rather abrupt end, and the spot appears to have been abandoned for a few hundred years. It was resettled thereafter by a new people possessing traditions quite different from their predecessors. At first its architecture was much more rudimentary than in the previous period. The earliest settlement of these new Jerichoans was formed of half-subterranean pit dwellings such as are usually characteristic of people just becoming sedentary. The urban tradition of Jericho persisted, however, and in the course of time the new Jerichoans learned how to build solid houses, with stone foundations and walls of mud bricks.

Two major waves of these people seem to have arrived at Jericho, each one surviving there for a rather long time, and at a certain point their local culture was influenced by the Yarmukian.[1]

Until now, the Pottery Neolithic culture of Jericho has been found in its full form only at its type-site, but elements of it have been uncovered at various sites both along the Jordan River and on the hilly slopes of western Judea.

At Tell Eli, to the southeast of the Sea of Galilee, only a few miles away from Shaar Hagolan, Moshe Prausnitz found Jerichoan pottery in the same level as the Coastal culture. This level overlay two levels of Pre-pottery Neolithic and had a general chronology similar to the Jerichoan.[2]

---

[1] Kathleen Kenyon comments that she believes that Pottery Neolithic B is probably a branch of Yarmukian culture.
[2] I am grateful to Moshe Prausnitz for allowing me to see and mention this unpublished material.

Jerichoan shards in a context of Coastal culture were found also at Wadi Raba [3] and at Tuleilat Batashi.[4] Again an isolated shard occurs in a cave near the tell of Lachish, in southern Israel.[5]

At Jericho, the latest date for Pre-pottery culture obtainable by Carbon-14 tests is 5850 ± 200 B.C. Thereafter no dates can be determined until Proto-Urban times.[6] At Jericho there is no evidence of the typical Chalcolithic culture (Ghassulian) that appeared in the immediate vicinity at the beginning of the fourth millennium B.C. The Jerichoan must have ended before the beginning of the fourth millennium B.C., and probably persisted from the late part of the sixth through the fifth millennium B.C.

At Byblos an evolved phase of the Coastal culture was dated by radiocarbon at around 4600 B.C.[7] Allowing for earlier phases, the settlement probably grew up at the end of the sixth or the very beginning of the fifth millennium B.C. The contemporaneity of the Jerichoan and Coastal cultures, therefore, seems established both by Carbon-14 datings and cultural evidence.

Jerichoan pottery falls into two distinct types: the coarse ware and the finely decorated ware. The coarse ware was made of a clay with many irregular grits, and straw was added to the clay in considerable quantities to provide the necessary cohesion. The use of straw is revealed by the negative prints left both on the surface and inside the shard. It was fired at a low temperature and as a result the ware was soft and crumbly. The fine pottery was made of a finer and better-fired clay, but straw was still used. A cream-colored slip covers the surface and over this there is sometimes a decoration of red slip, usually a combination of chevrons or triangles. Sometimes a lustrous burnish is added.

In the course of time, pottery became more sophisticated, and some influences of Yarmukian culture were felt. In the ad-

[3] J. Kaplan: IEJ, Vol. VIII, No. 3 (1958), pp. 149 ff.
[4] J. Kaplan: *Eretz Israel*, Vol. V (1958), pp. 9 ff.
[5] O. Tufnell *et al.*: *Lachish IV* (London: Oxford University Press; 1958), Fig. 1 and p. 300 (cave 6019).
[6] Kenyon: op. cit., p. 56.
[7] W. 627, U. S. Geological Survey.

Neolithic figurine from Tel Aviv
(excavated by Kaplan)

Coastal Neolithic pottery from
Hazorea and Tell Abu Zureiq,
with various types of impressed
decoration and amber-burnished
rims

vanced phases of Jerichoan Pottery Neolithic incised herringbone decoration, a Yarmukian characteristic, became one of the common patterns.

After the beginning of the Jerichoan, the celts made with a transverse blow and the deeply winged arrowheads typical of the Pre-pottery cultures became extremely rare. The mortars and stone bowls of the Natufian and Pre-pottery Neolithic complex were replaced with crudely worked stone vessels which imitated the shape of wooden vessels. The flint industry also changed abruptly and its relative importance drastically decreased. It produced a greater number of deeply toothed saw blades and sharply pointed awls similar to those found at Shaar Hagolan. These people seem to have been nomadic, or semi-nomadic, when they first arrived, but in a short while they learned how to adjust themselves to their new environment and their new resources and how to build permanent houses. They acquired the heavy material industry of sedentary villagers.

When the Jerichoan culture was finally destroyed, Tell es-Sultan, the tell of Jericho, was abandoned for a certain period. Most scholars believe that this hiatus in the life of Jericho corresponds to the time in which the village of Tuleilat Ghassul flourished near by, and that the Jerichoan settlement at Jericho was destroyed when the Ghassulians first came to this region at the beginning of the fourth millennium B.C.

NEOLITHIC PALESTINE—A SUMMARY

The earliest Pre-pottery Neolithic culture developed out of the Natufian. Various patterns of this Pre-pottery Neolithic evolved in Palestine, and the best known is the Tahunian, whose people lived mainly in the central mountains of Palestine and later spread out to the south and east. The Tahunian persisted quite late, while various regions of Palestine were being settled by newcomers who brought with them new types of material culture with different and already evolved traditions. The newcomers were well advanced in the making of pottery when they arrived, and probably some Tahunians learned their techniques.

Sometime late in the sixth millennium B.C. a new group of people entered Palestine, probably coming from the east, and settled down at Shaar Hagolan, near the Yarmuk River. The Yarmukian culture was at least in part contemporary with the Coastal and Jerichoan cultures; some of its elements appeared in the Jerichoan levels at Jericho, and isolated Yarmukian-like shards, flints, and works of art have been found over a rather large area, including the settlements of the Coastal culture in the Esdraelon Valley.

While the Yarmukians were settling down and developing their culture in the central Jordan Valley, another culture was spreading from the north into Palestine, mainly along the coast. Its people occupied parts of the Esdraelon Valley and the Coastal plains and a few other places.

A third group of people, who probably came from the east, settled down at Jericho. The center of Jerichoan culture was at Jericho, but its artifacts extended to Tuleilat Batashi, Wadi Raba, Lachish, and probably all of southern Judea, and up the Jordan Valley to Tell Eli.

This is merely a foundation for further research, and many questions remain unanswered, the most puzzling ones certainly being: Who were the Yarmukians and the Jerichoans? Where did they come from? Among the three Full Neolithic cultures of Palestine—the Yarmukian, the Coastal, and the Jerichoan—which were partially contemporary with each other, we do not know which was the first to appear. But each of them exhibited different traditions and probably had a different origin. All of them possessed evolved traditions of pottery making by the time they arrived; therefore pottery must have been made elsewhere long before it first reached Palestine.

THE MEGALITHIC MONUMENTS

During the Age of Early Farming, some people in Palestine customarily built Megalithic graves. This widespread type of tomb consisted of several large stones placed in such a way as to form a sort of large table, with standing monoliths sustaining it. Frequently the stones weighed several tons and were carried over considerable distances. Usually the tomb was covered by a small mound, or cairn, either of earth or of small stones. Often these cairns were the only visible sign of the Megalithic graves. Usually they are come upon in large clusters in rather limited areas, so that one may suppose that the people who built them lived within these limited areas.

In Palestine, the Megalithic monuments are usually found in marginal and semi-marginal regions. Most of them are concentrated in the upper Jordan Valley, on the Jordanian Plateau, in the central mountains, and in the southern deserts. Where the incipient-farming cultures were most developed there are few or none of these monuments. In Palestine, Megaliths are more numerous in the interior and decrease in number going westward.

Megalithic tomb with lines of small cup marks on the table stone, from the upper Jordan Valley

One of the large megalithic tombs from Kibbutz Shamir in Upper Galilee.

They do not seem to have ever existed in the coastal region.

Scholars are very much undecided about the origin of these widespread monuments. The Megalithic tombs of western Europe were built in ways very similar to the Palestinian ones. They first appeared there late in the fourth millennium B.C. Palestine is the only place in the world where these monuments seem to have been built at an earlier date.[8]

A certain recurrence of structural details is seen in the European and Near Eastern tombs. In both regions there are similar stone circles surrounding the monuments, cairns covering them, numerous cup marks carved on the roofs, and similar size and shape.

In Palestine, so far, we know very little regarding the burial rites performed by the Megalithic builders. We know that smaller tombs of this type at Adeime, in the Moab region, contained single and double graves and only rarely served to inter a

---

[8] This idea was first suggested by W. F. Albright in *The Archaeology of Palestine* (5th ed.; Baltimore: Pelican; 1960), p. 64.

larger number of individuals.[9] So far not a single undisturbed
monument of the larger and probably older style common in the
northern regions has been excavated, and we have no idea of
the number of bodies that might have been buried in them.

These monuments can be seen from far away, as they are
located in prominent spots. Many of them appear to have been
re-used for burials in later times, and most of them have been
dug up by treasure hunters in the last few centuries.

I have mentioned a Mesolithic funerary monument at
Einan which seems to be a prototype of the Megalithic tomb
(see page 172). At Wadi Dhobai, on the Jordanian Plateau, some
Megalithic structures were excavated, and seem to be connected
with a Pre-pottery Neolithic flint industry.[1] At present not one
of the standard Megalithic monuments in Palestine can be given
so early a date. The smaller graves at Adeime, which probably are
degenerative examples of Megaliths, date from the early or middle part of the fourth millennium B.C. (see page 310), and it is
possible, though yet unproved that the standard large Megalithic
monuments of northern Palestine go back to Neolithic times.
As we shall see, in the Negev a very late example of this sort of

[9] M. Stekelis: Archives IPH, Vol. XV (1932).
[1] J. d'A. Waechter and V. M. Seton-Williams: JPOS, Vol. XVIII (1938).

Rock-cut Megalithic tomb in the Golan region
    of northern Jordan, with porthole entrance

Megalithic monument at Shamir

Cup-marked stone in field of megaliths at Shamir

grave was built late in the third millennium B.C. (see page 365).

Four major groups of these monuments are known in Palestine—in the northern Jordan Valley and the Hula Plain, in the Golan and Bashan regions of Jordan, in the southern Jordan Valley and around the Dead Sea, and in the Negev.

The most impressive group is that of the northern Jordan Valley and the Hula Plain. Various Megalithic fields, or concentrations of Megalithic monuments, are found there, but the largest is that of Kibbutz Shamir, where over a hundred monuments are concentrated.

In this group there are two types of monuments. One is a short gallery grave with three or four supports on each of the long sides of the tomb and a similar number of large slabs across the top. The average size of these monuments is about five by fifteen feet. The second type are simple "dolmens" [2] roughly square in form, with single slabs on three sides and a single slab as a roof. Most of these monuments have the remains of stone cairns around them. Many have clusters of small cup marks engraved on the top of the roof slabs. A few Megalithic circles and other rough buildings have been found in the fields of the northern Jordan Valley, some of them with remarkable uniform pebble floors.

Numerous Neolithic flint implements have been found in the vicinity, but later pottery also has been found there, and because most of the tombs were probably disturbed and re-used in later times, it is very hard to date them at the present time.

The second major group of Megalithic monuments is concentrated mainly in the Golan and Bashan regions of Jordan, where over four thousand dolmens have been reported, some as far south as Moab. Most of these monuments are simple square dolmens, with a single tablelike slab as the roof. Some have a square or oval entrance cut through one of the side supports. Their date is unknown.

Of the two other major Megalithic groups, one is a small

[2] This is a Breton word meaning "table stones."

degenerate type of cist grave, or small "dolmen," best illustrated by the Adeime necropolis. It has yielded some pottery that probably goes back to the early or middle part of the fourth millennium B.C. (see page 310). The other major group consists of a different kind of cist cairn, usually round, having an average diameter of about twenty-four feet and a height of about three feet, and being a sort of elevated platform, built of flat stones, in the middle of which is found the tomb. This type is found mainly in the southern regions of Palestine, in the Negev, Moab, and Edom, where it is frequently associated with menhirs, or standing monoliths, and other Megalithic constructions. From the pottery with which it is associated we learn that this group is much later than the others, and dates from late in the third millennium B.C. (see page 365).

Pottery from the cist graves at Adeime (after Stekelis)

III

The Chalcolithic Cultures

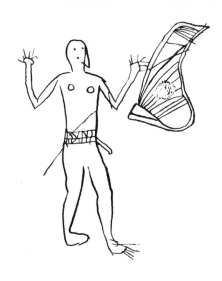

THE CULTURAL AREAS

THE TRANSITION from semi-nomadic to fully sedentary life
was not, as some believe, a single continuous process of change.
In Palestine, several different populations passed through this
transition in practically every period during the last ten thousand
years.

We have seen how sedentary village life began in Natufian
times, mainly at Einan, where a group of hunters and fishermen
settled down in round huts on the shores of Lake Hula. At
Jericho, a people successfully built a town and fortified it with
huge walls long before the discovery of pottery and the development of systematic agriculture. In the following chapters we shall
see how throughout history various waves of peripheral nomads
invaded the fertile areas and settled down in sedentary villages.

In Palestine, and indeed all over the Fertile Crescent, this cultural process was most vigorous during the fourth millennium B.C., in the Chalcolithic period. Then we witness the colonization of vast areas, the first settlement of many sites in northern Palestine which were to become tells, or city mounds, and the spread of farming settlements throughout the south.

The transition from Neolithic to Chalcolithic is not a sharp one; the division was made by archaeologists on the basis of differences in material culture. Material culture in its various aspects (pottery, flint implements, bone tools, art, the pattern of settlement) underwent gradual changes. Some hamlets evolved into real villages, and new regions of Palestine were settled. The border of settlement was pushed forward toward the arid regions, and new land was cultivated.

The Chalcolithic people of Palestine relied mainly on two major economic activities: agriculture and stock raising. Both activities already had a tradition thousands of years old, and were well evolved. Society became more complex and there were several kinds of social organization: they ranged from small rural communities very similar to modern Arab villages in the same regions, to what seem to be the seasonal settlements of whole clans, and to the homesteads of extended farm families.

Grindstone and grinder from Tell Abu Zureiq

In Chalcolithic times, as during the Neolithic, Palestine's culture was not uniform. Ecological factors again strongly influenced local variations. The cultures of the North and the South of Palestine were devised by different peoples, and within each of these two major divisions various subgroups evolved side by side.

The Northern Chalcolithic peoples occupied most of the territory previously settled by the Neolithic peoples (where city mounds were to evolve at the beginning of the Urban Age). The Southern cultures are found in semi-arid regions on the edge of the desert.

Environment was more varied in the North. There the Chalcolithic people encountered stony hills and thick forests, valleys with plots of cultivable land, plains with grassland and marshes. The Northern people lived in permanent villages; some used stone and mud bricks for building houses. They also lived in caves, huts, and wooden buildings. Many of their settlements persisted after the end of the Chalcolithic and became towns, whereas most of the settlements of the Southern people were abandoned at the end of this period and were never resettled again.

The Southern cultures occupied a region of good loess soil where it is unlikely that vegetation was thick and where cultivable fields were abundant and virgin. They did not have to clear forests, and for a few years they were able to grow rich crops on land near by. When the fields were exhausted they could use new ones a little more distant; but in the course of time they had to move their settlement. These people usually built their hamlets along the principal wadies, where some water could be found.

On the whole, the pattern of settlement and social organization seems to have been more uniform in the North. In the South, one gathers the impression that many innovations were attempted by the various groups. Moreover, the material culture and the art of the South is less traditional and more varied; it is very inventive, and in this period the South seems to have had more influence on the North than the North had on it. But the

House-shaped ossuary from Hederah
(after Sukenik and Avigad)

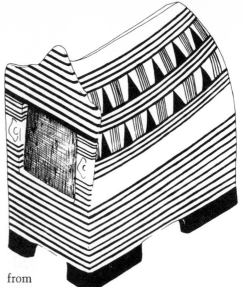

Chalcolithic hut-shaped funerary urn from
Azor. The nose-like projection at top center
over the entrance probably symbolizes the
funerary divinity; to its left is a pointed tool,
probably a pick.

Southern cultures were to disappear, whereas those of the North, with the help of exotic influences infiltrating from Syria, were to survive and to become the core of urban societies.

Between the beginning of the fourth millennium and the thirty-third century B.C., after the Coastal and Yarmukian Neolithic cultures and before the Proto-Urban cultures, northern and central Palestine underwent a gradual evolution which, with some innovations, seems to adhere to Neolithic traditions.

The Northern cultures had two principal varieties: one mainly along the coast, the other more in the interior. On the coastal plain, and in some of the larger valleys opening on the Mediterranean, the basic traditions of the Coastal Neolithic gradually acquired new characteristics. Here various groups of people seem to have coexisted. Some had close cultural ties with the Lebanese-Syrian coast, whereas others had comparatively stronger ties with the Southern cultures.

An interesting custom of the Coastal cultures was the burial of the dead in pottery (and perhaps also in wooden) urns. These urns, rather small in size, were stored in artificial caves dug into earth, into Kurkar, a type of coastal sandstone, or into other soft rock. This is the first trace in Palestine of the custom of using man-made caves for burials.

Most of the urns were shaped like houses, and they are the first indicators of a funerary rite which later became very widespread throughout Eurasia. The deceased was first cremated, and his ashes and unconsumed bones were collected in the "House of the Dead." The bones and ashes were inserted into the miniature house through an "entrance" which was then closed by means of a doorlike hatch. The urn was then lowered into a collective grave, where it joined the ashes of other deceased members of the group, and where eventually a "village" or a group of "houses" was assembled under the earth. In this way, the living gave their dead an afterlife similar to the life they were used to.

The first of these urn burials in collective caves was discovered twenty-five years ago at Hederah, on the Plain of Sharon, by Elazar L. Sukenik, late professor of archaeology at the Hebrew University.[1] More recently, very similar burials were found by Jacob Kaplan, an archaeologist from Tel Aviv, at Bnei Braq and Givatayim, in the same region; but the best preserved and most impressive of them was excavated by Jean Perrot at Azor, near Tel Aviv.[2] This was an artificial cave about 36 by 26 feet, in size, and the entrance was through a lateral shaft. The cave contained about fifty burials and yielded a great variety of extremely interesting urns. They have a median size of roughly 24 by 20 by 12 inches and their shape varies from that of a simple jar, to house-like, animal-like, and manlike urns. Some urns copy the form of imaginary animals or monsters with a highly suggestive effect.

We know very little at present about the beliefs that gave rise to the strange forms of some of these urns, but the imaginary animals and monsters were probably mythological figures.

The houselike urns have great variety, and almost every one differs from the others. Most of them, however, have a roughly rectangular ground plan with a square entrance on the short side. The entrance side is decorated with manlike figures with strange prominent noses, and sometimes with emphasized eyes resembling solar symbols. Some of these eyes even have rays painted all around them. They bear a strange resemblance to "guardian spirits" frequently depicted in Neolithic and Chalcolithic Europe.

The decoration of these urns reveals many details of the structure of buildings, of architectural fashions of the period, and of the materials used. Most of them have walls painted to imitate wood, and roofs painted to imitate straw. Some roofs are decorated with patterns clearly imitating palm leaves. All the

[1] E. L. Sukenik: JPOS, Vol. XVII (1937).
[2] See IEJ, Vol. VIII, No. 2 (1958), p. 133; IEJ, Vol. IX, No. 2 (1959), p. 266.

Oculi face with prominent nose and
solar eyes, on a funerary urn at Azor

Chalcolithic "fruit bowl" from
Tell Abu Zureiq

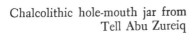

Chalcolithic hole-mouth jar from
Tell Abu Zureiq

urns take the form of small, presumably one-room houses unlikely to have sheltered more than a minimal family unit. The
decorations in fashion at the time, painted and in relief, include
geometric patterns with band motives, triangles, and stars.

These burial methods and the pattern of habitation and the
conceptual traits that go with them were, as far as we now know,
restricted to the coast. Though both at Hederah and at Azor
many of the accompanying pottery vessels are quite similar to
those of the South, the general pattern of the Southern culture
is rather different. Neither the burial methods nor the architecture of this Coastal culture has been detected in the South,
which, conversely, has its own localized cultural traits.

As already mentioned, what principally characterizes the
coastal region in Chalcolithic times is a continuation and evolution of Neolithic Coastal material culture. Incised ware and
amber-burnished pottery apparently remained in use for long
periods at Hazorea and other Esdraelon sites, and at Wadi Raba,
near Petah Tikva. At Tuleilat Batashi, in the Sorek Valley, this
pottery persists with other pottery indicating a date in the fourth
millennium B.C.[3] At Meser, at the entrance of Wadi Ara, near
Hederah, incised ware of the traditional Coastal type is still
present in small quantities in a level of advanced Chalcolithic.[4]

North of Israel, in Lebanon, a similar local evolution can
be followed. The second level of Byblos in part continued the
material traditions of the earliest settlement. Byblos B had
apsidal and rectangular houses like those built throughout Palestine in Chalcolithic times. Cremation and burials in jars are
common. Some urns were interred within the inhabited area,
often in artificial caves cut into the soft rock. One cave contained
as many as twenty-six adult skeletons and strongly resembled the
caves of the Coastal culture of Palestine.[5]

The site that illustrates best the Chalcolithic of interior

[3] See J. Kaplan: IEJ, Vol. VIII, No. 3 (1958), pp. 149 ff.
[4] M. Dothan: IEJ, Vol. VII, No. 4 (1957), pp. 217 ff., Pl. 40-g.
[5] M. Dunand: Fouilles de Byblos (Paris; 1939), pp. 373–81, 434–45.

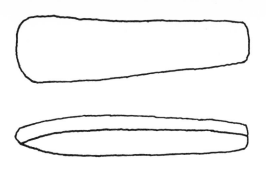

Chalcolithic copper ax from Meser (after Dothan)

Palestine is Tell el-Fara, near Nablus, where the French archaeologist Father De Vaux has directed the excavations ever since the end of World War II.[6] Both the pottery and the flint industry show strong Yarmukian and Coastal Neolithic traditions. Incised ware in the tradition of the Coastal Neolithic culture still appears in small quantities, and at least one potsherd has an incised herringbone pattern which recalls the Yarmukian. Other artifacts, chiefly small bowls with fine sharp rims, hole-mouth jars with red paint, and fragments of butter churns, have similarities with the Southern Chalcolithic. What best characterizes the Chalcolithic culture in interior northern Palestine is the abundance of incised and relief decoration on pottery, most often in a rope or a fingerprint pattern, in lines and in ribbons, which will be seen again in quantity and further developed in the earliest phase of the early Urban Age.

The flint implements are better shaped and richer than in the Southern culture, and include arrowheads, toothed saw blades, sickle blades, round scrapers, and blades with sharp retouching on their backs of a rather clear Yarmukian tradition. This Chalcolithic culture appears to have spread widely all over the central mountains of Palestine and the valleys crossing them. In each place it took on some localized characteristics while keeping its own general traits.

The interior Chalcolithic culture occurs in the lowest levels of the Megiddo mound, in the Esdraelon Valley (Levels XX–

[6] Called "Enéolithique Moyen" by Father De Vaux; see mainly RB, Vol. LIV (1947), pp. 397, 406, Pls. 12–14.

XIX), mixed with other, more archaic elements.[7] Further to the east, at Beth-Shan (Level XVI), it is well represented,[8] and it appears in various sites throughout the valley surrounding the tell of Beth-Shan.[9] More to the south, in central Palestine, at Lachish and Gezer, this culture seems to be impregnated with more Southern influence.[1]

At Megiddo and Gezer, the people of this culture inhabited structures built on bedrock and in caves, and customarily carved pictures on stones. One of their principal subjects was the ox, large herds of which were probably kept by these people. Other domestic animals depicted were goats and dogs. Wild animals included deer, foxes, jackals, and birds. Other interesting carvings likely to belong to the end of this period, or to the beginning of the Proto-Urban period, show a lyre player and the use of various weapons, including bows and arrows, lassos, spears, and perhaps boladors. Some engravings also illustrate details of the local fashion, and show that both men and women wore short garments around their hips and strange pointed hats on their heads. Men were bearded and had prominent long noses. The most emphasized garment was the belt, which was worn by almost all the figures.

This artistic style and that of the Coastal cultures are quite different. This fact typifies the high degree of localization characteristic of the Chalcolithic, which we shall encounter again in the Southern cultures, where some localities developed a rather personal art. After the end of the Chalcolithic, cultural areas become larger and a gradual unification of cultural traits begins in Palestine.

[7] G. Loud: *Megiddo II* (Chicago: University of Chicago Press; 1948), Pls. 1–3, 92–96, 166–7, etc.
[8] G. M. Fitzgerald: *The Museum Journal* (Philadelphia), Vol. XXIV, No. 1 (1935).
[9] See N. Tzori: PEQ, 1958, pp. 43–51.
[1] O. Tufnell *et al.*: *Lachish* IV (London: Oxford University Press; 1958), Pl. 11; R. A. S. Macalister: *The Excavation of Gezer*, Vol. III (London; 1912), Pls. 28–9, etc.

Chalcolithic carving of horned animal from Megiddo (after Loud)

The lyre player of Megiddo, from a stone carving (after Loud)

Chalcolithic carving of human figures, from Megiddo (after Loud)

Chalcolithic cave graffiti from Gezer (after Macalister)

It is not yet clear how the Chalcolithic cultures came to an end in northern Palestine. Late in the thirty-fourth and in the thirty-third century B.C., important Northern cultural influences reached northern Palestine, contributing to the creation of a new material culture there. The old culture did not die overnight. It seems rather that its traditions mixed with the new ones, and they will be found together in the earliest levels of the Urban Age.

THE SOUTHERN CULTURES

While the Coastal and Interior Chalcolithic cultures were flourishing in northern and central Palestine, in the South, at the margins of the desert, other human groups settled and colonized new strips of land. The Southern Chalcolithic culture can be divided into four major provinces, all of which share some general traits in their ceramic and flint industries, though each has a different pattern of settlement, a different art, and a different economic basis and social organization. From west to east these areas are: the Wadi Shallale region, in the western Negev; the Beersheba Plain; the Judean Desert; and the region of Moab. Each of these provinces is no greater than twenty-five miles in length, and they are the smallest cultural areas ever detected in Palestine.

In the first of these provinces over thirty Chalcolithic sites are known, concentrated along Wadi Shallale and the smaller wadies flowing into it.[2] They usually appear as small aggregations of roughly round and oval hut floors, similar both in kind and in size to the Pre-pottery huts found at Nahal Oren, Wadi Dhobai, and elsewhere. At other sites, there seem to be pit dwellings dug halfway into the soil, surrounded by dug silos. The material cul-

[2] Surveys led by me with the help of members of Kibbutz Beeri in 1952–5 added further information to the investigations of E. Macdonald. See E. Macdonald: "Prehistoric Fara," in Beth-Pelet, Vol. II (London: Quaritch; 1932).

ture shows at first very strong Tahunian traditions and slowly evolves into the general pattern of the Southern Chalcolithic culture. The oldest settlements of the Southern culture now known are in Wadi Shallale, which seems to have developed directly from the Tahunian culture.

The earliest phases lack ceramic ware and have a typical Tahunian flint industry. Late in the fifth millennium b.c., flint implements very similar to those of the Tasian and early Faiyum cultures of Egypt were abundantly produced. The transition from Neolithic to Chalcolithic was a gradual one, and probably was a consequence of both local development and external influence. There was a great deal of intercourse along the coast, and the Shallale culture kept in continuous contact with the Coastal culture to the north and with the various Pre-Dynastic cultures of Egypt to the south.

In fact, there is more evidence of contact with prehistoric Egypt here than in any of the three other Southern provinces. Some flint implements were made by a technique of pressure flaking typical of Pre-Dynastic Egypt. Several tools were made of light-brown chert, which is not found in the Negev and which is extremely similar to raw material used in prehistoric Faiyum. A schematic violin-shaped figurine found near Kibbutz Gilat is made of gray granite from Sinai or Egypt. Round and flat maceheads of various exotic hard stones were also probably imported from Egypt, from Sinai, or from Arabia.

Throughout the Chalcolithic period, flint implements were more abundant in this province than in the other three, and the frequency of arrowheads sharply contrasts with the rarity of these objects in the other provinces. One gathers a general impression of small half-sedentary, probably seasonal, settlements that numbered between four and ten households each. Large circles made of stone and battered earth are also found in some of the settlements. Animal pens presumably, they seem to point to the economic importance of herding. Farming and hunting too must have occupied a significant place in the local economy, and some

Flint knife from Wadi Shallale

Egyptian-type flint celt from Wadi Shallale

Rough flint ax from Wadi Shallale

sort of exchange of goods, or trade, obviously was regularly carried on by these people.

When the people of the Beersheba culture first arrived in the second province, they already had all their cultural characteristics. Various levels show some evolution in the architecture, but their art, their pottery, their flint industry, and the rest of the material culture do not seem to have undergone important changes during the four or five hundred years in which the Beersheba culture existed (probably around 3700–3200 B.C).[3] The pottery here is better shaped and richer in form than at Wadi Shallale, but the flint industry is poorer both in variety of form and in relative quantities.

The architecture is very different from that known today from Wadi Shallale. In the earliest phases of the Beersheba culture the people lived in subterranean dwellings or artificial caves dug into the compacted loess. Several chambers are connected with one another by corridors, and the number of individuals sheltered by each of these clusters of caves is certainly several times that of those who dwelt in the oval huts of Wadi Shallale. Most of the chambers had bell-shaped silos dug into the floors, fireplaces, and other arrangements needed for daily life. This pattern of settlement obviously signifies a social organization quite different from that of Wadi Shallale, and also different from that of the other two provinces of Southern Chalcolithic. From the pattern of settlement we learn that the society must have been organized in large clans which were apparently divided into various extended families. It is likely that they lived by some kind of garden agriculture similar to that of some African tribes of today (see page 232).

In the late phases of the Beersheba culture, its people had learned to build houses on the surface. Some of these buildings

[3] See J. Perrot: IEJ, Vol. V, No. 1 (1955), pp. 17 ff.; No. 2, pp. 73 ff.; No. 3, pp. 167 ff.; No. 4, pp. 246 ff.; Vol. VI, No. 3 (1956), pp. 163 ff.; No. 4, pp. 226 ff.

Chalcolithic clay churn in the Beersheba Museum

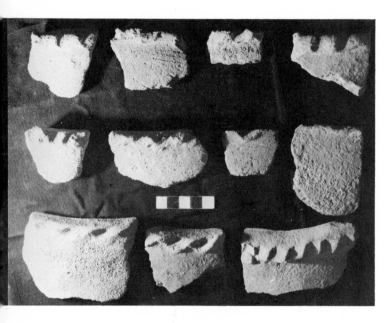

Chalcolithic pottery with decorated rims from Wadi Shallale (collection of Kibbutz Beeri)

Plan of Chalcolithic building at Khirbet Bitar, Beersheba (after Dothan)

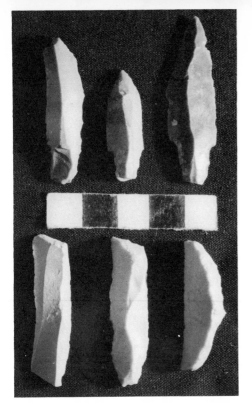

Flint arrowheads (above) and blades with blunt backs, from Wadi Shallale (collection of Kibbutz Beeri)

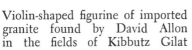

Violin-shaped figurine of imported granite found by David Allon in the fields of Kibbutz Gilat

Half-sunken basement of hut at Bir Abu Matar. Holes in the floor are bell-shaped granaries.

are extremely large, an obvious indication of their public or collective nature. Some characteristics of the Beersheba province find parallels in Pre-Dynastic Egypt. The bone and ivory figurines have particularly similar artistic and figurative traits; similar ivory and bone flat objects, known as plaquettes, are also found. However, the pottery and the flint industry are definitely different.

These figurines and the other art of Beersheba are one of the major characteristics of this culture. Perrot also found pebbles painted with red crosses and other schematic signs, and a rich collection of pendants and other ornaments, in bone, shell, copper, and clay.

As for the Chalcolithic culture in the third province, the Judean Desert, Tahunian influences are found in the flint industry at a few sites explored by René Neuville and A. Mallon; [4] the pottery is similar to that of Beersheba, but in addition there are horn-shaped drinking cups, decorations of appliqué bands with fingerprints, and other designs typical of Ghassul and the other

[4] *Syria*, Vol. XII, No. 1 (1931), pp. 24 ff.

Ivory handle portraying a bird, from Bir Safadi

Chalcolithic wall at Bir Safadi

Chalcolithic sites of the Moab region. Less is known about this province than about the other three, and most of the available information derives from very recent explorations by Yohanan Aharoni, Yigael Yadin, and other archaeologists of the Hebrew University. Most of the Chalcolithic sites of this province are caves located halfway up the canyonlike walls of wadies emptying toward the Dead Sea, and usually are extremely hard to reach. Some of these caves are the very ones in which the Jewish warriors of the Roman period hid from the Roman legions, and in which the famous scrolls and manuscripts of the Dead Sea were found. Though we know very little of the history of this period, it seem likely that such places were chosen for reasons of security, as neither herding nor agriculture could be easily carried on there. A few open-air sites were also discovered, including one at Ain Geddi with a very large building, probably a fortification, over 165 by 70 feet in size.[5]

It has been argued that this Judean group is the latest of the four, and that the Chalcolithic peoples of the Southern culture found shelter in these hidden caves and in this desert region when the Proto-Urban populations first invaded Palestine. There are no certain proofs at present for or against this theory, but at least one factor seems to be against it: The Proto-Urban peoples do not seem to have been interested in this province of the Southern Chalcolithic culture. South of Lachish, Jerusalem, and Jericho, Proto-Urban remains are extremely rare, and in all central Palestine they are found mainly in big centers near the most important water sources. As we shall see, the Proto-Urban people in northern Palestine were in part contemporary with the Southern Chalcolithic people. These cave dwellers of the Judean Desert left in their shelters a great deal of cloth, basketry, and other perishable materials that have been preserved there thanks to the extremely dry climate. They form a highly interesting paleoethnological record, one unequaled for peoples of that time or earlier elsewhere in Palestine.

[5] J. Naveh: BIES, Vol. XXII (1958), p. 46.

Ivory female figurine from the Beersheba culture. One of the inlaid eyes
is missing. Holes above eye sockets
probably were used for attaching hair

Ivory statuette from Bir Safadi
(Detail shown enlarged)

Figurine with strange hairdress from Beersheba

Basalt "fruit bowl" from the Chalcolithic
settlement at Bir Safadi (after Perrot)

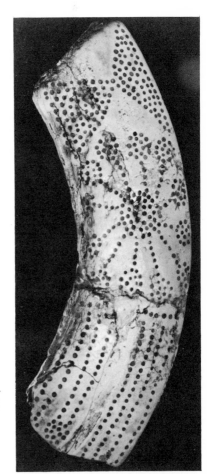

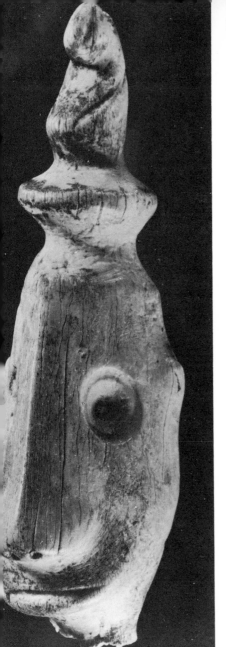

Carved bone decorated with stip-
pled pattern (Beersheba culture)

ory carving from Beersheba

These sites near the western shores of the Dead Sea are related to several other caves in the upper Judean mountains, at Umm Qatafa, Umm Qal'a, Erq el-Ahmar, and various other spots in the region of Wadi Kharaitun, studied in the early thirties by Neuville and Mallon.[6]

The fourth and best-known province of the Southern Chalcolithic culture is that of the eastern Jordan Valley and Moab, whose principal exhibit is Tuleilat Ghassul, a site composed of five small tells near Wadi Jarfa, northeast of the Dead Sea, which was excavated in the thirties by Fathers A. Mallon and R. Köppel of the Pontificium Institutum Biblicum.[7] Several other sites were found by Nelson Glueck in eastern Palestine showing the wide spread of the Ghassulian assemblage throughout the Jordanian mountains.[8]

Ghassul is the only site of the Southern culture for which the claim of a persistent, fully sedentary village life is justified. Each of the various neighboring tells had a cluster of buildings,

[6] *Syria*, Vol. XII, No. 1 (1931), pp. 24 ff.
[7] A. Mallon, R. Köppel, *et al.*: *Tuleilat Ghassul*, Vols. I and II (Rome; 1934, 1940). Father North has recently resumed excavating and a third volume is expected to appear in a short while.
[8] AASOR, Vols. XXV–XXVIII (1951), Sites 145, 161, 168, 183, 206, 219, 227, 249, 263, 306.

Violin-shaped figurines from Tuleilat Ghassul

Drawing of a mask, from a wall fresco at
Tuleilat Ghassul (after Mallon and Köppel)

some of which had walls in common and formed irregular blocks
surrounded by narrow streets and asymmetric squares. One of
the tells, the top layer of which has been fully excavated, disclosed a group of seventeen rather homogeneous houses. Their
average area is about 165 square feet, and they have one to three
rooms with floors frequently plastered or paved with pebbles,
and a walled courtyard for each. Each house had one or more fireplaces, usually located in the courtyard, and several storage pits
and silos in which the excavators found grains of corn, dates,
and olive stones. There were small basins, which must have
contained supplies of water and other liquids. This is the first
agricultural village found so far in Palestine similar to the modern farming communities.[9] Probably many contemporary Arab
villages look like Ghassul once did, and this is a reminder that
the foundations of modern life were already well established in
Ghassul about 5,500 years ago.

The houses were built of sun-dried mud bricks erected over
pebble basements, and they probably had roofs of wood and
straw. Some of the walls were painted with extremely interesting
polychrome frescoes portraying geometric patterns, stars, lines

[9] The town of Jericho does not seem to have been a farming community (see
pages 246–7).

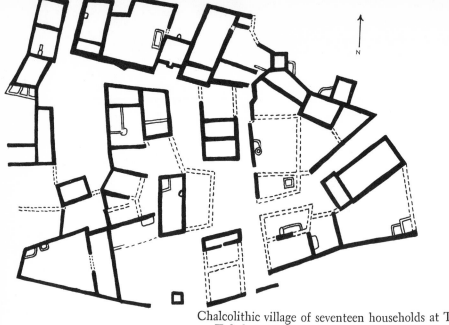

Chalcolithic village of seventeen households at Tell 1, Tuleilat Ghassul (after Mallon and Köppel)

Basalt bowls, pestle, and grindstones from Tuleilat Ghassul

Bone objects from Tuleilat Ghassul

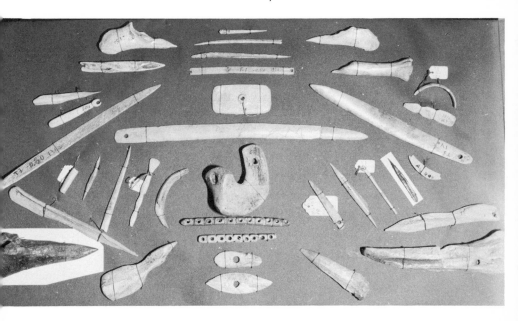

of human figures, masks, and strange monsters or demons indicative of a rich mythology and a fertile imagination. A few frescoes are more realistic; a particularly beautiful one depicts a long-tailed bird.

The cist-grave cemetery of Adeime, in the vicinity of Ghassul, was excavated by Moshe Stekelis, and its pottery was found to be vaguely similar to that of the top level of Ghassul.[1] However, the Adeime designs are undoubtedly more archaic and include incised ware of a kind unknown at Ghassul, and no painted patterns of the Ghassulian type occur, so that the cultural relationship between Adeime and the excavated layers of the nearby settlement of Ghassul is doubtful. Various burials in jars found below the houses at Ghassul seem to illustrate better the funerary customs of the late Ghassulians. All these are single burials, however, and no collective burials of the Coastal type have yet been found in any one of the four provinces of the Southern culture.

Probably the most interesting aspect of the Southern cultures is the evidence of a metal industry. Copper was extracted from the Araba Valley, from Nahal Timna, near Aqaba, and from other sites over sixty miles away from the settlements. Recent investigation by Benno Rothenberg has discovered at Timna a Chalcolithic ore tunnel similar in shape to the Beersheba subterranean dwellings; it had been excavated for a copper mine. In the vicinity were found Chalcolithic pots, grindstones, mortars, and pestles. At Beersheba, Perrot uncovered what seems to be the workshop of a coppersmith.

At Beersheba metal tools included round maceheads, flat axes imitating the shapes of flint axes, rings, handles, and ornaments. Metal craft spread quickly over the whole Southern area in this period. Metal objects similar to those from Beersheba and Ghassul were also used by the Coastal people. They were

[1] M. Stekelis: Archives IPH, Vol. XV (1935).

found at Meser, in Wadi Ara,[2] and more to the north at Byblos
(Layer II), where M. Dunand also found silver ornaments of
the same period which show no Mesopotamian inspiration and
seem to be the product of a local metallurgical industry. As
pointed out years ago by V. Gordon Childe, Syria-Palestine appears to have been an independent center of early metallurgy.[3]

An impressive detail of the Southern culture is the distance
of over sixty miles between the metal mines and the workshop.
This implies the regular transportation of metal ores on a trip
through the desert which took three days, and which raises the
question whether this could be done without the help of animals. There were enough domesticated oxen, and quite likely
donkeys were already serving men in Palestine by that time.
According to Thérèse Josien, the horse was available as well.

Pottery was extremely well made and well fired. The forms
are more elaborate and more varied than perhaps in any other
culture in Palestinian archaeology. There is a rich variety of handles, which are attached to different places on the bodies and
necks of the vessels. Pots on elevated bases and on legs, horn-
shaped cups, bowls, hole-mouth cooking jars (with rimless round
openings), large pithoi and flat basins, show the same fertile
imagination revealed by the art. Elongated churns with handles
on both sides and with small necks are also present, and they
occur more frequently and more typically in the Beersheba province than at Ghassul. These churns were used to make butter
and cheese and emphasize the importance of dairy products in
the local economy. Jars with spouts also are less common at
Ghassul than at Beersheba, whereas horn-shaped drinking cups
are very common at Ghassul and rare at Beersheba.

The decoration of pottery is quite different from that found
in Northern cultures. It consists chiefly of patterns of painted

[2] M. Dothan: IEJ, Vol. VII, No. 4 (1957), Pl. 37.
[3] See V. G. Childe: *New Light on the Most Ancient East* (4th ed.; London:
Kegan Paul; 1952), p. 224.

red lines, triangles, zigzags, squares, and nets, and of superimposed bands of rope patterns, fingerprint decoration, and "snakes," sometimes covered with small homogeneous incisions. Also some separately modeled animal figurines are sometimes applied to vessels. Incised decoration, which is rather common at Tell el-Fara and at other Chalcolithic sites of northern Palestine, is very rare throughout the Southern Chalcolithic.

The flint industry consists chiefly of fan scrapers, large, thin flakes with a semicircular retouched edge; of adzes with flat retouching along the length of the tool and frequently with a polished cutting edge; and of abundant but atypically shaped knife blades and sickle blades. Arrowheads and toothed saw blades which are characteristic of Neolithic times, and frequently persist in central Palestine in Chalcolithic times, have almost disappeared here.

The question of the climatic conditions of the area at this time has occupied various scholars. Some authorities believe today that no climatic change at all has occurred since Mesolithic times, but this supposition seems to be in contradiction with archaeological evidence. A discussion of this would lead too far afield; it will suffice to mention that most of these Southern settlements are located in sites where water is available today for only two or three months a year. Others, such as Ghassul, have no water at all, and so large a village could not possibly survive

Chalcolithic basalt hammer-stones from Tuleilat Ghassul

Basket imprints on the bottom of pots from Tuleilat Ghassul

Pottery from Tuleilat Ghassul

today in its geographical location. Moreover, olive stones were found by the excavators in the storing places of Ghassulian households, and it is likely that the Ghassulians cultivated olive trees, which cannot grow today in the same area. Despite the strong opposition of several authorities, I am therefore inclined to believe that the climate was not precisely the same as it is today.

Ghassul was destroyed and abandoned before 3300 B.C. In the Judean Hills and the Negev, the Southern culture probably persisted little longer. At Khirbet Bitar, near Beersheba a radio-carbon test dated a late phase of this culture at around 3325 B.C. (W. 245, U. S. Geological Survey). By then northern Palestine was already dominated by new cultures characterized by "gray-burnished" and "red-painted" pottery.[4] The makers of this new industry built the foundations of many of the early walled towns of Palestine, and with their arrival the Age of Early Farming came to an end.

[4] Called by various scholars "Late Chalcolithic," "Proto-Urban," or "Transition to the Bronze Age." No sharp cultural changes occur between this phase and the following one (Early Bronze Age I), which developed out of it.

Typical adz, fan-scraper, borer, and two retouched blades from Tuleilat Ghassul

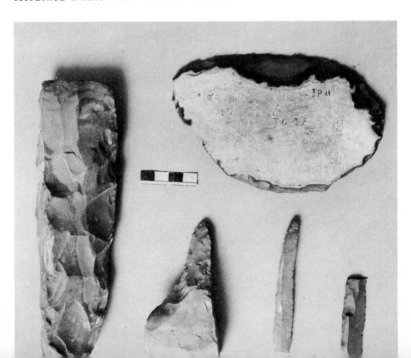

PART·FIVE

THE
URBAN AGE

I

The Origin
of the New Age

THE SEQUENCE OF CULTURES

P EOPLE HAVE TRIED to shift from village to urban life in
Palestine from Early Neolithic times to the present day, but we
know of only one example from before the beginning of the
Urban Age of a fortified urban settlement that was able to grow
and flourish—Jericho. Unique economic circumstances had
brought that city into being nine thousand years ago, and though
it is possible that Jericho was not the only fortified urban settlement of Neolithic times, towns developed as a common pattern
of settlement only at the beginning of the Urban Age (at the end
of the fourth millennium B.C.).

The Urban Age started with the phase which archaeologists
call Proto-Urban (or Final Chalcolithic), and continued throughout the period called Bronze Age in the traditional terminology.
This terminology turned out to be obsolete, as bronze was not

introduced into common use until about one thousand years after the beginning of this period. On the other hand, the term "Bronze Age" is usually used in Europe and elsewhere for societies which had no urban settlements, and whose economic, social, and political bases were different from those we find in the Near East at this time. The term "Urban Age" appears to define this epoch better.

In fact, the paramount characteristic of this age, from the archaeological point of view, is the urban settlement, or the large fortified city, which long survived or was rebuilt time and again on the same spot. In the course of their histories, these towns surrounded by defense walls were destroyed and rebuilt several times, each time leaving a stratum of debris on the previous one, and thus slowly forming those artificial mounds which Near Eastern archaeologists call "tells."

Archaeologists divide this age into three major periods: "Early Urban" (including at its beginning the transitional phase called "Proto-Urban" and at its end the "Intermediate Period"), "Middle Urban," and "Late Urban." Their dates were approximately as follows:

Early Urban : 3300 to 1850 B.C.
Middle Urban : 1850 to 1550 B.C.
Late Urban : 1550 to 1200 B.C.

Archaeologists detect during the Early Urban period a great deal of warfare, of destruction and rebuilding of settlements, of changes in the way of life and in the social organization of the various peoples who lived in Palestine.

In Palestine copper was used throughout this period, whereas bronze, which is an alloy and requires a more sophisticated technology, was extremely rare. Large quantities of bronze tools and weapons began to be made only at the very end of the Early Urban period, and larger ones only at the beginning of the Middle Urban period. Anatolia at this time shared various

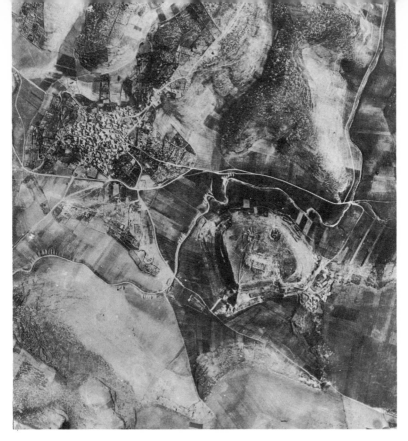

Aerial view of Tell ed-Dweir, the site of Lachish. Between the Arab village (upper left) and the tell is a wadi.

The Tell of Beth-Shan

traits and cultures with Palestine, and there this period is called the Copper Age. In both areas flint implements were still in common use, and consisted mainly of long knifelike blades with parallel, straight, very elegant flaking. These blades are frequently referred to by the unfortunate term "Canaanite." They were used as blades of daggers and knives and as heads of spears and arrows, and only very gradually did metal replace flint in these weapons.

Wood, skin, calabash, and other materials were used to make vessels, but pottery is the one which is best preserved. From the beginning of the Urban period, pottery fashions appear to have changed constantly. The shapes of the vessels and their decoration are the best illustration of the constant change in the aesthetic concepts of their makers.

The following table shows the major subdivisions of the Early Urban period, and the names given by archaeologists to the various successive styles of pottery:

THE EARLY URBAN PERIOD
(ca. 3300–1850 B.C.)

SUB-PERIODS	TYPICAL POTTERY	APPROX. DATE OF START	DATE CLUES
Proto-Urban (*Transitional*)	Gray-burnished (mainly in the North)	3300	Carbon 14 ca. 3260 at Jericho
Early Urban I	Band-slip and metallic (Early Bronze I)	3100	Jemdet-Nasr period in northern Mesopotamia and Syria
Early Urban II	Metallic and Abydos (Early Bronze II)	2900	Egypt, First and Second Dynasties
Early Urban III	Khirbet Kerak (mainly in the North) (Early Bronze III)	2700	Egypt, Third to Sixth Dynasty
Intermediate I	Enveloped handle jars (Early Bronze IV)	2300	Sargon of Akkad
Intermediate II	"Caliciform" (Middle Bronze I)	1950	Egypt, Early Twelfth Dynasty

Early Urban flint cores and blades
from Givat Haharuvim, near Hazorea

Unearthing pottery at Hazorea

This table gives an oversimplified bird's-eye view of the sequence of cultures, but as we shall see more in detail, several groups of people lived in Palestine side by side during this period, a great many tribes and peoples moved about, and the result was a rather complex assemblage of different cultures.

We know that not all the peoples lived in towns. Villages, hamlets, and isolated farms also existed in Palestine in this period, and various nomadic and semi-nomadic populations wandered between them and kept busy with pastoral, trading, and hunting activities. The highly varied patterns of culture and tradition are illustrated best by the variety of funerary customs. Cremation, inhumation in excavated graves, artificial funerary caves, and Megalithic monuments of various sorts were all employed. Some people buried their dead in collective tombs, others in cemeteries, still others in isolated graves. These various funeral rites suggest different views of death and of life, of the personality of man and of the community.

New tribes and peoples arrived in Palestine continually throughout the Early Urban period. Physical anthropologists have found different types of skeletons in Early Urban Palestine. The dominant race was the Proto-Mediterranean, which presumably was descended directly from the local Natufian Mesolithic people; but "Eurafrican" dolichocephalic, Alpine-like people and Armenoids are also found.[1] At Jericho, in three collective tombs studied by Gottfried Kurth,[2] over eight hundred individuals have been found and they seem to belong to two distinct groups: one is the short-statured, dolichocephalic Proto-Mediterranean, which is probably of local origin; the other, stronger and taller, with more archaic traits, resembles a type found at Yumuk Tepe and in other Anatolian sites and is believed to have originated more to the north. At Megiddo, both Mediterranean and Negroid types have been recognized by Aleš Hrdlička,[3] and

[1] D. Ferenbach: IEJ, Vol. IX, No. 4 (1959), pp. 221 ff.
[2] G. Kurth: Homo, 1955, pp. 145 ff.
[3] See P. L. O. Guy: Megiddo Tombs (Chicago: University of Chicago Press; 1938), p. 192.

at Tell Assawir both Proto-Mediterraneans and Alpine-like types are present.[4]

Obviously the racial intercourse was no less rich and varied than the cultural one. The picture we obtain is that of a great racial and cultural symbiosis equaled in no other historic or prehistoric period. But this was probably a common condition in most of the Near East throughout the third millennium B.C., a condition reflecting the role of this area as the meeting point of peoples and ideas which undoubtedly played a very important part in the formation of Near Eastern civilization.

THE SOCIAL, ECONOMIC, AND POLITICAL BACKGROUND

The two most important characteristics of the new age are that society was much more "sociable" than in all the previous periods, able to develop daily contacts with other societies and cultures; and that it was a society of full-time specialists.

Contact and intercourse between various human groups is a necessary condition for cultural development. An isolated human group without external contacts has a rhythm of evolution conditioned by the experience of that group only. The transmission of information enriches the knowledge and the experience of the group with the knowledge and experience of other groups and individuals, and thus the rhythm of cultural evolution is frequently modified by the range of external contacts.

Hamlets and farming villages had fewer external contacts than towns. Trade, warfare, and all the other means of intercourse between groups had a broader range of possibilities the larger the group.

The building of towns caused a considerable revolution in the internal relations of the group. The town—a large number of people living together, seeing one another constantly, and having certain obligations to coexist and to collaborate—broadened the daily contacts of each individual, awakened new social and

[4] D. Ferenbach: IEJ, Vol. IX, No. 4 (1959), p. 221.

intellectual ideas, united men in the common interests and experiences of a large group, and required the systematic specialization of labor.

The complex urban society needed various kinds of specialists and opened to the individual many different fields of occupation and the possibility of choice. The building of fortifications, temples, and other public buildings required masons; making the tools of daily use, such as pottery vessels, metal weapons, and implements, became increasingly complex tasks and required the work of specialists. The development of trade required specialization in the tasks of trading and transportation. The increasing size of population units, and the rise of such profitable activities as trade, stimulated competition and antagonism between people disputing the ownership of lands or natural resources. Professional soldiers were needed to defend the community, its trade, and its welfare.

Metal was increasingly becoming a necessity for making tools and weapons, and people started deliberately to look for metal deposits and to exploit them. These early "miners" formed another group of specialists who must have been attached in some way to a center from which they were sent out.

The complex social, political, and economic organization demanded leaders and administrators to plan and co-ordinate the activities of the group, to defend it in the event of war, and to make sure that the various specialists could attend to their tasks and satisfy the needs of society.

The centralization of power, the rise of a leading class, the

Copper ax from the gray-burnished period, Beth-Shan. Length is about four inches

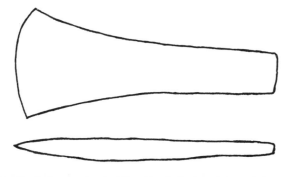

great energies devoted to the building of fortifications, temples, palaces, public water reservoirs, storage places, granaries, and other buildings for collective or official use, made it necessary for some individuals to become attendants and servants. The capturing of war prisoners eventually led to the institution of slavery, a way of obtaining cheap and abundant labor.

The multiplication of economic, social, and political needs was accompanied by a similar increase in the spiritual and ritualistic needs of the population. Each urban settlement had a religious center. At first this was just a shrine, but it quickly evolved into a temple, and the temple into a sacred area with various buildings. Professional priests took care of the religious needs of the population, becoming another type of specialist. The society that was born with the Urban Age was much more complex than the previous ones. In it we can see the prototype of the urban society of our day.

The Early Urban period was not an age of gradual and homogeneous evolution. From beginning to end there was general progress in the building of cities, in the material culture, and in daily life. But this was the result of the mixture and superimposition of different cultural traits, behind which were the various waves of newcomers of diverse origin arriving in Palestine. Tribal life was still going on in most regions; and in the vicinity of the cities some people still lived in villages, hamlets, huts, and tents.

The characteristic political pattern of the Early Urban Age in Palestine was that of the city-state. Walled cities were surrounded by their lands and by an agricultural population living in nearby farms and hamlets. At the beginning of the Early Urban period, the economic and social organization in the large settlements of Palestine was very similar to that found in Mesopotamia at the same time. The major city mounds, such as Megiddo, Beth-Shan, and Beth-Yerah, were located in highly strategic points, dominating highways and important valleys. Isolated hamlets were scattered about in the vicinity.

Isolated tombs also show that the agricultural population was spread all over the country. The city was the residence of the leaders and the specialists, who lived upon the surplus products of the agricultural population; it was the center of commercial and intellectual activities, the place which carried on international intercourse and which extended its protection and its taxes over its land.

The birth of the city and the development of trade started an opposite trend to the one observed in previous times. From Paleolithic times to Chalcolithic times more and more human beings settled down in particular places, and culture became more and more localized. Cultural provinces had become smaller and smaller, and with this increasing regional partition, human contacts within each province had become more constant and more regular. But with the spread of urban societies, contacts extended over the regional frontiers and slowly spread to more distant places.

Although in Neolithic times Palestine, in economy and culture, had frequently marched ahead of nearby lands, during the Chalcolithic period, in the fourth millennium B.C., other Near Eastern regions, mainly Mesopotamia, northern Syria, and Egypt, were able to foster larger cultural areas and more trade and contacts, and to evolve faster than Palestine. At the beginning of the Urban Age, late in the fourth millennium B.C., Palestine found itself at the margins of the two major centers of the urban civilization: Syria-Mesopotamia and Egypt.

I have previously mentioned the influence of the size of a settlement upon cultural development. The people who first succeeded in building up urban centers and who first pushed ahead with the specialization of labor were able immediately to speed up the tempo of evolution and to leave other peoples behind. Progress was so fast in Egypt and Mesopotamia at the beginning of the Urban Age that the pattern of city-state lasted there for a only a very short time, soon giving way to a pattern of states made up of several towns each involving an even more complex administration and political organization. Where the beginning of urban societies was delayed, this cultural advance was also delayed.

Early in the third millennium B.C., Upper and Lower Egypt became unified under a single Pharaoh. In Mesopotamia, city-states started to expand in the fourth millennium B.C., but the first large empire was formed only under Sargon, king of Akkad, in the second half of the third millennium B.C.

Mesopotamia and Egypt developed the traditional antagonism that was to color the history of the Near East during the third millennium B.C. Economic motives, drives for expansion, and probably also the ambitions of local princes inspired this "cold war." While Palestine was still in the Urban Age, Egypt and Mesopotamia were regarded as the two giant powers of the world.

It is interesting to look at this political situation today from a perspective of over four thousand years and to recall what has happened to these two centers of civilization since. Most of the technological advances of the last two and a half millennia were achieved elsewhere, largely among the Indo-Europeans, who were then a barbaric and semi-nomadic people living somewhere on the northern periphery. The ethical principles of our modern world were to come to us from the Hebrews, who were then one of the small nomadic bands in the eastern desert only very sporadically in contact with nearby peoples.

In Mesopotamia and Egypt, the use of conventional symbols eventually led to one of the major discoveries of civilization, when pictographic signs evolved into writing at the beginning of the third millennium B.C. This marked the moment when these two countries passed from prehistory into history. Thanks to written documents, our knowledge of the history of these two countries thereafter is vast, and from the beginning of the third millennium B.C. on, we have precise information about the administration of towns and temples, about contacts between various groups of people, about the rule of high priests and princes, and about other relevant events.

Palestine did not achieve literacy until the second millennium B.C., but pictographic signs were in current use. They usually were simple symbols, such as stars, crosses, squares, and other geometric patterns, and schematic figures of animals and human beings; they are found mainly on seals and property marks. These two pictographic devices probably had a large variety of purposes. Both were used as signatures and trademarks, and are best illustrated by the impressions on pottery vessels containing trade goods. Actual seals of stone, bone, ivory, metal, and pottery came into rather frequent use in the course of the Early Urban period, and one would suppose that they were extensively used also on perishable materials.

While Mesopotamia and Egypt entered fully recorded history during the third millennium B.C., in Palestine the Early Urban Age can be considered the Proto-historic period. A little historical information about Palestine is indirectly provided by Egyptian and Mesopotamian documents, but on the whole, these reveal very little about the causes of cultural change, warfare, and the destruction and rebuilding of settlements in that country.

For the Hyksos period historical information will become more abundant, and then Palestine will gradually enter history.

Oculi-face seal impression on metallic ware, from the Plain of Antioch (after Braidwood)

Impression of a seal on metallic ware from Megiddo, Level XIX (after Loud)

A large number of letters from local princes will disclose details about the Late Urban period, but written history, in the form of records and annals, will not appear in Palestine until it is conquered by the Hebrews.

THE URBAN SETTLEMENTS

Archaeologists call "urban" only those settlements of the Urban Age which were surrounded by a fortified wall and which had the other characteristics of city mounds, or tells. The buildings of these settlements usually were set much closer together than those of open villages, as the mound and the fortifications limited the available space. Because of this crowding, the narrow streets and squares soon required some sort of general planning.

Towns usually have other signs, besides the evidence of the fortifications, of public enterprise and centralized leadership. The frequent use of the same walls by two or more adjoining houses and other aspects of urban life imply a certain amount of co-operative labor. Towns usually had shrines or temples— of moderate size at the beginning of the Urban Age, but later increasingly important. They frequently also had larger buildings which might have belonged to the leader, or might have had a collective or public use. They had canals for draining or collecting water, and occasionally water reservoirs, granaries, and other public storage places.

In these towns of the Early Urban Age, family life does not seem to have been very different from that of many Near Eastern villages today. However, the presence of fortifications, temples, palaces, and other public buildings suggests that the social life in the city and the structure of society must have been considerably different from those of contemporary Near Eastern villages.

Little is known so far about the precise town planning of Early Urban cities, but at Ay, Beth-Yerah, Megiddo, and the other excavated tells, a considerable part of the excavated area within the walls was occupied by public buildings. Most of them were built along the fortifications, the inner sides of which were used as the rear walls of such buildings as storehouses, granaries, and temples.

Sometimes, as at Ay, around a central square, there were palaces, temples, or other buildings of official or public use. Private houses appear to have occupied only a minimal area within the city, and it is likely that these were reserved as residences for officials and specialists, such as leaders, priests, administrators, soldiers, masons, blacksmiths, potters, and traders, while the bulk of the agricultural population probably lived in hamlets outside the city wall.

Some architectural trends can be traced, although family dwellings did not change very drastically during Early Urban times. Some peculiar architectural characteristics crop up at certain times, but nothing suggesting large collective habitations nor other buildings implying special social organization have ever been found in Palestinian urban centers. Thus the towns were essentially an accretion of households based on family affiliations.

The round huts of Pre-pottery Jericho belonged to the formative period of the town. Later, when solid walls were built, the inhabitants realized that square ground plans were better suited to urban centers because they saved space and permitted better planning. This shift from round to square ground plans when villages were changing into towns was repeated again and again, particularly in the Proto-Urban period, when within a span of three hundred years all the major tells of northern Palestine became walled urban centers. In this transitional phase houses frequently had a round wall at one end and two corners at the other. We call these "apsidal" houses, and they are very common throughout the Near East in the formative urban phases. The sequence of basement hut, apsidal house, square house, repeats itself, with local variations, at slightly different times in Beth-Shan, Beth-Yerah, Megiddo, and elsewhere in

Mouth and handle of Early Urban
zoomorphic juglet, from Beth-Yerah

Palestine. This was a formative period, a period of trial and adjustment to new living conditions, and therefore there were many architectural innovations.

After the transitional period family houses usually were built like those we have seen in the Chalcolithic village of Ghassul. The center of family life must have been the cloistered courtyard, where fireplaces and other conveniences show that most daily activities were carried on there. Except during the three annual rainy months, the two or three rooms were probably used more for storing supplies than as living quarters. It is also quite probable that, as in many Palestinian Arab villages today, the houses also served as shelter for the few chickens owned by each family, for the donkey, and for the dogs, and one of the rooms was probably reserved for the livestock.

When the city was particularly crowded, some wealthy families were able to build two-story houses in which the upper floor probably was the private quarters of the family, while the ground floor was used for storage, cooking, and other daily activities.

Early Urban clay figurine of
mother and child from Beth-Yerah

Early Urban paved street at Beth-Yerah

In all these towns the main centers of social life probably were the temple and the plaza in front of it. These ceremonial centers had the important function of being places where the population could assemble when necessary and thus were instrumental in unifying the people and in creating the civic spirit needed for urban life.

In the Chalcolithic village of Ghassul, several rooms with walls covered with mythological frescoes have been found (see page 307), but nothing in the ground plan, or in the artifacts found in these rooms, seems to indicate that they were temples or that they were used by the whole community and not by a single household. No temples have been found so far dating from any part of the Chalcolithic period.[5] As previously mentioned, they are found in Neolithic Urban Jericho, and reappear in the Proto-Urban period. In Palestine temples have been discovered only in fully developed urban sites, and thus must be considered a typical cultural trait of the Early Urban period. As one of the public institutions of the town, at least in the beginning, they adjoined other public buildings, and in consequence were frequently attached to the fortifications. Two good examples of temples adjacent to the defensive walls were found in the tell of Megiddo (Level XIX), in the Esdraelon Valley, and at et-Tell, the site of the Biblical town of Ay, not far from Jerusalem.

In the course of time, the religious centers became increasingly prominent, and this is best illustrated at Megiddo, where a holy area developed in the heart of the settlement and persisted there for several centuries. Several sacred structures were built around a plaza, and in a rear corner there was a *bama*, or circular altar, probably some sort of holy of holies, hidden by a surrounding wall.[6]

[5] A strange, very large building recently found at Ain Geddi might be an exception, but only future excavations will be able to verify this. See J. Naveh: BIES, Vol. XXIII (1958), p. 46.

[6] G. Loud: *Megiddo II (Seasons 1935–39)* (Chicago: University of Chicago Press; 1948), p. 64, Fig. 143.

Two imposing buildings dating from the Early Urban Age have been discovered in Palestine; both have been considered to be temples by some scholars, but others disagree; and both are still puzzling to archaeologists. One was discovered at Ay by the French expedition directed by Judith Marquet-Krause. What was found is obviously only a small part of a much larger structure. The other was found at Beth-Yerah, on the shores of the Sea of Galilee, by an expedition directed by professors of archaeology at the Hebrew University.[7] It is built of flat and roughly square stones in a style resembling that of the Ay "palace."

The fragmentary building at Ay is a little over 110 feet long; in its center is a hall approximately 40 by 23 feet which had a roof supported by four massive central columns. This building was erected in the period characterized by a well-fired pottery called metallic ware (see table, page 320), but its ground plan has the same general "apsidal" shape as the private houses of earlier phases. It seems to have been two-storied, and the size of its central room obviously was planned for a considerable gathering of people; it was built on the highest spot of the city, in a very dominant position. Shmuel Yeivin, who participated in its excavation, thought at first that it had been a fortified sanctuary,[8] but the French archaeologist René Dussaud and other scholars preferred to see in it a princely residence of the town's leader.[9] Its ground plan bears some resemblance to that of temples found at Megiddo and elsewhere, but nothing like altars or ceremonial objects were found in this building; on the other hand, no living quarters were found in it either. Until other similar buildings are found in a more illuminating context, this structure will probably keep its secret.

---

[7] J. Marquet-Krause: *Les Fouilles de 'Ay (et-Tell)*, 1933–35 (Paris; Institut Français d'Archéologie de Beyrouth; 1949), Pl. 93; B. Maisler, M. Stekelis, and M. Avi-Yonah: IEJ, Vol. II, No. 4 (1952), pp. 218 ff.
[8] S. Yeivin: PEQ, 1934, pp. 189 ff.
[9] R. Dussaud: *Syria*, Vol. XVI, No. 4 (1935), pp. 346 ff.

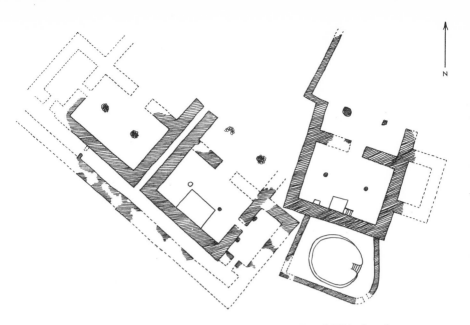

Plan of the sacred area at Megiddo, Level XV, showing
three temples and the oval high place (after Loud)

The city wall of Jericho, built of mud bricks in Early Urban times

The sources of the Jordan at Tell el-Kadi

The second puzzling structure was found at Beth-Yerah, and was attributed by the excavators to a phase characterized by the Khirbet Kerak ware (see table, page 320). It is an imposing building roughly square in shape, over 130 by 115 feet in size; it has a courtyard, an elongated central hall over 30 feet long with an entrance in the middle of the long side, and two central columns to sustain the roof. Surrounding the courtyard and the hall there are nine puzzling circular structures, eight of which were partially preserved. All had four partitions, and a narrow passage, some leading to the courtyard and some to the hall. In the courtyard, a fireplace with an incense stand was found. The entrances to the courtyard and to the central hall are on the eastern side, and the building is oriented exactly east-west. These facts seem to suggest the ritual character of the structure.[1] On the other hand, the circular cells are similar to those found in ancient granaries elsewhere.[2]

When this building was discovered, the excavators were divided in their opinion regarding its nature; some believed it to be a sanctuary, and others considered it a granary. Now it seems that both these ideas were partly correct, and that the courtyard and the elongated room were in fact a sanctuary and that this was surrounded by round granaries. Temples of the same period surrounded by granaries are well known in Mesopotamia.[3] This building sheds new light on the social structure of Early Urban Palestine. The storing of crops in temple granaries under the supervision of the religious authorities implies a theocratic leadership at Beth-Yerah similar to that known for the same period in Mesopotamia.[4]

Fortifications are the most important and best-known type

[1] IEJ, Vol. II, No. 4 (1952), p. 228.
[2] S. Marinatos: *Bulletin de Correspondance Hellénique*, Vol. LXX (1946), p. 342, Fig. 4.
[3] See P. Delougaz: *The Temple Oval of Khafajeh* (Chicago: University of Chicago Press; 1940); P. Delougaz and S. Lloyd: *Pre-Sargonid Temples in the Dyala Region* (Chicago: University of Chicago Press; 1942).
[4] See H. Frankfort: *The Birth of Civilization in the Near East* (London: Williams and Norgate; 1951), pp. 49 ff.

Partial view of building with circular structures, at Beth-Yerah

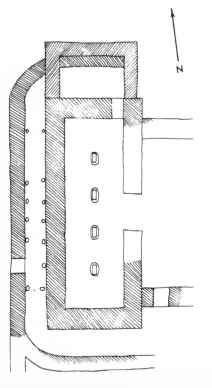

Plan of the so-called "Fortified Temple" at Ay (after Marquet-Krause)

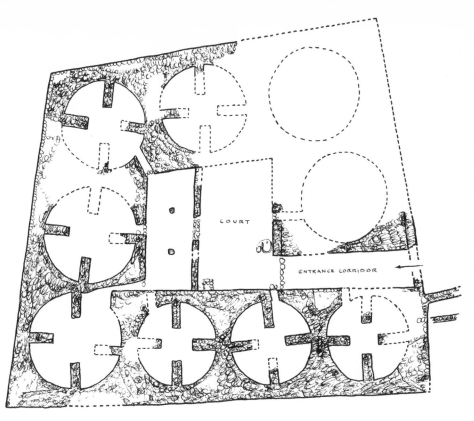

Reconstructed plan of the building with circular structures,
at Beth-Yerah (excavated by Stekelis and Avi Yonah)

Early Urban stone defense wall, at Beth-Yerah (excavated by Bar-Adon)

of public building. Again Jericho was unique in that this expression of urban life also appears there earlier than at any other known site. Pre-pottery Jericho had a very strong defensive wall reinforced by a moat.[5] The earliest fortifications elsewhere date from Early Urban times.

The best sequence of fortifications in Palestine was uncovered by the excavations of the Chicago Oriental Institute at the city mound of Megiddo. There (Level XIX) the earliest ring wall was about 10 feet thick and was built of mud bricks on a foundation of well-arranged pebbles and other natural stones.[6] Shortly thereafter, at a time when Mesopotamian and Egyptian contacts became increasingly close and international trade grew in importance, the first wall of Megiddo was not strong enough, and a second was built. This time it was entirely of stone and was over 13 feet thick. At about the same period, other tells were surrounded by fortifications. A massive ring wall was found at Beth-Yerah. There it was built of mud bricks, as was the first wall of Megiddo, but it was much better constructed and reached a thickness of as much as 26 feet.[7]

In central Palestine, the excavations of Ay have uncovered an extremely interesting and complex defense system, with what is believed to be a gateway and a semicircular tower beside it.[8] In southern Palestine, at Tell Gath, Shmuel Yeivin and his co-workers have recently discovered another defensive wall, which seems to belong to the same general period as the examples just described, or slightly before. It is the earliest example of offsets and recesses known in Palestine. Such walls are known, however, in Egypt from pictures dating from the Old Kingdom.[9] This kind

[5] K. Kenyon: *Digging Up Jericho* (London: Benn; 1957).
[6] Loud: op. cit. Kathleen Kenyon is today reluctant to accept the traditional idea that this was a defensive wall.
[7] IEJ, Vol. II, Nos. 3–4 (1952), pp. 218 ff.
[8] Marquet-Krause: op. cit., Pl. 6. Another very early gateway, probably the earliest yet found in Palestine, was recently discovered at Tell el-Fara by Father De Vaux.
[9] Yigael Yadin stresses that the nearest Egyptian depiction is from the lower register of the Nar-Mer palette. See also W. M. F. Petrie: *Desharsheh* (London: Kegan Paul, 1898), Pl. 4. The depiction of the siege of a Palestinian town goes back to the twenty-fourth century B.C.

of military architecture became very popular in later times, as it probably proved to be more efficient and useful for defense than the straight wall.

All this gives us a general idea of what life in these cities must have been like. The cities were accretions of households surrounded by defensive walls, and in the center the temples and the other public buildings served the needs of the community and of the leaders. Private life went on in cloistered courtyards; public life, mainly in and around the temple and the other public buildings. The various specialists thronged the city and conducted their daily activities in it. The agricultural population of the surrounding districts came to town to exchange their produce for other goods, and to take part in the social and religious activities. In the narrow streets, people went by with their donkeys and their other animals, while at the gate and along the walls soldiers took care of the security of the settlement.

I I

The Early
Urban Cultures

THE PROTO-URBAN CULTURES [1]

THE END of the fourth millennium B.C. was a time of change and gestation and of great political activity and migration throughout the Fertile Crescent and Egypt. Egypt was then in late Pre-Dynastic and in Proto-Dynastic times, and Mesopotamia was in the proto-literate period. In both these countries, cultural patterns were quickly spreading out and dominating large areas. In the countries along the Levantine coast of the Mediterranean, several regions were already well settled by sedentary agricultural populations and there were rather unified cultural areas spread along the Syro-Cilician coast, the upper Euphrates Valley, the valleys of the Orontes and Jordan rivers, and along the coast of Lebanon and Israel. But in between these areas cultural patterns

[1] I wish to thank Robert H. Dyson, of the University Museum, Philadelphia, who read and commented on this chapter.

were not sharply delimited and some regions were not yet settled by farmers. The sedentary regions at that time were oases of early farming around which nomadic and semi-nomadic groups still were wandering.

Open grasslands, deserts, and rocky hills began from the upper Euphrates, the Orontes, and the Jordan valleys; they were free territory through which bands of people could move at will and where distance still had a totally different meaning from what it had in the regions of sedentary life. The wandering bands came into occasional contact with farmers, and sometimes they settled down at the margins of sedentary regions. The archaeological remains in such regions frequently reveal the sudden arrival of a new culture whose origins are not always easy to trace.

While the last phases of the Southern Chalcolithic culture still persisted in the Beersheba region, in the North of Palestine several new cultures were emerging. Some of these "Proto-Urban" cultures remained rather localized and after a short while were absorbed by more vigorous nearby cultures, whereas others were able to spread over and to dominate large regions. The most important of these, which finally succeeded in sweeping over large

Cup marks on a rock near Hazorea

Late Chalcolithic jar with ledge handles, from Teil Abu Zureiq

parts of northern Palestine, was a culture characterized by shiny, lustrous, burnished gray pottery called by archaeologists "gray-burnished ware." The color and the lustrous burnishing were produced by techniques of baking in a particular manner in closed ovens, and of polishing the pots before the baking. These techniques were previously unknown in Palestine.

What seems to have happened is that new groups of people had arrived in Palestine, carrying with them their own traditions. In various major settlements of northern Palestine the old Chalcolithic material culture persisted to a minor degree side by side with the new culture. With the new wave of people came new aesthetic values and new techniques which conquered the country, and it would seem that the Chalcolithic people of the large farming villages in the mountains, on the Esdraelon and Beth-Shan plains, and in the Jordan Valley absorbed, or were absorbed by, the new culture.

The makers of the "gray-burnished ware" reached northern Palestine quite suddenly, and thereafter slowly spread southward along the Jordan Valley and the coastal plains. This culture reached the lower Jordan Valley before ca. 3260 B.C.,[2] and shortly thereafter it got to Maadi, near the Nile Delta in Lower Egypt.

Flint and bone were little used by the newcomers, and their stone bowls and mortars seem to copy the shapes of wooden artifacts. Another outstanding characteristic of the new pottery is the abundance of knobs and other protuberances used either as handles or purely as ornaments. The vessels frequently have bodies with keel-like ridges and rims turned outward. Deep bowls and "fruit vessels," or vessels on stands, with a more elaborate and finer form than those found in Middle Chalcolithic times are typical. Pots with spouts also occur. The best examples of larger jars come from Beth-Shan, Megiddo, and Tell el-Fara, where they frequently have bands of appliqué decoration. Many of the shapes

---

[2] Kathleen Kenyon comments that "Proto-Urban A" reached Jericho before ca. 3260 B.C., but the gray-burnished is not found at Ain es-Sultan, but at nearby Tell el-Aleiyek.

are exotic, whereas others appear to be advanced developments of earlier designs. The typical gray burnishing appears mainly on the small vessels, whereas the larger ones sometimes have bands of reddish slip which will become increasingly predominant later on.[3]

By examining the traces of this gray-burnished ware outside of Palestine, some general idea of the possible place of origin of its makers can be obtained. This culture reached Egypt from Palestine, and it probably reached the lower Jordan Valley from the North. The Esdraelon Valley was its main center in Palestine, but along the Mediterranean coast of Lebanon and Syria, few traces of it were found. That coast was then inhabited by other vigorous peoples, well settled and well organized, and it is unlikely that the makers of the gray-burnished ware passed through such stable and thickly populated regions. This culture was of northern origin, and its seems to have reached Palestine through inner Syria. Its traces are in fact found on the edges of the Syrian Desert. Gray-burnished ware has been found at Hama, on the Orontes, but only in small quantities amid the remains of a locally evolved culture. It also occurs in small quantities at Tepe Gawra and at other sites of the upper Euphrates. But nowhere in the Levant does it appear with the same homogeneity and abundance as in northern Palestine.

The people of this culture probably came originally from somewhere north of the Syrian Desert, and their culture apparently spread and flourished in two main regions. One was Palestine, the other was northern Anatolia, where a very similar gray-burnished ware is found. These two regions are about four hundred miles apart, and this culture does not seem ever to have succeeded in establishing itself in the stretch between.

[3] The excavators of Megiddo were able to follow a micro-evolution of this culture. See R. M. Engberg and G. M. Shipton: *Notes on the Chalcolithic and Early Bronze Age Pottery of Megiddo* (Chicago: University of Chicago Press; 1934). Very detailed studies of the material culture of this period have recently been undertaken by Kathleen Kenyon and G. E. Wright. See K. Kenyon: *Excavations at Jericho*, Vol. I (London: British School of Archaeology in Jerusalem; 1960); and G. E. Wright: *Eretz Israel*, Vol. V (1958), pp. 37 ff.

View of one of the temples, with the *bamah*
in the background, in the holy area of
Megiddo. The base of a column can be
seen in front of the temple.

This culture is believed to have appeared in northern Anatolia later than in Palestine, though this belief has not been fully
verified.[4] There was an important concentration of it in the valleys near and along the central strip of coast of the Black Sea,
between the towns of Bafra and Sinop.[5] From there the culture
of the gray-burnished ware spread southward and eastward, reaching Lake Van, where it flourished without drastic change for
practically the entire duration of the Early Urban period in Palestine.

[4] Robert H. Dyson comments as follows: "According to Burney the material
from northern Anatolia may be related typologically to Troy I (usually beginning
about 2900 B.C.). This is a rough estimate and the difference in date between
a 2900 and a 3200 B.C. date, given the lack of excavations, etc., is probably not
very significant."
[5] T. Özgüç: *Türk Tarsh Kongresi*, 1943, pp. 393–419; ibid., Belleten IX (1945),
pp. 361–400; C. A. Burney: *Anatolian Studies*, Vol. VI (1956), pp. 179 ff.

Early Urban stone bowl from Kinnereth

Jar with crisscross red paint
from Beth-Yerah

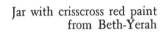

Early Urban stone bowl
from Har Haharuvim

Red painted pottery from Jerusalem and Gezer, now in Palestine Museum

THE EARLY URBAN CULTURES

In the course of the thirty-second century B.C. the gray-burnished ware was gradually replaced in northern Palestine by a new type of pottery decorated with parallel and crisscross patterns made by bands of slip. At first these two types of pottery were contemporary with each other, but later the gray-burnished diminishes, leaving the new type as dominant. In the South of Palestine the gray-burnished ware never became a dominant pattern of culture; there it seems that the Southern Chalcolithic gradually evolved into a new culture, characterized by a red-painted pottery decorated with parallel and wavy lines, which appears to be roughly contemporary with the "band-slip" pottery of the North.

At this time, Palestine had thrust upon it the peculiar task of transmitting cultural traits between the two major centers of Near Eastern civilization, Mesopotamia and Egypt. This was a period in which organized trade started to grow and contacts began to multiply. In Palestine houses and public buildings were then built by architectural methods learned from Mesopotamia, and mud bricks, a Mesopotamian device, became an important building material.[6] A new kind of pottery gradually turned up, the "metallic ware," which bore strong similarities to pottery found along the upper Euphrates and in other northern Mesopotamian regions. This metallic ware is a very hard and extremely well-baked pottery which has a characteristic metallic ring when struck and was frequently decorated with a comb-like impressed pattern.[7]

Additional evidence of trade is supplied by the seal impressions which now start appearing on Palestinian vessels. They are of the same kind as those used in Mesopotamia, in the Jemdet-Nasr period (about 3100–2900 B.C.). These seal impressions were

---

[6] Kathleen Kenyon comments: "Except in the hill country."
[7] The term "metallic ware" was used by the excavators at Megiddo to define only a few specific shapes of vessels. Here this term is used in a broader sense, to define all the contemporary pottery possessing the described qualities.

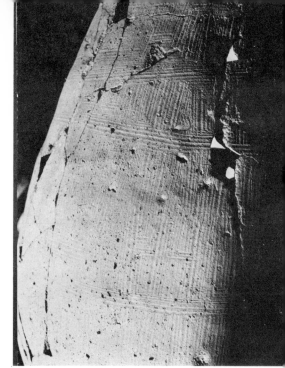

Metallic-ware jar with comb-mark decoration
from Beth-Yerah

Imported vessels of alabaster and stone from Kabri

trademarks, and were used in much the same way as the labels that modern vineyards put on the bottles of wine they produce and sell. The same seal impressions are scattered over a fairly large territory—throughout Palestine, Syria, and the upper Euphrates Valley—and this probably indicates the wide extent of trade in agricultural products achieved by then.

At about this same time (in the Late Gerzean period) Palestinian jars made their way also into Egypt, and it is likely that they had been brought there as containers for some sort of imported liquid. Trade developed very fast throughout the Levant. Caravan routes connected Mesopotamia with Syria and Palestine and with Egypt. By then sea voyages began to be made on a considerable scale. Large boats were able to remain at sea for many days, and professional sailors had enough experience to navigate correctly both day and night.

It seems that by the end of the fourth millennium B.C., or at the very beginning of the third, the "Sea Way," the international coastal highway, already was being used for long-distance trade. Recently this fact was stressed by an interesting discovery made at Kabri, a site along this highway in northern Israel. Moshe Prausnitz found there a group of alabaster and other stone vessels of Proto-Dynastic Egyptian types, Anatolian obsidian objects and tools, and other goods that imply long-distance trade. It is likely that Kabri was a stopping place or trading station on the already prosperous highway.

In the thirtieth century B.C., when Egypt became united under the first Pharaonic dynasty, oil, wine, perfumes, grains, and honey became important objects of trade. Various harbors were rapidly expanding along the Levantine coast, from the Nile Delta to the Plain of Antioch. In Lebanon, the harbor of Byblos was becoming a large town and an important trading center. A few fragmentary documents give us an idea of the dimensions this trade was gradually assuming. An Egyptian notation dating back to the twenty-seventh century B.C. reads in part as follows: "Bringing forty ships filled with cedar logs. Shipbuilding of cedar

Abydos vase, center, and two other
Early Urban pots from Jericho

Egyptian pottery of the
First Dynasty (after Petrie)

Appliqué decoration representing a snake,
on Early Urban pottery from Beth-Yerah

wood. One 'Praise-of-the-two-Lands' ship, 100 cubits [long] and of meru wood, two ships 100 cubits [long]. Making the doors of the royal palace of cedar wood." [8]

The need for metals and for other trade goods drove prospectors to search for ores and potential mines in the deserts. At the beginning of the third millennium B.C. the Egyptians were already busy with mining enterprises in the Sinai Peninsula. Copper and turquoise were extracted "industrially"—that is, in large quantities and with well-organized and trained labor—and were transported on donkeys to the Nile Valley by way of the caravan route crossing the Tih Desert.

The main evidence of Egyptian connections in Palestinian material culture in the twenty-ninth century B.C. is provided by the recurrence of a peculiar kind of red-buffed one-handled vessel standing on a wasp-waisted cylindrical base, usually called an "Abydos vase" after its type-site in Egypt, where it was found in the tombs of the First Dynasty. Flat dishes and bowls with rims turned inward and downward, large jars, oval jars, and flasks of the kind that have a rimless hole mouth (or opening), are the most characteristic pottery shapes of this period, which also persistently shows affinities with the same period in northern Mesopotamia.

Trade was largely responsible for communications between one country and another, but by this time large-scale military activities probably also played their part. It seems that Egypt in this period made its earliest attempts to penetrate into Asia through military expeditions. Yigael Yadin has considered the Nar-Mer palette, one of the magnificent ceremonial slating palettes of the period, to be a proof of earlier military activity. The two figures at the bottom are interpreted by Professor Yadin as two Asiatic people fleeing from their fortresses and fortified enclosures.[9] Recent excavations at Gath seem to show that daily

[8] From the Palermo Stone; see ANET, p. 227. (100 cubits equals about 170 feet.)
[9] See Y. Yadin: IEJ, Vol. V, No. 1 (1955), pp. 1 ff.

The Hierakonpolis panel of King Nar-Mer. In the top section, the name of the king is shown on the façade of a palace, with a head of Hathor on each side. The central section shows the king, wearing the white crown of Upper Egypt, smiting a prisoner. The prisoner's head appears again above him on an oval bowl holding six papyrus stalks; a falcon holds the head with a rope. Behind the king is a servant or slave. In the bottom section, two Asiatics, each with his own symbol, are shown in flight. Height about twenty-five inches.

contacts between Egypt and southern Palestine occurred as early as the First Dynasty. On one jar found in Egypt, the seal of a king who lived in the twenty-ninth century B.C. reads: "The Seth: Pre-Ibsem, who carries off Asia," and this has been read as evidence of Egyptian military activities in Asia as early as the Second Dynasty.[1] Military activities intensified, and from the Fifth Dynasty (about 2550 B.C.) there has come down to us a drawing of ships carrying Asiatic prisoners to Egypt and a scene of Egyptians attacking an Asiatic fortress.[2] But it is not until the Sixth Dynasty, in the twenty-fourth century B.C., that the first clear historical text relating to military campaigns in Syria-Palestine is available. It concerns a military commander called Uni, sent by Pharaoh Pepi I to "punish the Asiatics," whose story was written on his cenotaph at Abydos.[3]

Egyptian trade and political influence increased, and was particularly marked along the coast; but the interior of Palestine enjoyed fewer of these international contacts and went more its own way—a way of relatively independent agricultural and pastoral economies.

In addition to its intercourse with Egypt and Mesopotamia, Palestine appears to have maintained some contacts with regions farther north, with Anatolia and Caucasia. Objects of Anatolian provenience were found in a tomb of this period at Kinnereth, near Beth-Yerah, on the Sea of Galilee. Two battle-axes of Caucasian origin were found at et-Tell, the site of Biblical Ay, not far from Jerusalem.

A new kind of pottery, the Khirbet Kerak ware, suddenly appeared, probably sometime in the twenty-seventh century B.C., approximately in the same area in which the gray-burnished ware of the late part of the fourth millennium B.C. had been concentrated. At a few sites, mainly at Beth-Yerah, Beth-Shan, and

[1] W. M. F. Petrie: *The Royal Tombs of the Earliest Dynasties*, Vol. III (1901), Pl. 22.
[2] See *Cambridge Ancient History*, Vol. I, pp. 226, 289–90.
[3] ANET, p. 227.

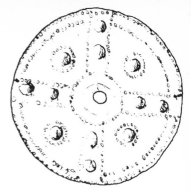

Gold plaque from Kinnereth
(after Maisler-Mazar)

Khirbet Kerak ware with incised
geometric decorations, from Beth-Shan

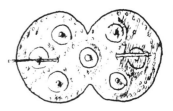

Gold brooch from Alaça-Hüyük
(after Kosay and Amiran)

Perforated hammer ax from Ay

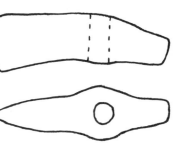

Khirbet Kerak ware with geometric
decorations in high relief, from Beth-
Yerah

Affula, the advent of this culture marked a considerable decline of the previous culture. Elsewhere, for example at the mound of Megiddo, this new culture was less predominant and was mixed with the local culture. In still smaller quantities this pottery invaded the South of the country. It is, however, much more common in the North. It is present everywhere, in the layers of its period, north of the Esdraelon Valley; but farther south it is to be seen only in the major centers, and only in minor quantities.

This pottery had none of the painted and incised decorations common in the local Palestinian cultures. Instead, it had decorations in high relief, and was coated with a thick slip and a red-and-black shiny burnish. The representative vessels of this ware are deep bowls with carinate, or keeled, bodies and outward-flaring rims, one-handled deep bowls, little one-handled jugs with flat bases, trumpet-shaped stands, strange lids with knob handles on top, and fireplace cranes which frequently have schematic human faces engraved or in high relief.

There are some Khirbet Kerak pots at most sites, but oddly enough they did not in any way influence local potters. This culture remained separate even though it must have been in frequent contact with the other cultures of the region, and it took root at only a few large and well-fortified sites.

Whereas in Palestine some vessels had been partially or completely made by means of the wheel for the previous four hundred years, the Khirbet Kerak ware was entirely handmade, and both its forms and its decoration are totally exotic. Plastic decoration in relief had not appeared on pottery since the gray-burnished ware, and the carination and the out-flaring rims of the bowls also have some distant suggestion of the gray-burnished ware.

The interesting aspects of this puzzle were first stressed by William F. Albright and G. Ernest Wright,[4] but a more extensive discussion did not come until 1950, when Sinclair Hood, a British scholar, and later Ruth Amiran, an Israeli archaeologist, empha-

[4] W. F. Albright: AASOR, Vol. VI (1926), p. 28; see G. E. Wright: op. cit.

Spiral decoration on Khirbet Kerak ware from Beth-Yerah

Anthropomorphic stand from Khirbet Kerak levels at Beth-Yerah

Biconic stand of red-burnished Khirbet Kerak ware from Beth-Yerah

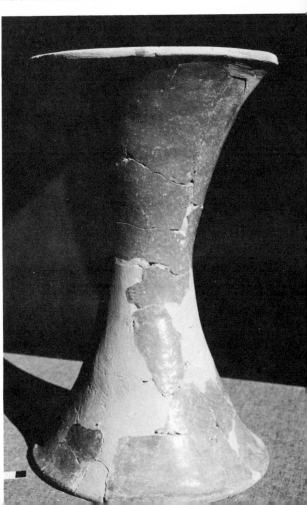

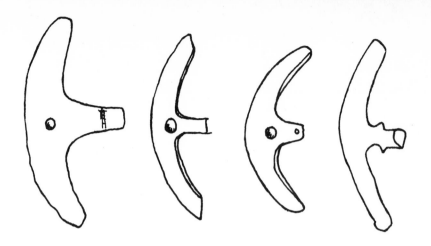

Crescent-shaped axes from Tell el-Hesi, Jericho,
Soli, and Satir Hüyük, one-fifth actual size

sized the Anatolian resemblances of this pottery.[5] Anatolian influences in Palestine in the third millennium B.C. were well known
from several earlier sporadic finds. At Kinnereth, Professor Benjamin Mazar located a golden plaque of probable Anatolian origin
in a tomb with other foreign objects, and Judith Marquet-Krause
uncovered at Ay two stone battle-axes of northern origin.[6]
Crescent-shaped copper axes were found at Jericho and Tell el-
Hesi identical in design with Anatolian and northern Mesopotamian tools of the same period.[7]

The Khirbet Kerak culture is well known in inner Syria, from
Hama on the Orontes, from Aleppo, and from the Plain of Antioch, Ugarit, and various other sites along the coast. Excavations
in the site of Tabara el-Akrad, on the Plain of Antioch, have
revealed four major strata of Khirbet Kerak immediately following the Jemdet-Nasr period. Here this culture seems to have
started earlier than in Palestine.[8] It also occurs in central Ana-

[5] S. Hood: *Anatolian Studies*, Vol. I (1950), pp. 113 ff.; R. B. K. Amiran:
IEJ, Vol. II, No. 2 (1952), pp. 89 ff.
[6] J. Marquet-Krause: *Les Fouilles de 'Ay (et-Tell)*, 1933–5 (Paris: Institut
Français d'Archéologie de Beyrouth; 1949), Pls. 37–8 and 68.
[7] F. J. Bliss: *A Mound of Many Cities: Tell el-Hesi Excavated* (London: 1894),
p. 35, Fig. 69; Kenyon: op. cit., Fig. 1.
[8] See S. Hood: *Anatolian Studies*, Vol. I (1950), p. 113.

tolia,[9] but its most important concentration outside of Palestine is in the Kura-Araks basin in Transcaucasia.[1] It does not occur in southern Anatolia, where a very different culture was strongly established at the time.[2] Sinclair Hood has interpreted its sudden spread throughout Syria and Palestine as the result of the migration of a people who came from the desert regions of the Northeast.

After their arrival, these people do not seem to have penetrated further into Palestine; but where they did settle they preserved their exotic culture for at least three hundred years. Then it began to absorb more and more local influences until its identity disappeared. In some cases, as at Beth-Yerah, its end came with the destruction of a town, marked by a level of charred debris and ashes. The end of this culture is roughly contemporary with the Egyptian military expedition to Asia described by Uni, officer in the army of Pharaoh Pepi I.

Toward the end of the Khirbet Kerak culture, late in the twenty-fifth or early in the twenty-fourth century B.C., it seems that Palestine went through a period of strong economic development.

This was a time of expansion for towns, of founding new urban and farming centers, and of colonization; the strip of land from Gezer to Beersheba was then settled with cities. For example, at the lowest level of Tell Beit Mirsim, William F. Albright found that in the course of this period an open farming village evolved into a fortified town. Tell Gerar, Tell el-Hesi, and other southern tells also show the first signs of urban settlements at about the same time.

Archaeological findings point to two major trends. One is the spread of permanent settlements and of sedentary populations; the other is the tendency of nomadic and semi-nomadic popu-

---

[9] H. Kosay: "Ausgräber von Alaça Hüyük," *Vereine der Türkischen Geschichts Kommission*, Vol. V, No. 2a (1944).

[1] B. A. Kuftin: *Vestnik Gos. Muzeya Gruzi*, Vol. XIII B (Tiflis; 1953).

[2] See *Iraq*, No. 44 (1949); *Anatolian Studies*, Vol. IX (1954), p. 175; *Anatolian Studies*, Vol. VIII (1950), p. 157.

lations in transition to reach the edges of the fertile regions and to attempt to settle down.

Apparently at first all this happened quite harmoniously. The country flourished and the various local peoples lived in peace; but after a short while new cultural and political forces suddenly appeared on the scene, and Palestine became again the stage of active migrations and of warfare. We have come to the end of the twenty-fourth century B.C., a time when everywhere in the Fertile Crescent and in Egypt, large migrations and great changes took place.

THE INTERMEDIATE CULTURES

The waves of various desert peoples moving into Palestine reached flood proportions during the last three centuries of the third millennium B.C. In Egypt the Old Kingdom came to an end, and the continual arrival of barbaric people from Asia brought a time of decadence, of abandonment of the old values, and of warfare, called the "First Intermediate" period.

In Mesopotamia the old civilizations were coming to an end, and the infiltration of marginal peoples into the fertile and prosperous land renewed the vigor of the inhabitants and stimulated the establishment of a new civilization. Shortly before the year 2300 B.C., a Semitic population which had previously lived in peripheral regions, the Akkadians, led by a king named Sargon, extended their hegemony over most of northern Syria and Mesopotamia.

Sargon, the mighty king of mysterious origins, probably the most legendary figure of the ancient Near East, invaded Akkad from the hilly regions, as is recorded in one of the Mesopotamian epics. According to legend, his father was unknown and his mother was a prostitute. A text known from later inscriptions describes his birth as follows: "My mother conceived me, in secret she bore me, she set me in a basket of rushes, with bitumen she sealed my lid, she cast me into the river, which rose not over

me. The river bore me up and carried me to Akki, the drawer
of water . . ." [3] Further on, the same epic reads: "The black-
headed people I ruled, and governed, mighty mountains, with
chip-axes of bronze I conquered . . ." Sargon's reign started
sometime before 2300 B.C., and in his time the use of bronze in
industrial quantities was introduced into Mesopotamia. The people who arrived with him were much better metalworkers than
any who had lived before them in the fertile regions of Mesopotamia. With him, historical annals and real, full history began in
the land of the Tigris and the Euphrates, which was then united
under a single ruler.

Sargon's life contains the secret of the origins of the Semites,
who in his time made their first appearance in history. Yet it is
highly probable that the Semites had already become an important ethnic element everywhere in the area conquered by him and
in the peripheral regions on the southern edges of the Fertile
Crescent.

Shortly after the Akkadians flourished in Mesopotamia, several nomadic peoples entered Palestine. They occupied most of
Jordan and the Negev.[4] They settled territory that had never
been inhabited before by sedentary populations, and the remains
of their settlements show that they were only partly sedentary.
The most important trait of their small settlements is large herd
pens, which show that herding must have been one of their principal occupations.

The same process that we have already followed several times
repeated itself once again. These semi-nomadic bands entered

[3] See ANET, p. 119.
[4] See L. H. Vincent: BASOR, No. 95, p. 6.

Copper blade of sword or spearhead,
from Megiddo, Level XVIII (after Loud)

fertile Palestine, destroyed towns, and settled near or on their ruins, taking advantage of the devices already developed by the previous inhabitants. In a short while they were acclimated to the new way of life and had learned how to build their own houses and fortifications. At the end of this book we shall observe another such wave, in which the Hebrew tribes conquered Palestine.

The broad ethnic movements on the edges of Palestine after the Sumerian civilization had come to an end, when the Akkadians were conquering large parts of the Near East, have been frequently associated with a people called Amurru in many Near Eastern texts, and with the Amorites in the Bible. "Amorite" is a Semitic name, and the people of this name originally were nomads living in the Land of Martu,[5] west of Sumer, somewhere in the regions between Mesopotamia and Palestine. According to a Sumerian song, in early times the Amorites were hut or tent dwellers, ate uncooked meat, and were dangerous bandits.

They probably were part of the extremely varied population which inhabited the marginal lands south of the Fertile Crescent during the third millennium B.C. In later times they grew immensely in number and in power, and various groups of them settled down in different parts of the Near East. At the beginning of the second millennium B.C., several local Amorite princes and kings were established in Mesopotamia. They had typical western Semitic names, like Abam-ram (Abraham) and Jacob-el (Jacob). The most famous of their royal families was the dynasty of Shemu-abu, which made of Babylon the center of a very great empire between the eighteenth and sixteenth centuries B.C. King Hammurabi belonged to this dynasty, which had one of the most outstanding codes of laws of antiquity, whose moral concepts are in many ways similar to those of the Bible.

Groups of Amorites were in Palestine by the time of the Hebrew Patriarchs, and until the Hebrew conquest they formed

[5] The Sumerians called the Amorites by the name of Martu.

an important part of the population. In the Bible the Amorites are mentioned as one of the several peoples inhabiting central Palestine;[6] in the Book of Joshua [7] they show up again as one of the groups of people living in the hills, while the Canaanites are said to live on the plains and along the seacoast.

These Amorites are an important factor in the early historical documents of the Egyptians, Mesopotamians, and Hittites, and they continued to be such as late as the Iron Age. Sargon marched to conquer the Land of Amurru shortly before the nomads just mentioned first invaded Jordan and the Negev, bringing new cultural elements to fertile Palestine. And it is likely that all these ethnic movements and political activities were somehow related to one another.

We do not know whether all these cultural groups called Amorites were a single people, but it seems likely that they were groups of tribes which had been pushed out of their homelands and thus propelled into Palestine. Some of them settled down there near other peoples, while some disappeared from the Palestinian corner of the Near East after a short while.

This was the period in which the last major Megalithic monuments in Palestine were built. At the sites of Bab ed-Dra, Ader, Lajjun, in Jordan, and in various localities of the Negev, the newcomers erected rough Megalithic monuments called massebahs, or menhirs (standing monoliths), and small cist graves surrounded by round stone cairns.

Rows or series of menhirs are also common in this period (the end of the third millennium B.C.) in fertile regions. They occur at Gezer in the middle of the town. At Ugarit, in Syria, they are related to the Temple of Dagon, a marine divinity, while at Assur a field of menhirs was located just outside the town. The cairns, however, have been found only in the desert. These Megalithic monuments have nothing to do with the dolmens of Golan

[6] Numbers 13: 29.
[7] 5: 1; 10: 6.

and Bashan, or with the Chalcolithic cist graves of Adeime, but they seem to have a common inspiration, suggesting some further evolution of the traditions of the earlier Megalithic groups.

Menhirs occur at various sites in Jordan in the vicinity of funerary monuments, and seem to have some connection with the cult of the dead or with commemorative practices, but this was certainly not their only use and purpose. They are frequently referred to in the Bible, and their erection was a part of the religious customs of the Hebrew Patriarchs. Jacob, after he had his dream in Beth-El, "awaked out of his sleep, and he said, Surely the Lord is in this place, and I knew it not. . . . and rose up early in the morning, and took the stone he had put for his pillows, and set it up as a massebah, and poured oil upon the top of it." [8]

These menhirs were used to solemnize a pact that had been made between Jacob and Laban. This description is particularly interesting because it shows that not every menhir had a direct religious purpose: "And Jacob took a stone, and set it up as a massebah. And Jacob said to his people, Gather stones; and they took stones, and made a heap: and they did eat there upon the heap." [9] This ceremonial meal on the cairn ratified the treaty between Jacob and Laban, and friendship was established once again. The place was called Gal-'ed, or "cairn of witness."

The Biblical descriptions show that these cairns and these menhirs were customarily used at the time of the Patriarchs, and they must have had a long traditional use among many dwellers in the arid regions. It is very interesting to note that they turn up for the first time in the desert regions of Palestine shortly after the Semitic Sargonid dynasty founded the Akkadian Empire, that is, late in the third and early in the second millennium B.C., just when the Hebrew Patriarchs seem to have first appeared in Palestine (see pages 380 ff.).

[8] Genesis 28: 16–18.
[9] Genesis 31: 45–6.

Basalt stele from Shihan, Jordan, in high relief. The "warrior" wears a short kilt of skin held by a belt, and holds a spear. To his left is an animal.

Pot with a high-looped handle decorated with red burnishing, from Tell Assawir (after Dothan)

Intermediate I pottery *in situ* in one of the tombs of the Hazorea necropolis

The occupation of the arid regions of Palestine by semi-nomadic settlers lasted only a short period, and many of them disappeared as mysteriously as they had come.

In Jordan, two remarkable steles have been attributed to this period by William F. Albright; one is the stele of Shihan with the high relief of a warrior carrying a spear, with a haircut similar to those of the Beni Hassan Asiatics; [1] and the other is the Balu'ah stele, which was re-used at the beginning of the Iron Age but still shows the original inscription above the later panel.

The burial methods and settlement patterns in the fertile regions were varied, but all peoples reaching Palestine in this period paid very special attention to the cult of the dead. Single burials and, less commonly, collective ones are found, each in several variant types. An interesting attempt was made by Kathleen Kenyon to discern tribal traits in the type of tomb used and in some details of the material culture. [2] Graves were given much more attention by these people than habitations, and appear to have demanded the concentration of a great deal of energy and constructive ability. Shaft graves are common, and several distinct kinds can be distinguished. At Hazorea, I have excavated a cemetery of this period in which at least three distinct types of shaft graves were present. Some of these graves were dug in an irregular shape, and have a very deep shaft leading to an approximately oval chamber. Others were precisely cut, with a large square entrance shaft and approximately square burial chambers. In this cemetery, and in various other sites of northern Palestine of the same date, the pottery is characterized by an abundance of small jars with spouts of a form practically identical with that of modern teapots. Red burnishing is found on some of these vessels, which somewhat resemble the pottery of the Sargonid period in northern Mesopotamia.

In Palestine most of our knowledge of the material culture of this period comes from tombs. Settlements were much more

[1] Yigael Yadin comments that he thinks that this stele is later than is currently believed, and that it shows affinities with Hittite art.
[2] K. Kenyon: *Archaeology in the Holy Land* (London: Benn; 1960), p. 143.

Various types of pottery, copper tools, and pendant ornaments from the Hazorea necropolis

Various types of Intermediate I pottery from the Hazorea necropolis

Two pots *in situ* in a tomb at Hazorea

primitive and less stable than during the previous millennium. At Jericho more than eight feet of debris was accumulated in a ditch before the first houses were built; at Lachish these people dwelt in caves; at Tell Beit Mirsim, Albright found an open village with very poor buildings, while most of the material from Tell el-Ajjul, Megiddo, and other major tells comes from tombs. However, judging by the number of tombs and by the area these open settlements occupied, numerically these peoples formed important groups.

One of the later cultures of this period (late in the twentieth and in the nineteenth century B.C.) was far more civilized than those heretofore described. It reached Palestine along, or on the border of, the fertile coastal strip, and seems to have flourished at Hama, on the Orontes, and at other northern Syrian sites before it reached Palestine. This is the culture characterized by calix-like pots, which archaeologists refer to by the unfortunate name of "Caliciform culture." In Palestine this culture very rarely turns up as pure and uniform as it does in Syria; usually it is mixed with many local elements and it is impossible as yet to decide whether it came to Palestine as the result of larger ethnic movements. However, a few tombs have yielded a quite uniform Caliciform material culture, and this indicates that the objects found were not simply imported goods and that human groups with a traditional Caliciform culture lived in Palestine.

Though the Intermediate period is well known from many excavations, the types of material culture are so varied in it that it is not yet possible to analyze the sequence of its sub-phases. What seems to have happened, however, is that several peoples making different sorts of pottery lived in Palestine at the same time, eventually coming into contact with one another and exchanging pottery and other materials.

The most powerful and the best-organized of these invaders, the Hyksos, arrived after the end of the Early Urban Age and also penetrated into Egypt and ruled vast areas for two hundred years. But even before their time, during the dark age called First Inter-

Pendant and necklace
from Tell Assawir
(excavated by Dothan)

Intermediate "caliciform" ware from Tell el-Ajjul (after Kenyon)

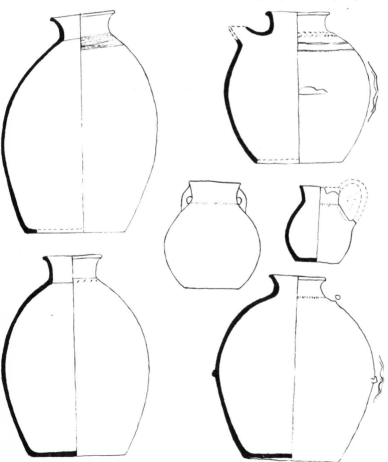

mediate (between the Old and Middle Kingdoms), other waves
of Asiatics strongly influenced Egypt.

There can be little doubt that all these extremely broad
ethnic and cultural movements occurring throughout the Near
East in Akkadian times were interrelated, and that all were part
of a very large political chain reaction. The Sumerian civilization
came to an end; the Semitic Akkadians spread out and founded
the largest empire ever seen up to that time; and powerful Egypt
was invaded by Asiatic barbarians. All this happened within three
generations.

We shall meet again, in later times, the continuation of the
turmoil begun in this period, which was a sort of Middle Ages for
Syria, Palestine, and Egypt—an age of barbaric invasions, or warfare, and of declining art and culture—but one which prepared
the way for a new era in most countries of the region. It lasted
almost five hundred years before giving way to a new culture and
to a new, dynamic, and well-organized people.

In the course of the nineteenth century b.c., more sophisticated weapons, building methods, and pottery molded by new
traditions were slowly introduced into the Early Urban cultures
and finally replaced them. In the middle of the eighteenth century b.c., power in Syria, Palestine, and Egypt was seized by the
people whom the Egyptians called Hyksos, or "rulers of the foreign countries."

Cooking pots from Level XVI at Megiddo (after Loud)

III

The Hyksos
and the Hebrew
Patriarchs

ARCHAEOLOGY, HISTORY, AND THE BIBLE

WHEN THE early part of the second millennium B.C. is reached, historical evidence increases considerably in importance. Political and military events begin acquiring names and dates. Long Biblical descriptions are an important complement to royal archives, letters, and annals found by archaeologists in the capitals of Near Eastern kingdoms and empires and in their vassal cities. An enormous quantity of pictorial material from Egypt, Mesopotamia, Syria, and Anatolia provides direct and vivid information on the daily life and the history of the people living in and near Palestine. The material culture found in excavations is such that we can reconstruct the trends of economic activities, of social and political contacts, of religion, technology, architecture, writing, art, and fashion, with great precision in terms of time and space.

The time dealt with in the last chapters of this book is subdivided by archaeologists into the Middle Urban period (Middle Bronze II in the traditional terminology) and the Late Urban period (Late Bronze Age in the traditional terminology). It starts in the course of the nineteenth century B.C., during the rule of the Twelfth Dynasty in Egypt, and comes to an end with the Israelite conquest of Palestine during the thirteenth and the early part of twelfth century B.C. The date of its end varies slightly in different parts of the country, as the conquest appears to have taken place at different dates in various regions.

These periods can be divided into four major phases, as follows:

				EGYPT
MIDDLE URBAN	I	*Before Hyksos rule (M.B. II A)* *	*19th to late 18th century*	*Late 12th Dynasty*
	II	*Hyksos rule (M.B. II B-C)*	*Late 18th to middle 16th century*	*13th to 17th Dynasty*
LATE URBAN	I	*"Bichrome" Transition (L.B. I A)*	*Middle 16th to early 15th century*	*Early 18th Dynasty*
	II	*Egyptian rule (L.B. I B and L.B. II)*	*Early 15th to 13th century*	*Late 18th and 19th Dynasty*

* The technical abbreviations in parentheses are those used by archaeologists for the particular phases.

A curious and interesting fact characterizes the history of Palestine during these periods: the presence of two separate traditions and histories, the one concerning the inhabitants of cities, the peoples who had most of the military, political, and economic power, of whom archaeology, royal archives, and descriptions of Egyptian military campaigns tell us most; the other concerning the marginal units which included the Hebrews and other similar groups, the peoples who had become an important ethnic factor in the area at the end of Early Urban times.

Bronze hairpin from Level XIV at Megiddo (after Loud)

Archaeology helps us only a little in the study of the latter groups, but many ancient texts provide very rich and detailed information, and the Bible devotes many chapters to them. Strangely enough, the two histories remain very much separated from each other, and usually the texts enlightening us on the one do not deal with the other. However, there are several exceptions to this rule, and there are also documents which provide a link.[1]

As a result of this separateness, there were two distinct ways of life and cultural patterns—that of the permanent settlers and that of the nomads—which were able to exist near each other and come in contact with each other, and still preserve their own values and principles.

The three main sources for these times are texts, archaeology, and the Bible. The books of the Bible that concern the Hebrew Patriarchs cannot be considered mere legend; however, they cannot be called history, for one very important requisite for history is missing here. The Biblical accounts do not provide the missing links which would enable us to place the kings and their people in a precise historical framework. As yet not a single one of the personal names found in the Patriarchal stories can be surely identified with a figure mentioned in historical texts. Had we not substantial archaeological evidence for a more precise dating, the stories of the Patriarchs could have taken place at any time after the great ethnic movements began in Sargonid times (around 2300 B.C.) practically until the conquest of Palestine in the thirteenth century B.C. In fact, archaeology and rock pictures provide evidence of groups similar to Abraham's *hamula*, or clan, which wandered in the Syrian Desert, Jordan, the Negev, and Sinai throughout this long period. The life described by the Biblical stories is that of traditionally semi-nomadic peoples. As we shall see, it is possible to place the Patriarchs in a relatively small time

[1] For example, the Tell el-Amarna letters; see page 430.

period; but this does not mean that a similar way of life was not carried on in the area before and after.

The Hyksos rule started in Palestine shortly after the middle of the eighteenth century B.C. and lasted about two hundred years, but Hyksos culture seems to have infiltrated before the beginning of the political conquest. Material culture of the Hyksos type appeared and evolved in Palestine during the nineteenth century B.C. and in Egypt during the Twelfth Dynasty,[2] and we can say quite safely that by the beginning of the eighteenth century B.C. the groups of people known as Hyksos must have already been a political factor of first importance in the area. Several towns were destroyed at that time in Palestine, and Hyksos pottery and weapons were already predominant.

The arrival of the first bands of Hyksos seems to go even further back, to the twentieth century B.C.; the earliest mention of them is probably in the story of Sinuhe, an Egyptian who lived in Syria or Palestine with an Amorite tribe and who advised them on the military tactics to be followed "when they became so bold as to oppose the rulers of the foreign countries." [3]

The short period which lasted from the appearance of the new material culture to the beginning of the Hyksos rule corresponds to the time in which Egypt was ruled by the strong kings of the Twelfth Dynasty, and it marks a short peak of Egyptian influence in Syria-Palestine. At the time, the town of Byblos, on the Mediterranean shore of Lebanon, was an important harbor and had daily trading contacts with Egypt. Trade in cedar timber

[2] R. Weill: *XIIᵉ Dynastie: Royaume de Haute Egypte et domination Hyksos dans le Nord* (Cairo; 1953).
[3] See J. A. Wilson in ANET, p. 20; these Egyptian words are probably the origin of the word "Hyksos."

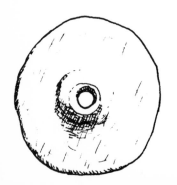

Clay models of wheels from Level XVII at Megiddo (after Loud)

from Lebanon was flourishing, and rings, scarabs, and other Egyptian objects are abundant in local tombs.

Mining was intensified at Serabit al-Khadem, in Sinai, where copper and turquoise were extracted for the Pharaoh. We know of at least one Egyptian military expedition to Palestine-Syria in the middle of the nineteenth century b.c.[4] Egypt was the nominal ruler of these countries, and for a short while controlled them economically and politically.

The sphere of Egyptian control in Asia is indirectly revealed by the strange documents discovered in Egypt called Execration Texts. These are vases and figurines inscribed with the names of vassal rulers. By means of magic, breaking the vase would destroy the ruler whose name was inscribed on it. Through these execration figurines the Pharaoh kept his vassal princes at his mercy. This is a good example of a kind of magic ritual which had been in common use in the Near East throughout the ages. Similar magic is still found today among the Bedouins.

Two groups of Execration Texts of this period have been studied so far. The first, now in Berlin, goes back to the middle of the Twelfth Dynasty, and the second, now in Brussels, belongs to the late part of the Twelfth Dynasty. The proper names in these texts supplement archaeological findings to a great extent in the reconstruction of the history of this period, and they reveal that Egyptian control extended north of Byblos and Damascus and included Palestine and southern Syria.

The Execration Texts are the earliest direct historic documents on the political activities of urban centers in Palestine. The earlier texts indicate that several centers had more than one leader. The places mentioned seem to be tribal settlements governed by family chiefs. The second group of texts, only two generations later, indicate that most settlements had only one chief by then. From this it can be conjectured that Palestine was then undergoing an important change in its social and political

[4] Inscription of Khu-Sebek; see ANET, p. 230.

structure, and that the tribes which had settled down at the end of the Early Urban period were acquiring some sort of centralized leadership.

At the same time, archaeology shows that urban centers were growing more rapidly and strengthening themselves in fertile Palestine. The improvement in building methods and town planning and the growing number of public buildings and structures all seem to point to this increase in the centralization of power.

At the same time the nomadic and semi-nomadic tribes also were increasing in importance, and the two separate histories unfolded side by side. They will provide us with the clue for understanding the political events preparatory to the Hebrew conquest.

THE HEBREW PATRIARCHS

The earliest information we have regarding the Hebrews fits into the general framework of the massive migrations of people at the end of the Early Urban Age. Probably the Hebrews were just one small group among many on the move, and they must have been one of several related Semitic groups that migrated westward along the southern edges of the Fertile Crescent.

There can be little doubt today that we have to look for the origins of the Patriarchs in or near Mesopotamia. The Biblical story of Genesis has little resemblance to either Canaanite or Egyptian mythology, whereas it is closely related to similar Mesopotamian accounts. The stories of creation, the Garden of Eden, the Flood, the Tower of Babel, and the rest cannot but be of Mesopotamian origin, and these stories must have been known to the Hebrews in Patriarchal times.

The story of the Tower of Babel also has some importance in connection with the possible date of migration of the Patriarchs from Mesopotamia, as it is likely that this tale refers to a time previous to the destruction of Babylon by the Hittites in the middle of the sixteenth century B.C.

Other hints of the dates of the Patriarchs are provided by the Bible and by archaeology. From the Biblical story it appears that the city of Hebron, also called Kiriat Arba, was founded when the Patriarchs were already in Palestine.[5] From the Book of Numbers [6] we know that Hebron was founded "seven years before Zoan in Egypt," and Zoan, the Hyksos capital in the Nile Delta, was built early in the Hyksos rule, late in the eighteenth century B.C.[7] This would indicate that the Patriarchs arrived in Palestine before the eighteenth century B.C. On the other hand, archaeology shows that places such as Beersheba and Gerar (identified with Tell Beersheba and Tell Abu Hureire, respectively), which were settled towns at the time of the Patriarchs, were abandoned in the late Chalcolithic period and remained deserted from the end of the fourth millennium B.C. to the end of the third. The Patriarchs must have lived *after* these towns were resettled.

The Amorites and other peoples had settled down in Jordan, the Negev, and the Jordan Valley late in the third millennium B.C. William F. Albright and Nelson Glueck were able to date these settlements rather precisely, and to show that they quickly dwindled and finally disappeared in the Jordan Valley during the nineteenth century B.C. Thereafter this region remained almost deserted (except for some important centers such as Jericho) for several centuries. Now it seems very likely that Abraham lived in that period, for during his life a significant decrease in population must have taken place in this area. In Genesis [8] we read that "the plain of Jordan . . . was well watered everywhere, before God destroyed Sodom and Gomorrah, like the Garden of God [Eden], like the land of Egypt . . ." Then something happened which was not clearly understandable to the nomads; we do not know whether it was a war, earthquake, or some other phenomenon,

---

[5] Genesis 13: 18; see 23: 2 and 35: 27.

[6] 13: 22.

[7] Or rather rebuilt and named Avaris. Zoan (or Tanis) was its name in Israelite times. Late in the fourteenth century B.C. Pharaoh Rameses II erected a stele to commemorate the 400th anniversary of the city.

[8] 13: 10.

but the Bible tells us that "God rained upon Sodom and Gomorrah brimstone and fire . . . and overthrew those cities, and all the plain, and all the inhabitants of the cities, and that which grew upon the ground. . . . the smoke of the country went up as the smoke of a furnace." [9] After that the Jordan Valley became the silent herding ground of pastoral nomads. From these various hints it seems likely that Abraham arrived in Canaan during the twentieth or nineteenth century B.C., bringing with him his own traditions and transmitting them to future generations there.

The Biblical description of this migration provides us with several interesting details. It reads as follows: "And Terah took Abraham his son, and Lot the son of Haran his son's son, and Sarai his daughter-in-law, his son Abraham's wife; and they went forth with them from Ur of the Chaldees, to go into the land of Canaan; and they came into Haran, and dwelt there. And the days of Terah were two hundred and five years: and Terah died in Haran. Now the Lord had said unto Abraham, Get thee out of thy country, and from thy kindred, and from thy father's house, unto a land that I will show thee. . . . And Abraham took Sarai his wife, and Lot his brother's son, and all their substance that they had gathered, and the souls that they had gotten in Haran; and they went forth to go into the land of Canaan; and into the land of Canaan they came."[1]

From this description we learn that the place of origin of the Hebrews was Ur of the Chaldees, a region in the southwestern part of Mesopotamia, probably not far from the city of Ur excavated by the British archaeologist Sir Leonard Woolley. The migration started in the company of other groups of people belonging to the same general family. Abraham was the "brother" of Haran, and this is also the name of a land in northern Mesopotamia at which these Semitic tribes first arrived and where Abraham's brother remained with his tribe.

[9] Genesis 19: 24–8.
[1] Genesis 11 and 12.

It is not unlikely that this first part of the great migration took place at about the same time that the Semitic Akkadians were infiltrating into large regions of northern and central Mesopotamia and expanding their hegemony there.

The second part of the migration, from Haran to Canaan, was undertaken by a smaller group. Abraham (the father of the Hebrews) was accompanied on this part of the journey by Lot, father of two peoples who occupied large marginal regions in Jordan: the Moabites and the Ammonites.[2]

Once arrived in Canaan, the Hebrews led by Abraham parted from the Moabites and the Ammonites led by Lot. While the Hebrews penetrated into western Palestine, the land of the Canaanites, their brother tribes settled in the Jordan and Araba valleys and in eastern Jordan.[3] This account seems to be based on very much the same facts discovered by archaeologists. One may recall that rock pictures indicate contacts between the Palestinian marginal regions and Mesopotamia at about this period, and that musical instruments and customs of Mesopotamian or northern Syrian origin are depicted in the Negev (see page 209).

The arrival of the Hebrews in Canaan did not cut them off completely from Haran, their country of origin, and when Jacob had to take a wife, Isaac, his father, son of Abraham, asked him to go there and choose a wife among his cousins (the marriage of cousins was favored among the Semites of Patriarchal times as it is today among the Arabs). The encounter between him and Rachel, his future wife, after his long journey into the desert is one of the most moving descriptions ever written. It throws light not only on the daily life but also on the intimate behavior and feelings, the strong family bonds, as well as the landscape of almost four thousand years ago: ". . . Rachel came with her father's sheep: for she kept them. And it came to pass, when

---

[2] Genesis 19: 36–8.
[3] Genesis 13: 12.

Jacob saw Rachel the daughter of Laban his mother's brother, and the sheep of Laban his mother's brother, that Jacob went near, and rolled the stone from the well's mouth, and watered the flock of Laban his mother's brother. And Jacob kissed Rachel, and lifted up his voice, and wept. And Jacob told Rachel that he was her father's brother, and that he was Rebecca's son: and she ran and told her father. . . . when Laban heard the tidings of Jacob his sister's son . . . he ran to meet him . . . and brought him to his house."[4]

The Book of Genesis allows us to follow in detail the family and tribal structure and the birth, marriage, and burial customs of the Hebrews. It also provides information about foreign relations, behavior toward servants and slaves, and the roles of the father, the mother, and other members of the extended family.

The Bible also yields an enormous amount of information on the political situation, the social organization, the economic bases, and the moral values and religious beliefs of this period.

At that time various tribes lived in the Jordan and Negev semi-arid zones. Some of them lived in "towns," others led a nomadic or semi-nomadic way of life. The situation is extremely similar to that discerned by archaeologists for the late part of the third millennium B.C. These peoples appear to have been of various ethnic origins. Each group had a leader, a king or a prince; their names are frequently cited, and show a wide range of linguistic affiliation. They frequently make war on one another, form small confederacies, try to destroy other groups in order to take their land and their belongings. These conditions probably prevailed as long ago as the end of Early Urban times, and still persisted in part at the time of the Tell el-Amarna letters.

One of the most remarkable documents in the Book of Genesis is Chapter 14, which describes in a very vivid way some of the political activities going on at the time. The kings of Sodom, Gomorrah, Admah, Zeboiim, and Zoar, five settlements

[4] Genesis 29: 9-13.

in the Negev and the Araba Valley, appear to have been vassals of "Chedorlaomer, king of Elam," and after a while they decided to rebel. Chedorlaomer, probably the distorted name of a southern Mesopotamian figure, came with his allied kings and his army, and first attacked the nomadic and semi-nomadic people of the region. We find among these people Horites, Amorites, Amalekites, Rephaites, Zuzites, and Emites. Many different tribes, probably of different ethnic origins, appear to have lived at this time in the peripheral regions of Palestine, and presumably they were allied with the five rebel kings. After having chased away these tribes, the Elamite king directed his armies against the confederacy of the five kings, met them in the valley of Sodom, and defeated them.[5]

Genesis conveys the impression that the newly arrived peoples kept in touch with their land of origin in or near southern Mesopotamia, and that they at first recognized their vassalhood to a prince or a king there and paid him tribute until the day they decided to rebel. This account is interestingly reminiscent of what has been happening with European colonies ever since the American Revolution.

In these stories we see how one of these battles drove a people over considerable distances from Syria to the Negev, and from there to Jordan and to Sinai. All these were open territories through which nomads could move freely. This is vastly different from the picture we have of the fertile regions, where city dwellers fought their wars from the towers of their walls, or laid siege to an enemy city protected by walls, and where each tribe or budding community for the most part kept to its own territory.

The marginal tribes and the city dwellers lived very near each other. The Hebrew Patriarchs spread their tents near

[5] William F. Albright has dealt extensively with this chapter of Genesis and its historical implications. See AJSL, Vol. XL (1923), pp. 125–33; AASOR, Vol. VI (1934), pp. 62–6; BASOR, No. 88 (1942), pp. 33–6; BASOR, No. 163 (1961), pp. 48–50.

Shechem, Jerusalem, Hebron, Beersheba, Gerar, and other cities, and they came in frequent contact with the inhabitants. They moved freely around and between the cities and in the wilderness. They stopped near wells, sold the products of their herds and flocks, and traded other goods with their sedentary neighbors.[6]

The Patriarchs must have done some farming as well. We know that both Abraham and Jacob purchased fields in various parts of the hilly country[7] and that Lot, Abraham's brother's son, settled down in Sodom. We also know that both hunting and herding were daily activities by the time of Isaac, and that agricultural products such as wine, oil, grain, and lentils were part of their diet.[8]

The account of the Patriarchs has an interesting counterpart in the story of Sinuhe, the Egyptian official who went into voluntary exile in Asia at the death of Pharaoh Amen-em-het I, in the middle of the twentieth century B.C. He reached the land of Qedem, probably the Bashan and Golan of later times, where he met Ammi-enshi, an Amorite chieftain who led a life very similar to that of the Patriarchs. Sinuhe married the Amorite's daughter and became one of the tribe. The tribesmen ate figs, olives, and grapes; they cultivated barley and emmer, herded cattle, and went out to the desert to hunt. Milk and honey were plentiful, and bread and wine were part of the daily diet. The main weapons used by Sinuhe's fellow tribesmen were the bow and arrow and the dagger, but in his story he tells of having to fight a hero of a nearby tribe. The weapons of his adversary were a shield, a battle-ax, and javelins.

Sinuhe gives us the same picture of internecine warfare, of small intertribal battles, that we have read in Genesis: "Every foreign country against which I went forth, when I had made my attack on it, was driven away from its pasturage and its well.

[6] William F. Albright has recently stressed the importance of trade in the economic activities of the Patriarchs. See BASOR, No. 163 (1961), pp. 36–54.
[7] Genesis 25: 10; 33: 19.
[8] Genesis 25.

I plundered its cattle, carried off its inhabitants, took away their food, and slew people in it by my strong arm, by my bow, by my movements, and by my successful plans."[9]

While the Patriarchs were frequently moving about from Qedem to the Judean Hills and to the Negev, and from there to Sinai and to Egypt, Egyptians, according to the story of Sinuhe, were frequently visiting the Asiatic countries and traveling a great deal. The Egyptian language was probably understood by many Amorite chiefs. Asiatic visitors in Egypt were numerous by that time, and we can tell what they looked like from the *hamula* of a man called Abisha, depicted on a fresco at Beni Hassan in Egypt.

International trade was well developed at the time, not only between cities but also among the herders. Joseph was sold to a company of Ishmaelites coming from Gilead and "bearing spicery and balm and myrrh" down to Egypt.[1]

In the city of Mari, at the site of Tell el-Hariri, on the banks of the Euphrates (probably not far from the Biblical land of Haran), the archives of King Zimri-Lim, who lived in the eighteenth century B.C., report that commerce flourished and that caravans continually traveled between Syria and Mesopotamia. Mari was conveniently located on the caravan route, and trade was an important source of its wealth. In the times of the Patriarchs, Mari was the capital of an empire stretching from the frontiers of Babylon to the borders of Syria. Its rulers could afford the palace of three hundred rooms in which the royal archives were discovered. The more than twenty thousand clay tablets from Mari throw a dramatically new light on the history, daily life, religion, economy, laws, and customs of the central regions of the Fertile Crescent in this period. They tell us also a great deal about the nomads, some of whom have familiar Semitic names such as Ben-Yamin (or Benjamin). Some of these western Semitic nomads had a way of life surprisingly

[9] After J. A. Wilson's translation in ANET, pp. 18 ff.
[1] Genesis 37: 25.

Abisha, an Asiatic desert chieftain, coming to Egypt with his people and bringing kohl, or eye make-up (after a fresco on a tomb at Beni Hassan)

Limestone seal from Level XIV at Megiddo (after Loud)

Seven-branched oil lamp from the Canaanite *bamah*, or sacrificial platform, at Nahariyah (excavated by Dothan)

similar to that of the Hebrew Patriarchs as described in the Bible.

The Abisha fresco at Beni Hassan shows us how just such a group of Asiatics looked when they reached the cultivated and sophisticated Nile Valley, with their goods, their donkeys, their wives and children, their tools, weapons, and musical instruments. In addition, it suggests that these nomads of the desert did some mining and were bringing stibium, a dye highly valued as a body cosmetic, to Egypt.

According to the Biblical accounts, the three central figures of Patriarchal times were Abraham, Isaac, and Jacob. They have been considered by some scholars to be actual historical figures; by others, dynasties or ruling families. In my view they were individuals—powerful, half-legendary figures who led the Hebrew tribe. Probably they were not its only leaders, but the names of no other such outstanding figures have reached us.

One of the most discussed dates in early Hebrew history is that of Jacob's migration to Egypt. Most authorities agree that this must have happened during the time of the Hyksos rule, when the city of Avaris, in the Delta, was the capital of the Hyksos empire. It was located in the immediate vicinity of the land of Goshen, where the Hebrews are said to have lived as slaves. If we accept the Biblical tradition that the Hebrews stayed in Egypt 400 (or 430) years, the date of their migration would be about 1700 B.C.[2] It is very surprising that not the slightest record or even hint of the long stay of the Hebrews as slaves in the land of the Pharaoh exists in any historical Egyptian text, especially in view of the many thousands of Egyptian documents of that time we now possess—documents in which groups of slaves are often referred to by their ethnic names. On the other hand, the tales of the Bible are too detailed, too vivid, too realistic to be imaginary; Moses and other names in Leviticus are of Egyptian origin; and the Biblical descriptions of Egyptian life are accurate.

[2] Genesis 15: 13; Exodus 12: 40.

Many were the people coming to Egypt by that time; the Hyksos period had probably led to the Nile Valley many Asiatics in the service of "the rulers of foreign countries." When the Hyksos rule came to an end, the status of many of these strangers must have changed drastically. It is likely that we have to think of the Hebrews in Egypt in such a context. The end of the Hyksos rule and the start of the Eighteenth Dynasty probably coincide with the beginning of the Hebrew captivity. We do not know what part of the Hebrew tribe went down to Egypt, and what part of it remained in the land of Canaan, but large bands of peoples called Habiru, or Apiru, who had a way of life very similar to that of the Hebrews in Patriarchal times, remained in Palestine throughout the Canaanite period, and it seems that they ultimately took an active part in the conquest of Canaan.

WHO WERE THE HYKSOS?

Few problems have preoccupied Near Eastern archaeologists as much as that of the origin of the Hyksos. These people, now known by their Egyptian name, imposed their rule upon Palestine and Egypt for two hundred years, and introduced their exotic culture into these countries. A great deal is known about the Hyksos—about their material culture, their customs, their beliefs, their towns and fortifications, their methods of waging war, their social and political organization—but their origin is still obscure.

After they had come to rule Egypt and Palestine, they adopted many of the local customs. In Egypt they used the Egyptian writing and the Egyptian language and most of them acquired Egyptian names. Others had Semitic names, such as Yakub, Hur, Nahman; and others had Indo-European ones, such as Bnon, Khyan, Edire, and Og.[3] Some of the words for traditional titles and ranks are Indo-European. *Maryan*, their name

[3] M. G. Posener: *Syria*, Vol. XVIII, No. 2 (1937); Mironov: *Acta Orientalia*, 1922.

for hero or noble, meaning "the people in power," is a purely Indo-European word. And in a later period, for which we have more precise information about local rulers in Palestine after the Hyksos had been defeated, some rulers have Indo-European names.

This linguistic mixture has puzzled many scholars and is the main factor in their uncertainty about the origin of the Hyksos. Some scholars have concluded that the Hyksos were northwestern Semites.[4] Others have suggested that they were Indo-Europeans.[5] Other scholars believe that the Hyksos were local rulers in Syria-Palestine who marched down to Egypt in the time of the Hebrew Patriarchs and conquered it. Still others see in them a Hittite or Caucasian people who joined in with the Hittite expansion in the eighteenth century B.C. Finally, some scholars have claimed that the Hyksos were a mixed people —ethnically, linguistically, and culturally—and that they suc-

[4] See W. F. Albright: *The Archaeology of Palestine* (5th ed.; Baltimore: Pelican; 1960), p. 86.
[5] T. J. Arne: *Excavations at Shah Tepe, Iran* (Stockholm; 1945).

Clay model of war chariot from Level H at Hama (after Inghold)

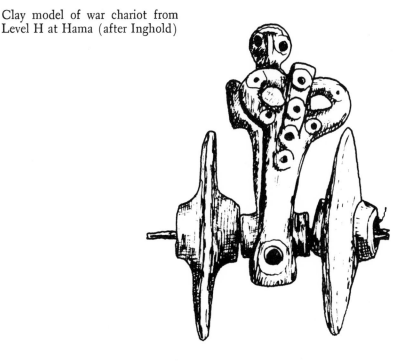

ceeded in conquering Palestine and Egypt, in instituting their centralized government, and in establishing their customs and their culture thanks to their superior weapons. And they were successful in spite of their lack of a common language. All these hypotheses are strongly defended, and most of them have convincing arguments to support them.

Whatever may be the truth, the problem is that by the time the Hyksos became rulers and entered history, some of them had probably already spent several generations among the peoples they had conquered. Before the date of our first detailed information about their possible descendants in Syria-Palestine, where they were probably not as well assimilated as they were in Egypt, the Hyksos rule had already ended.

It is very likely that the wave of people who invaded Palestine in the eighteenth century B.C. with their chariots and their well-organized army was a single body, well trained and quite used to discipline and to central rule. But apparently they were preceded by various smaller kindred bands who had settled in the region and had slowly mingled with the local population; they brought with them several dominant Indo-European traits of language, ways of life, artistic outlooks, religions, and beliefs.

The German scholar Kurt Galling believed that the Hyksos introduced into Palestine a totally exotic social structure and political organization. The existence of a noble class led by the king, and of a lower class constituting the rest of the free population, was in sharp contrast with the democratic patriarchal organization of the early western Semitic tribes, and Galling suggested that these new institutions might have been imported from Caucasia or Asia Minor.[6]

Although class stratification already existed in the urban centers of both Palestine and Egypt in the third millennium B.C., Galling's view is tempting, because the Hyksos rule appears to have brought to these countries a great many similar political

---

[6] K. Galling: ZDPV, Vol. LXII (1937), p. 107.

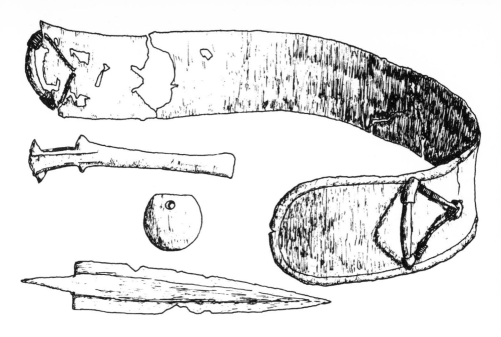

Belt, ax, dagger, and pendant from a Hyksos tomb at Tell el-Fara (after De Vaux)

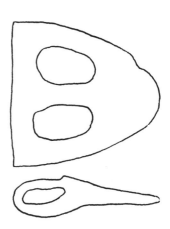

Bronze double-headed ax from Level
XIII at Megiddo (after Loud)

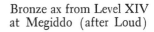

Bronze ax from Level XIV
at Megiddo (after Loud)

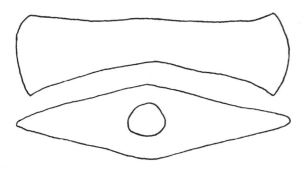

and social changes of foreign origin. Political organization, however, may change with the changing needs of society, and Galling's argument is not totally convincing, for the growth of a "noble" class probably was a necessity for a totalitarian government of the sort instituted by the Hyksos, and does not necessarily imply any special cultural influences.

Another argument parallel to Galling's was based on the weapons used by the Hyksos, which are definitely exotic in Palestine and Egypt. They included shaft-hole axes, daggers with a central rib, and other arms having strong affinities with the weapons of Caucasia and Persia.

These two arguments did not solve the riddle, as both the structure of government and the material culture are traits that can be transmitted from group to group, and do not necessarily define ethnic origins. Other cultural traits that could give a more intimate glimpse into the nature of Hyksos society had to be examined. Their religious beliefs, their psychological attitudes, and their aesthetic values turned out to be more useful indicators.

One of the cultural traits of the rulers of Palestine in the Middle Urban Age is their custom of burying the dead with their horses and donkeys. The best examples in Palestine of this custom were found by Sir Flinders Petrie at Tell el-Ajjul, "the tell of the chariots," near Gaza, where equines appear to have been sacrificed and buried near the warriors.[7] Recently another good example was discovered at Jericho. In the tomb labeled JS, Kathleen Kenyon found skeletal remains of two equines in the tomb shaft. This tomb, originally used in the Intermediate period, was re-used in the Middle Urban Age, and presumably the two equines were part of the second burial.[8] The burial of human beings together with horses or other animals is in sharp contrast

[7] W. M. F. Petrie: *Ancient Gaza, Tell el-Ajjul* (London: British School of Archaeology in Egypt; 1931), Vol. I, p. 4; Vol. II, p. 5; Vol. IV, p. 16. For dates, see W. F. Albright: AJSL, Vol. LV, No. 4 (1938), pp. 342 ff.

[8] K. Kenyon: *Excavations at Jericho*, Vol. I (London: British School of Archaeology in Jerusalem; 1960), pp. 307–8, 535–6.

with all we know of early Semite practices.[9] On the other hand, it is a well-known Indo-European practice. In Caucasia and southern Russia, both horses and models of wheeled vehicles are frequently found in tombs belonging to the third millennium B.C. [1] In Greece, in the Mycenaean royal graves, the actual horses and vehicles of the Asiatics and the vehicle models of the southern Russians were replaced with high reliefs carved on the funerary steles. Graves with horses and vehicles turn up in central Europe in the Urnfield culture, a culture which was established late in the second millennium B.C. and which is believed to have been Indo-European. This custom persisted in Europe among such later Indo-Europeans as the Celts and the Scythians.[2] Burying the dead with their horses and chariots or honoring them with their models or representations was a typical Indo-European custom. That the Hyksos also had this custom is very significant.[3]

Another hint regarding the origin of the Hyksos is provided by their peculiar decorative style. The principal Hyksos designs are found chiefly on their seals, their ornaments, and their pottery. They were the solar wheel, the spiral, the wavy and interlocked spiral, and other designs that were predominant among the early Indo-European populations of Greece and were later to become the symbols of all the Celtic populations of Europe.

The spiral is believed to have originated in the solar symbol and the solar cult. The turning solar disk evolved in many different shapes. It may be depicted in isolation or in repeated patterns.[4]

In Palestine the spiral is an imported decorative element. Before the Hyksos, some rare spirals are found in the decoration of the Khirbet Kerak ware, which was, as I have said, of Cau-

---

[9] See G. Contenau: *Man*, No. 194, p. 178.
[1] See M. Gimbutas: *The Prehistory of Eastern Europe*, Part I, The American School of Prehistoric Research, Peabody Museum, Harvard University, Bulletin No. 20 (1956), pp. 1–241, Pls. 1–50.
[2] See T. Powell: *The Celts* (London: Thames and Hudson; 1958).
[3] For chariots in Bronze Age Europe, see PPS, 1960, pp. 50–63.
[4] See J. Dechelette: *Revue Archéologique*, 1909.

Twelfth Dynasty scarab
from Egypt

Hyksos scarabs
from Level XII at Meg
(after Loud)

Hyksos jug with spiral decoration from Genosar
(excavated by Negbi and Epstein)

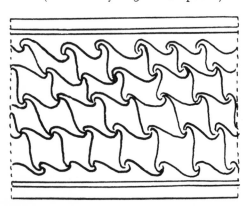

Hyksos cylinder seal from Egypt (after Newberry)

Jar from Level XIV at Megiddo. Painte
decoration is red and black (after Loud

casian origin. Thereafter, the spiral was virtually absent until the beginning of the Hyksos period. Then suddenly it became a dominant element in the decoration of seals and ornaments, and it also occurs on pottery.

Among all the thousands of decorative designs in the rock pictures of Sinai, the Negev, Jordan, Syria, and Arabia, there is not a single spiral dating from prehistoric times to the middle of the second millennium B.C. When we compare this with the importance of the spiral in Hyksos decoration, we realize how productive following the story of a decorative pattern can be.

In Egypt during the Old Kingdom the spiral was an extremely rare element of decoration, and when it appeared in the First Intermediate period it was probably imported from Asia. It was used more often during the Middle Kingdom, but not until the time of the Hyksos rule did it become the dominant decorative design.

West of the Tigris, for a very short period in prehistoric Elam, the spiral was used as a decorative design together with the swastika and other shapes. These same designs turn up again, sporadically, at the sites of Shah Tepe, Tepe Hissar, Tepe Giyan, and others in Iran. East of the Tigris, no center of well-developed spiral designs dating from Early Urban times has yet been found.

Solar wheels depicted on Hyksos pottery from Tel Aviv (after Kaplan)

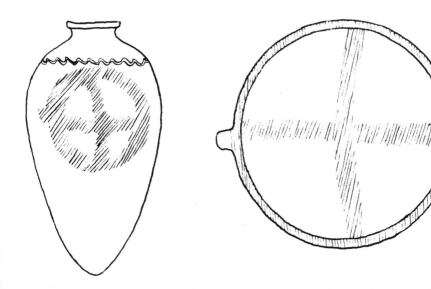

Even in such rich decorative repertoires as that of Early Dynastic Ur, in southern Mesopotamia, the spiral plays a secondary role. At Mari, the spiral decorates murals in the palace of Zimri-Lim, dating from before its conquest by Hammurabi in the eighteenth century B.C., but this is an isolated case and in the Euphrates Valley it never became an important decorative design.

The spiral is a very sporadic decorative element in Early Urban times throughout the Fertile Crescent, though it occurs in Caucasia and at Troy. The spiral came into widespread use in Palestine with the Hyksos, and it was diffused throughout Asia Minor at about the same time, early in the second millennium B.C., with the rise of the Hittite Empire.[5]

In the southern Russian steppe, mainly between the Dnieper and the Danube, spirals are a basic element of decoration in the Tripolye pottery, which dates from the third millennium B.C.[6] In Greece the spiral was already an element of decoration by the middle of the third millennium B.C., but it became a dominant element only during the second millennium B.C.[7]

Decorative designs are more than a random and unconscious gesture of the artist's hand. They illustrate a way of thinking and a psychological background. They are the fruit of culture and tradition, and in regard to spirals this is especially evident.

All in all, a great many exotic features were introduced into Palestine by the Hyksos, and they all seem to have come from a similar source. Their origin must be looked for somewhere to the east or north of the Fertile Crescent.

It seems that the original Hyksos were Indo-Europeans but that other peoples probably gathered around the Hyksos core; wherever these heterogeneous people went, they seem to have first adopted local customs and to have finally developed a complex culture with various acquired traits superimposed on it.

---

[5] O. R. Gurney: *The Hittites* (Baltimore: Pelican; 1954), p. 22; etc.
[6] See Gimbutas: op. cit., p. 99.
[7] See H. J. Kantor: *The Aegean and the Orient in the Second Millennium B.C.* (New York: Archaeological Institute of America; 1947).

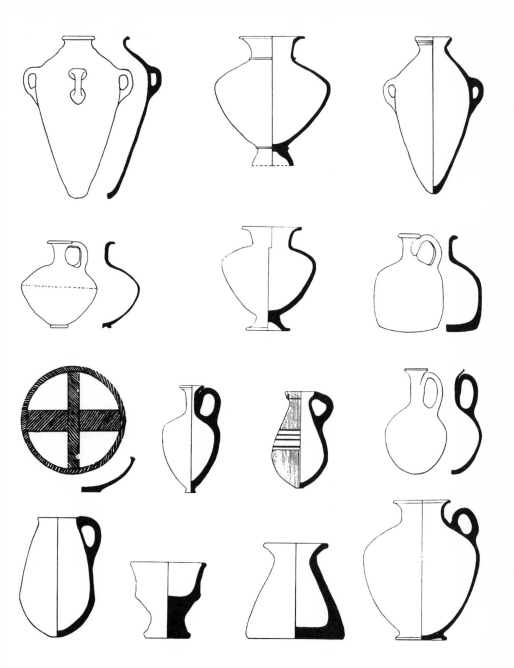

Types of Middle Bronze Age pottery in the Palestine Museum

The Hyksos are believed to have introduced into Palestine and Egypt the domesticated horse and the two-wheeled war chariot.[8] Since the use of these comprised two of their most characteristic cultural traits, it is interesting to trace back their origins and try to understand when, where, and how the ancestors of the Hyksos acquired them and what effect they had.

The war chariot and the domesticated horse reached Anatolia with the Hittite expansion, at about the time the Hyksos were conquering Palestine and Egypt. The same two traits reached Greece at the beginning of the Middle Mycenaean culture, in the sixteenth century B.C., and spread to Europe shortly thereafter.[9] Before the Hyksos, the Hittites, and the Middle Mycenaeans, traces of these traits are scanty, but there is some useful evidence.

Wheeled vehicles seem to have originated in Sumer (in the Uruk period) toward the middle of the fourth millennium B.C.[1] The use of wheeled wagons spread from southern Mesopotamia and reached the Indus Valley, Caucasia, and northeastern Syria by the second half of the third millennium B.C.[2] Only late in the third millennium or at the beginning of the second millennium B.C. do we meet with lighter vehicles, probably early types of war chariots. They are depicted on Anatolian seals and occur in the form of models at Hama on the Orontes and Qatnah in northern Syria.

At present we are unable to trace back further the origin of the light war chariot, but there were two prerequisites for such

---

[8] Walter B. Emery has found the earliest evidence of the domestic horse in Egypt, dating back to the seventeenth century B.C.; see ILN, September 12, 1959, pp. 250–1.

[9] See E. Anati: PPS, 1960, pp. 64 ff.

[1] P. Delougaz and S. Lloyd: *Pre-Sargonid Temples in the Dyala Region* (Chicago: University of Chicago Press; 1942), pp. 128–31.

[2] See V. G. Childe: PPS, 1951, pp. 128 ff. Actually the earliest vehicles that can be called war chariots are depicted on mosaic standards from Ur. However, they are four-wheeled and have solid wheels. They are much heavier than the later two-wheeled war chariots with spoked wheels.

an invention—a suitable terrain and fast horses. This vehicle, which turned out to be a tremendously powerful weapon, is unlikely to have been created by people living in mountainous, heavily forested, or desert regions. The inventors must have lived on broad flat plains, grasslands, or some other similar terrain. Large areas of this kind are not to be found in the Near East, and must be looked for either more to the north, on the southern Russian steppe, or more to the east, on the Iranian Plateau. For the second prerequisite, the fast horse, we would also have to search, before the end of the third millennium B.C., beyond the boundaries of the Near East, in the same places as in the case of the war chariot—most likely on the southern Russian steppe or the Iranian Plateau.[3] (Another possibility would be northern Syria, but neither historical documents nor archaeological discoveries allow us, so far, to put much faith in this conjecture.)

It is likely that the semi-nomadic horse-breeders of the steppes or the flat plateau were the people who could transform the slow ox-drawn wheeled vehicles into the light war chariots that gave them a tremendous superiority over foot soldiers. This was one of the weapons with which they invaded and conquered more civilized regions.

As we shall see in the following section, the fortification and defense methods used by the Hyksos also point to the same northeastern origins.

THE HYKSOS PERIOD

During the Intermediate period the Near East underwent great changes. Except for Mesopotamia, not a single region was then economically and politically stable, and this turmoil must have prepared the way for the Hyksos when they arrived with their new weapons and their well-organized armies.

[3] V. G. Childe: *New Light on the Most Ancient East* (London: Kegan Paul; 1952), p. 189.

Stone glacis and fosse from Hyksos period at Hazor

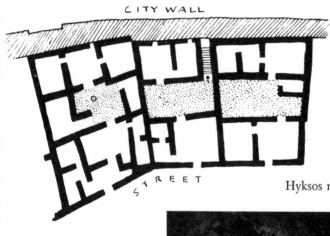

Reconstructed plan of three houses at Megiddo, Level XII

Hyksos mud-brick wall at Tell el-Fara

The Hyksos and their affiliated bands brought with them new types of weapons, military tactics, and military architecture. At Gezer, Beth-Yerah, and other Palestinian sites there is a characteristic feature of their military architecture, dating from early in the second millennium B.C.—a sloping glacis at the foot of defense walls. This is a construction of terre-pisée, stone, sun-dried bricks, or other materials extending outward from the fortification and forming an artificial slope which frequently ended in a moat. This glacis gives a totally new shape to the fortification, and indeed to the town and to the tell as a whole. In later times it reached enormous dimensions, sometimes extending to over a hundred feet out from the wall.

The reasons that led to the building of this new military device were in dispute among archaeologists until Yigael Yadin, of the Hebrew University, found the solution to the riddle. The most popular previous idea was that the use of war chariots had inspired the use of a glacis to keep the chariots away from the wall.[4] Yigael Yadin, a onetime chief of staff of the Israeli Army, observed that chariots can be decisive in open warfare but are of little use in attacking a walled city. He went on to show that the new weapon which inspired the change in defense work must have been the battering-ram.[5] This weapon was gradually adopted in Early Urban times, and a scene showing it in use in a breaching operation is depicted in a Fifth Dynasty picture from Egypt.[6] The term for battering-ram already existed in Mesopotamia during the third millennium B.C., but it seems that in Syria-Palestine and Egypt, it became an important weapon of attack only with the Hyksos.

The Hyksos rulers built enormous defense systems based on the glacis. In later times, the terre-pisée glacis was replaced

[4] K. Kenyon: PEQ, 1953, p. 90.
[5] Y. Yadin: BASOR, No. 137 (1955), pp. 23 ff.
[6] W. M. F. Petrie: *Desharsheh* (London: Kegan Paul; 1898), Pl. 4.

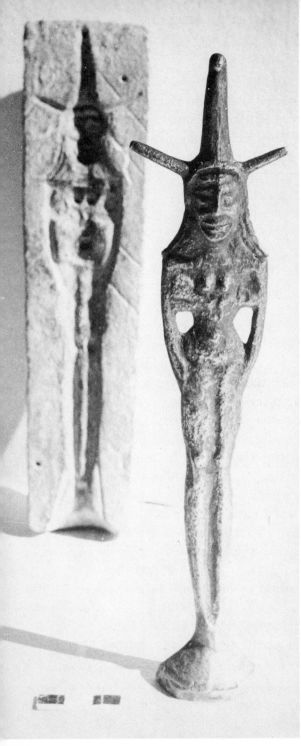

Mold of Astarte found at Nahariyah, and a contemporary cast made from it (excavated by Dothan)

Silver figurine from the Canaanite temple at Nahariyah (excavated by Dothan)

Figurine of bird from Canaanite temple at Nahariyah (excavated by Dothan)

Plan of Canaanite temple at Nahariyah, from the Hyksos period (after Ben-Dor)

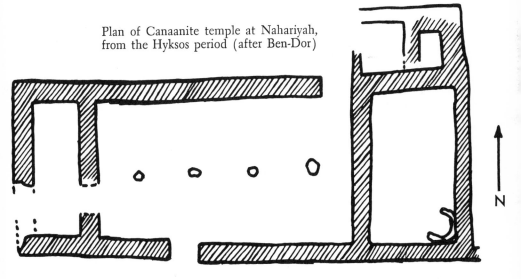

N

with stone walls of massive polygonal masonry with a sloping outer side.[7]

Very similar defense systems appear in some early Hittite towns in Anatolia[8] and throughout northern Syria, where the best examples are found at Karkemish, Alalakh, and Ugarit.[9] Palestine, however, has the greatest number of them, the best examples of which are from Tell Jarishah, Tell el-Ajjul, Jericho, and Tell Beit Mirsim. They also occur at Tell el-Yahudiyah and other sites in Lower Egypt.[1]

In the vicinity of some of these tells the Hyksos built huge fortified enclosures, usually of rough rectangular shape, surrounded by sloping ramparts of terre-pisée. Here probably the mercenaries were sheltered, as well as the various camp followers in the service of the nobles, who lived in the fortress. (As pointed out by N. Kalinin, there is a strange resemblance between these enclosures and the fortified camps of the semi-nomadic warriors of the Tatar steppe.[2])

The burial methods of Hyksos times were not uniform in Palestine.[3] Some older tombs were sometimes re-used, others with a vertical shaft and a burial chamber at the base seem to continue traditions of late Early Urban times. At Megiddo there are tombs of this period in which several individuals were buried together; other types of communal and single tombs were also found. However, the typical Hyksos tombs seem to be best illustrated by the communal tombs of Tell el-Fara, Jericho, Lachish, and other sites in central and southern Palestine, where the bodies were interred in artificial burial caves together with their grave goods and sometimes also with sacrificed animals.

---

[7] See Yadin: op. cit.
[8] M. I. Maksimova: JNES, Vol. X (1951), pp. 77 ff.
[9] T. Ave-Goderbergh: JEA, Vol. XXXVII (1951), pp. 53 ff.
[1] W. M. F. Petrie: *Hyksos and Israelite Cities* (London; 1906).
[2] N. Kalinin: "Expedition to the Occidental Provinces of the Tatar Republic, U.S.S.R.," *Gosudarstvennaia Akademia Istorii Materialnoi Kultury*, Vol. XLIV (1952).
[3] K. Kenyon: *Archaeology in the Holy Land* (London: Benn; 1960).

Tell Yahudiyah juglet from Affula
(excavated by Dothan)

Jar with figure of monkey
from Canaanite temple
at Nahariyah
(excavated by Dothan)

In recent years, Immanuel Ben-Dor, Yakob Ory, and other archaeologists from the Israel Department of Antiquities have found Hyksos tombs at Maale Hahamisha, near Jerusalem, and at other sites not connected with cities. This suggests that not all the Hyksos were concentrated in the fortresses and that some of them must have lived in shelters of which no traces were left.

The material culture of this period is today well known, mainly from excavations at Tell Beit Mirsim, Megiddo, Jericho, and Hazor. The evidence of pottery forms and of metal tools and weapons is from this time on supplemented by a great abundance of scarabs, the personal seals of officials and nobles, which frequently provide precise dating.

The pottery forms are marked by carination on chalices and goblets and by elongated and softly curved small jugs. Bowls with harmonious forms and ring bases (low cylindrical bases) show that many forms were inspired by metal prototypes. Coloring is frequent and varied; on small pots the most common is a dark gray which is often burnished. There is also a type of small jug, with a pen-shaped body and a small buttonlike base, dark and roughly burnished and with pitted triangles and other geometrical patterns; it is called the Tell el-Yahudiyah juglet, after the modern name of its type-site, which was once Avaris, the capital of the Hyksos empire on the Nile Delta. This juglet is found throughout Syria-Palestine, Cyprus, and Egypt in this period, and its distribution probably delimits the range of Hyksos influence.

Sporadic contacts were much more extended than that. To occasional intercourse with the Semitic rulers of Mesopotamia may be added overseas relations, one of which was dramatically disclosed by an alabaster lid inscribed with the name and titles of the Hyksos ruler Khyan, found at Knossos, in Crete, by Sir Arthur Evans.[4] Trade must have been highly developed by this time, and one may suppose that within the Hyksos sphere of

[4] *Palace of Minos*, Vol. I (London: Macmillan; 1922), p. 26.

influence communication was very active, as there are no fundamental regional variations in the material culture.

The Hyksos rulers were driven out of Egypt early in the
sixteenth century B.C., and the Pharaonic army, after a three-year
blockade of Sharuhen, a city-fortress in the Negev, occupied
Palestine and made it an Egyptian province. At this time, early
in the Eighteenth Egyptian Dynasty, Palestine was spoken of as
the land of the Canaanites, but its ethnic composition was extremely mixed, and the basically Semitic population included a
great many other elements. Exotic names of princes and chieftains were to continue to turn up later in the Tell el-Amarna
letters and in the other texts that throw light on the period of
Egyptian rule.

I V

The Late
Urban Period

THE BICHROME INTERLUDE
AND THE TIMES OF EGYPTIAN RULE

W E HAVE SEEN how several foreign peoples settled in
Palestine during the Early Urban period, and what complex
ethnic and cultural influences were superimposed at the end of
that period. The ancient Hebrews had a fairly good knowledge
of the three major peoples with whom they were in contact, the
Semites, the Hamites, and the Indo-Europeans; they were believed to be the descendants respectively of the three sons of
Noah: Shem, Ham, and Japheth. It is likely that people of all
three stocks lived in Palestine and the surrounding lands in
Canaanite times.

According to the Bible, the Canaanites were not Semites.
In the genealogical lists of Noah's descendants, Canaan appears

as one of the four sons of Ham, the father of the Hamites.[1] This does not necessarily mean that the Canaanites were not Semites, and many scholars are in fact convinced that they were. The identity of the Canaanites, and even the question whether they were a single population, of a single origin, is still very much disputed. The Bible sometimes describes the Canaanites as one people among the other inhabitants of the country; at other times the term is used as a collective name for all the sedentary dwellers in Palestine before the Hebrew conquest.

Palestine was called by many names; for the Akkadians it was part of Amurru (which, as is known, means "west" in Akkadian), or land of the Amorites; the Hurrites called it Arrapha, or Arrapkha; the Egyptians of the Middle Kingdom called it Retennu and thereafter included it in the broader geographical term Kharu, or land of the Hurrites. Canaan, or Canahn, was the name they frequently used for the Syro-Palestinian province they ruled during the Eighteenth and Nineteenth Dynasties (ca. 1550–1200 B.C.). It is also the name given to this area by the Hebrews, and is used in the Pentateuch.

During this period several languages were spoken in this small country, and five systems of writing gradually came into use. Akkadian cuneiform and Egyptian hieroglyphs were the international scripts of the period. Both already had a thousand-year-old tradition and were well established throughout the ancient Near East as the private means of communication of the governing aristocracy and the priestly class. But in the second millennium B.C., three local methods of writing were invented, and they occupy a paramount place in the history of writing. One is the syllabic script of Byblos, which probably was already invented by the late part of the third millennium B.C. and developed early in the second. Instead of the six hundred or more signs of the Egyptian ideographic writing, the Byblos syllabary was composed of about one hundred phonetic signs, which made the study and the use of writing a much easier task.

[1] Genesis 10.

Detail from a picture in the Great Temple of Medinet Habu, Egypt, showing prisoners of war captured by Rameses III. Left to right: a Libyan, a bearded Asiatic, a Hittite, one of the Sea People, and a Syrian.

The other two scripts were even more revolutionary, for they are the earliest alphabetic scripts ever to have been invented. One was used mainly in the Syrian harbor town of Ugarit; the other was probably invented and developed in southern Palestine. The Ugaritic script had borrowed the method of impressing characters on metal and clay tablets from the most widespread method of writing of the era, Mesopotamian cuneiform; but whereas the Mesopotamian was an ideographic script with a great number of characters, the Ugaritic cuneiform was composed of just thirty-two letters.

In the Palestinian script (or Proto-Sinaitic, as it is also called), most of the letters were also inspired by ideographic signs, but here the main influence came from Egyptian hieroglyphs. The twenty-two-lettered Palestinian alphabet is the father of the alphabets of modern languages. Hebrew, Phoenician, Greek, Etruscan, Roman, and all subsequent alphabets have derived from it.

The revolution in civilization brought about by this alphabet was spectacular. Thanks to its relative simplicity, writing has become common and is no longer the exclusive domain of the priestly and noble classes, as it was in Mesopotamia and Egypt. From the very beginning, the Palestinian alphabetic writing seems to have been a popular script. The ten inscriptions found so far in Palestine do not seem to include a single official document. In most cases they were inscribed on pottery vessels and other "popular" utensils of daily and religious use. A group of related inscriptions which was found in the mining region of Serabit al-Khadem, in Sinai, is believed to have been written by Palestinian captives or slaves. The language of these inscriptions is probably a colloquial Semitic dialect, and several had a votive character and were dedicated to Baalat, the Syro-Palestinian serpent goddess.[2]

While this "popular" alphabetic script was being invented and gradually coming into widespread use, government officials and the noble class persisted in writing in the official and traditional ideographic style for all international purposes.

The Hyksos rule must have been a time of adjustment and assimilation for the various peoples of the fertile regions of Palestine. The totalitarian government and the domination of the Hyksos nobility probably contributed to the growth of a sense of common interest among the peoples of lower status. The common labor, the common impressment as foot soldiers, servants, or slaves in the Hyksos armies, the common problems under the Hyksos rule, must have broken the barriers created by

[2] W. F. Albright: BASOR, No. 110 (1948), pp. 6–22. See also J. Leibovitch: *Annales du Service des Antiquités d'Egypte*, Vol. XL, No. 1 (1940), pp. 101 ff.

Spearhead from Lachish with early Semitic inscription

ethnic, cultural, and linguistic differences and slowly united the Palestinian population.

The end of the Hyksos rule did not bring very many changes in the social and political organization of the country. It became an Egyptian province; Egyptian tax collectors and administrators paid frequent visits to it, and Egyptian governors resided in the southern Palestinian city of Gaza. But the existing city-fortresses, their princes and rulers, and the small class of nobles living in the large, comfortable buildings were not much affected by the change. An overwhelming majority of the population was still very poorly sheltered and equipped. There was to be no major change in urban society until the Hebrew conquest. And in this conquest the feudal rule of local kings and the virtual enslavement of the majority of the population were to play important roles.

In contrast, the material culture underwent a marked change

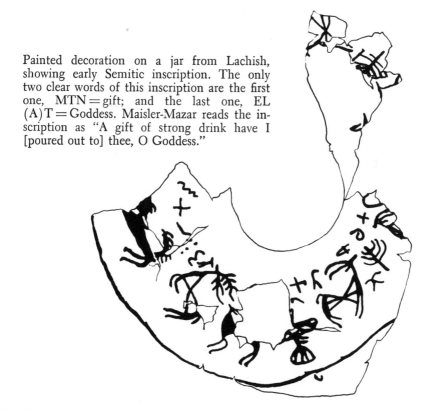

Painted decoration on a jar from Lachish, showing early Semitic inscription. The only two clear words of this inscription are the first one, MTN = gift; and the last one, EL (A)T = Goddess. Maisler-Mazar reads the inscription as "A gift of strong drink have I [poured out to] thee, O Goddess."

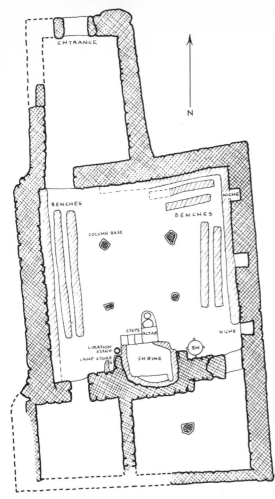

ENTRANCE

N

BENCHES

NICHE

BENCHES

COLUMN BASE

STEPS

ALTAR

LIBATION
STAND

BIN

LAMP STORE

NICHE

SHRINE

The third temple in the
fosse at Lachish

Aerial view of Canaanite temple at Hazor

at the end of the Hyksos rule, and it is likely that this happened because of three major factors: the influence of the farmers and other non-urban people living in Palestine and the neighboring regions; the Egyptian influence (which affected all other aspects of Canaanite life); and the movement of peoples and customs southward from Syria.

The same division into regions which we have encountered many times before, reappears now in a generally similar way. Southern Palestine and the central coastal region, with such important cities as Gaza, Gezer, and Apheq, and other urban centers farther north, such as Beth-Shan and Megiddo, were in close touch with Egypt. The hilly country and other interior parts were more autonomous in their material culture, and the northern coastal region and its ports were more closely tied to Syria and the North than any other part of Palestine.

Several marginal peoples in the deserts of Palestine and in surrounding regions appear to have maintained, as late as this period, traditions in art and material culture that must be regarded as a persistence of pre-urban ideas and ways of life. Some of these people still relied on hunting as one of their major economic activities, and carved pictures on the rocks of the desert. Others sculptured menhirs and steles in a very rough and coarse manner. Various groups of these menhir statues have been found in the Jordanian desert and elsewhere, but most of them could not be dated. A group of them, however, was found at Alalakh, in an archaeological level belonging to the fifteenth and sixteenth centuries B.C.[3]

[3] Sir Leonard Woolley: *Alalakh: An Account of Excavations at Tell Atchana, in the Hatay* (London: Oxford University Press; 1955), p. 238 and Pl. 44.

Woman's face on bichrome ware from Gaza (after Petrie)

During the seventeenth century B.C., while Egypt and Palestine were still under the Hyksos rule, in the northern Euphrates Valley there was a mass migration of people called Hurru by the Mesopotamian and Egyptian texts and Horites by the Bible. These people were probably of Armenoid stock. They came from an unknown land in the North, moved down along the eastern edges of the Hittite empire, and invaded northern Mesopotamia and northern Syria, where they adopted many of the customs of the local Amorites. When the Hyksos rule came to an end, some of their units advanced southward into southern Syria, Palestine, and probably also Cyprus.

Dating from this time, throughout Palestine there is a new type of two-color painted pottery with northern Syrian affinities which was popular for a short while and was most abundant at Tell el-Ajjul, near Gaza, and in other coastal sites. In Cyprus, a few pots of this kind have been found at Enkomi and other sites; but a considerable concentration of this ware found mingled with Cypriote pottery at Mila, an important ancient harbor on this island, might indicate that a foreign colony had existed there for a while. In Palestine, this pottery can be accurately dated, for it appears extensively only after the defeat of the Hyksos by Ahmose I, the first Pharaoh of the Eighteenth Dynasty, probably around 1550, and it vanishes abruptly after the middle of the fifteenth century B.C.

The best study of this ware is that of a British scholar, W. A. Heurtley, who believed it to be originally the creation of a single artist who lived in Tell el-Ajjul.[4] Recently Kathleen Kenyon has emphasized the resemblance between this bichrome ware and the pottery of the Horites, and has come to the conclusion that it was produced by those Horites who had come southward.[5]

Toward the end of the fifteenth century B.C., sea-borne trade increased rapidly. The coastal cities of Palestine have

[4] QDAP, Vol. VIII (1938), pp. 21–37.
[5] K. Kenyon: *Archaeology in the Holy Land* (London: Benn; 1960), p. 200.

Bichrome decoration on pottery
from Gaza (after Mackay and Murray)

Imported Mycenaean vase from the
necropolis at Tell Abu Hawam

Imported Mycenaean vase found
at Lachish

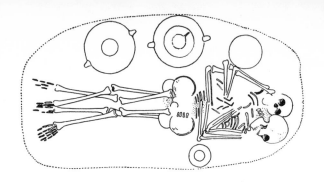

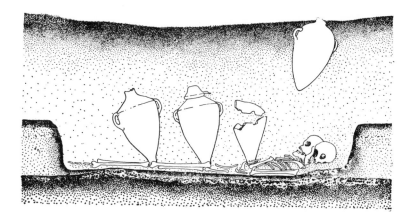

Plan and section of two tombs in the necropolis at Tell Abu Hawam

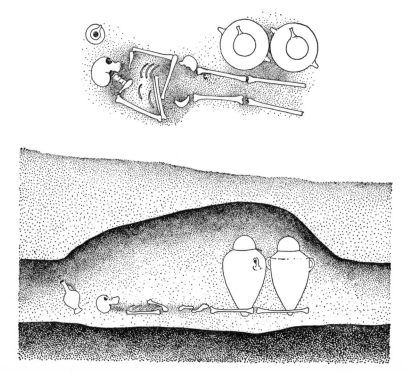

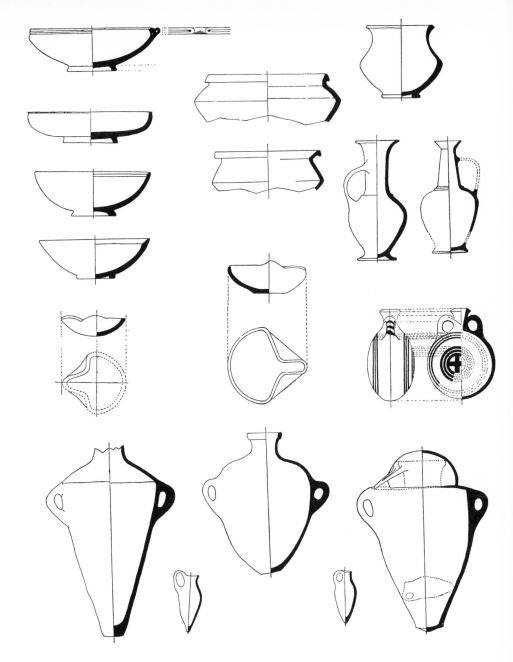

Canaanite pottery from the necropolis at Tell Abu Hawam

Imported Mycenaean clay figurine of bird (two views) found in necropolis at Tell Abu Hawam

yielded large quantities of Mycenaean, Cretan, and Cypriote pots, figurines, tools, and other objects. In this period Ugarit and Byblos, the two major harbors of the Levant in the second millennium B.C., had daily contacts with other parts of the Mediterranean shore. There trade and seafaring distinguished the way of life from that of the interior. Along with these Greek, Cypriote, and northern Syrian artifacts there must have come to the Palestinian coastal strip ideas and perhaps also people. Harbors were growing rapidly, and Gaza, Askalon, Jaffa, Tell Abu Hawam, Acco, and other places were becoming important centers of international trade. At about the time of the Hebrew conquest these towns were to become extremely powerful. In the twelfth century B.C. they were to be inhabited by the "sea people" who threatened Egypt and whose descendants were to reach North Africa, the central Mediterranean, and Iberia, found colonies all around the Mediterranean, and conduct a highly organized international trade.

In the period extending from the middle of the sixteenth century B.C. to the end of the thirteenth, the Egyptian rule in the Levant had several ups and downs; in times of Egyptian political weakness the princes of the Palestinian city-states refused to pay tribute to Pharaoh, and he would thereupon organize a

Basalt bowl decorated with wavy
spirals from Hazor (after Yadin)

Large Canaanite jar, covered with a milk bowl of Cypriot origin. The juglet was found inside the jar, at the Tell Abu Hawam necropolis.

Imported Mycenaean vase found at Lachish

Cult objects, some of Egyptian origin, found at the shrine of the Canaanite temple at Lachish. A scarab, a faïence vase, ivory perfume flask, ivory gazelle head, neck of glass vase, two cylinder seals, and a pottery bowl

military campaign, invade the country with his armies, defeat the rebelling princes, and reaffirm his rule over Canaan. Descriptions of several of these campaigns have come down to us, and they are highly important for the study of the history of the period, as they describe cities and name them, trace the routes followed by the armies, and throw light on the balance of power in Palestine.

Similar foreign influences also appear in the Canaanite art. The Canaanite culture was definitely not autonomous. Palestine can be considered in this period to be the southernmost region of an artistic province centered on coastal Syria. It was a much poorer region than those farther north and seems to have had very little independent creativity. Most of the known art objects of this period, in the form of ivory inlays, cult figurines, statues, and steles, were imported from the three major areas from which other influences reached Palestine: Syria, Egypt, and the central Mediterranean. At the same time, some of the decorations on pottery from Tell Beit Mirsim, Gezer, Lachish, and other southern towns seem to have been strongly influenced by the primitive art of the peripheral desert nomads who produced the rock pictures in the Negev and Jordan. Steles and orthostats (decorated standing slabs) were either imported or copied from foreign models. At Hazor, Beth-Shan, and elsewhere there are several basalt orthostats in high relief of northern Syrian inspiration, and Egyptian steles and statues were erected at Beth-Shan, Kinnereth, Jaffa, and elsewhere.

This lack of creativity and individuality in Palestinian art and material culture was the fruit of a political, economic, and ethnic situation that finally led to the end of Canaanite civilization. The roots of this situation were many; the local feudal system, the economic and cultural differences between neighboring peoples, and the Egyptian administration all played their roles in the Hebrew conquest.

An additional factor, which reflects the decadence of the Canaanites and which probably contributed to the death of their

Seated priest or divinity found in
Canaanite temple at Hazor

Canaanite divinity with snake
and solar symbol, from Hazor

Fourteenth-century B.C. basalt slab from Beth-Shan. In the upper panel, a dog and a lion. Below, a dog attacking a lion. Each lion has a star on its shoulder.

culture, was their brutal religion. In this field the rich iconographic and material remains from Palestine are abundantly supplemented by the mythological and religious texts discovered at Ugarit. Human sacrifice, which had been given up long before by the people of Mesopotamia and Egypt, was still in current use in Canaan. There the temples were also centers of the sacred prostitution of both sexes. Serpent worship and the concepts suggested by their ruthless divinities, who were framed in a mythology full of atrocity, fear, and brutality, were most likely reflections of the facts and rules of daily life.

THE BACKGROUND OF THE HEBREW CONQUEST

The peoples who had migrated to Palestine at the end of the Early Urban period had to some degree settled down in permanent settlements, and to some degree continued a nomadic or semi-nomadic way of life at the margins of the fertile regions and between the urban and agricultural settlements. From their arrival to the beginning of the Hyksos rule, there was a great deal of warfare.

During the strong Hyksos rule, the nomadic and semi-nomadic peoples markedly reduced their political activity, but they slowly reasserted themselves and became an increasingly important factor in the Palestinian balance of power after the Hyksos rule was over. Certain groups of these nomads without cities or land were called by ancient texts Habiru or Apiru.[6] When this name was first found on Egyptian clay tablets at the end of the nineteenth century, it aroused great interest in the scientific world, because some scholars believed that it referred to the Biblical Hebrews. Today, seventy years later, the discussion is still going on, and no general agreement has been reached. However, most scholars believe now that this term indicated a social status rather than an ethnic group.[7]

[6] I shall refer to them as Habiru even when the reading in a particular citation is Apiru.
[7] G. Bottero: *Le problème des Habiru* (Paris; 1954).

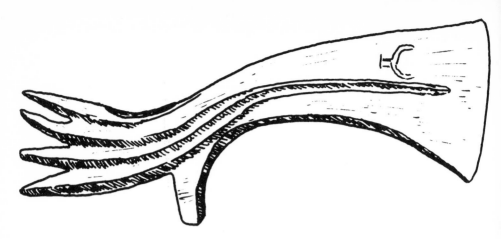

Thirteenth-century B.C. eastern ax found at Beth-Shan

The Habiru were already on the scene by Patriarchal times, according to the story of Sinuhe and other documents from Mesopotamia and Egypt. During the Hyksos period they also showed up in Anatolia. A text from Bogaz-Köy, the capital of the Hittite empire, states that they were there as mercenary soldiers. In the course of time they became increasingly dangerous. From a letter dating back to the times of Hammurabi, we learn that they had helped the inhabitants of a town called Talhaya, probably located in the upper Euphrates Valley, not far from Mari, to pillage the neighboring city of Lahaya, killing ten inhabitants and taking away five hundred cattle.

In other records they are spoken of as raiders, rebels, traders, captives, slaves, mercenary soldiers, and government employees. Most of them were of nomadic origin and lived in the desert, but they came in continual contact with sedentary peoples, either to serve them or to fight against them.

One of the most interesting texts referring to the Habiru was written by Idri-mi, a king of Alalakh, a city in northern Syria, who lived in the sixteenth century B.C. A revolution forced him to flee his capital on the Orontes River, not far from Antioch, and he came to Canaan. Here he met many other people who had fled their own country for political reasons. He calls them Habiru. He succeeded in organizing them, and seized some ships, sailed back to the mouth of the Orontes, and reconquered his kingdom.

These landless Habiru were becoming a great threat to the city dwellers. They were increasing in power and in number, and many of them had worked in the urban centers and were well acquainted with the political and social problems within the walls of the towns. Meanwhile, the rapid increase in the density of settlements throughout Palestine and the foundation of new cities all around the Beersheba region—where fortified sites appear now for the first time—doubtless were consequences of a considerable growth in population. The multiplication of settlements, which implies the use of more and more agricultural land to feed the inhabitants and a more systematic utilization of water sources, probably created an uneasy situation for the nomadic and semi-nomadic tribes who were accustomed to wandering on once open land and to using the wells near which new settlements were now being built. This situation must have contributed to a change in the attitude of the sedentary population

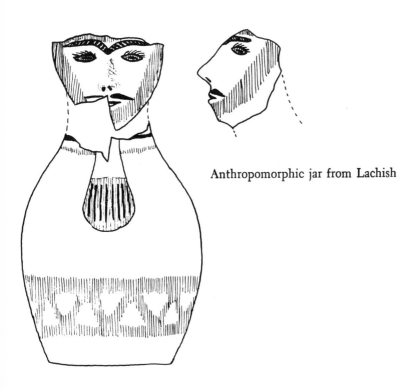

Anthropomorphic jar from Lachish

toward the nomads, who were becoming ever more threatening to the safety of farms and water supplies.

What seems to have happened is that the settled people tried to disrupt the thousand-year-old traditional pattern of friendly relations, alliances, and economic exchanges with the nomads, and to keep them out of settled territory which had become too crowded. On the other hand, some of these nomads and Habiru served in the armies of the Pharaohs and local chieftains, were skilled in the weapons and military tactics used by them, and were familiar with the defensive systems of the cities and with the problems and weaknesses of city society.

By the fifteenth century B.C. the nomads and the landless had multiplied, as had the inhabitants of the cities, and some of them banded together in powerful tribes. The city dwellers began to grasp the danger posed by the nomads and the mercenaries in their service, and the incompatibility between intensive settlement and agriculture and the wandering way of life of the nomadic bands.

The most dramatic description of these changing relations, and of the role played by the Habiru in the extensive upheaval that was to destroy the Canaanite civilization, is found in the royal archives of Pharaoh Ikhnaton, who ruled in the fourteenth century B.C. There are over 370 clay tablets written by the princes and local chieftains of vassal cities in Asia to the mighty ruler of Egypt, and they give us the names of the major Canaanite towns and chiefs who kept in correspondence with the Tell el-Amarna court.[8]

The picture they give is that of a very unstable situation, of total mistrust of one ruler for another, of continual skirmishing between one town and another, often with the help of Habiru mercenary soldiers. There were frequent revolts and many dissidents within the cities. These letters reveal that in Palestine plots

[8] For the general background see W. F. Albright: JNES, Vol. V, pp. 7–25; also JEA, Vol. XXIII, pp. 190 ff.

against a ruling prince were organized by the lower class, by the nobility, and by members of the prince's own family alike. They show that the pressure exerted on the cities by the pastoral nomads and by the Habiru was entering into a complex political framework in which three major factors played prominent roles. The first was the Egyptian rule, which managed things so as to keep Canaan under control and to maintain the flow of revenue from the vassal states. The second was the loss of power and authority by the nobles, who were divided and continually quarreling among themselves; they no longer looked upon Egyptian colonialism as oppression, but rather as protection for their privileged status, the only pillar of strength on their side in the forthcoming struggle. The third factor was the ever growing power of the people. New ideas of freedom were coming into their minds, and their daring vis-à-vis the nobles was increasing. The castles of the nobility were becoming the last strongholds of feudalism in a land in which the princes were only the nominal rulers, unable to master the situation any longer. The castles were small islands of the old regime in a sea of new ideas.

The situation oddly resembled that which preceded some of the European revolutions in the last few centuries. Many slaves and lower-class people were turning to the Habiru in the hope of regaining their freedom. We have evidence of at least one prince who turned his back on the feudal system and came over to the side of the landless Habiru.[9]

Our information comes from the nobles, the people shut inside their fortresses, watching from narrow windows what was happening in the streets and the fields. But their reports are explicit. Some passages taken from these letters will probably illuminate the situation better than any further comment: "Dagantakala to the king. Asks for rescue from the Habiru and the Shutu." [1] ". . . let my lord protect *his* land from the hand

[9] Tell el-Amarna letters, No. 254.
[1] W. M. F. Petrie: *Syria and Egypt, from the Tell el-Amarna Letters* (London, 1898), p. 134.

of the Habiru. If not, let the king, my lord, send chariots to fetch us, *lest our servants smite us.*" [2]

The revolt seems to have increased in scope. In this period the city of Jerusalem was governed by a prince called Abdu Heba. Several of his letters were found at Tell el-Amarna, and have been studied by William F. Albright. They are of great help in understanding the political situation and the state of mind of the feudal nobility in Canaan.

The nobles were caught between the onerous taxes levied on them by the Egyptian Pharaoh under the threat of the Egyptian army, and the growing ferment among their people. Abdu Heba was accused of rebellion against the Pharaoh, and in his answer to the Egyptian ruler, he explains things as follows: "Why should I commit transgression against the king, my lord? As long as the king, my lord, lives, I will say to the commissioner of the king, my lord, 'Why do you like the Habiru and dislike the governors?' and thus I am blamed in the presence of the king, my lord!"

The situation was such that neither the Pharaoh nor the administrators nor the princes and governors knew any longer on whom they could safely rely. Abdu Heba asked the Pharaoh for help: "O king, my lord, there are no garrison troops! Let the king take care of his land! The lands of the king have all rebelled. . . . May it please the king to send me garrison troops in order that I may enter and see the two eyes of the king, my lord." Apparently the nobles did not dare any longer to leave their castles without an escort of Egyptian troops.

Abdu Heba obviously realized that the real threat was from the Habiru, and that the only help he could realistically expect was from the Pharaoh, to whom he was a tributary. The letter goes on: "Lost are the lands of the king . . . all governors are lost. . . . The Habiru plunder all the lands of the king. If there are archers . . . the lands of the king, my lord, will remain, but

[2] Tell el-Amarna letters, No. 271; see ANET, p. 486.

if there are no archers the lands of the king, my lord, will be lost." [3]

The situation was becoming increasingly difficult, and in a later letter the same Abdu Heba wrote: "I have become like a ship in the midst of the sea . . . the Habiru conquer the cities of the king. There is not a single governor to the king, my lord. All have perished . . ." [4]

Archaeological excavations have revealed that most of the major Palestinian fortified towns were repeatedly destroyed. Lachish, Megiddo, Tell Beit Mirsim, and other sites were burned and rebuilt several times. Archaeology confirms what the Tell el-Amarna letters say: that the political situation was very unstable. The political situation was also unstable in Egypt during the reign of Ikhnaton, but his son-in-law, Tutankhamen, re-established order, pacified the dissidents and the powerful Egyptian priesthood, and was free to pay attention once more to the province of Canaan. The Pharaohs of the Nineteenth Dynasty pressed their military campaigns actively, and the rule of the feudal princes was reinforced for a short while. The towns were once more under full Egyptian domination, but the social and political problems of Palestine were not solved and the country was seething with people ready for the explosion.

The *coup de grâce* was probably given to the Palestinian princes by the unexpected return of a group of freed slaves from Egypt after four hundred years of captivity. Palestine was over-populated by that time, every strip of land belonged to someone, and there was no place for the newcomers except densely wooded regions in Galilee and central Palestine and in parts of the southern desert.

The conquest of Palestine was really the clash of two cultural worlds. At the moment of impact they represented two ways of life: on one side, the autocratic feudal system of a de-

[3] Tell el-Amarna letters, No. 286, ANET, p. 488.
[4] ANET, p. 489.

cadent noble class, based on slavery and on taxation imposed upon the agricultural population and supported by the imperial army of Egypt; on the other, the tribal democratic system of the nomads, to whom the oppressed class of slaves and servants, the landless mercenaries, and probably also parts of the vassal agricultural population adhered. The two ways of life could no longer continue to exist side by side.

It is not difficult to see, from the descriptions of the Tell el-Amarna letters and other ancient texts, that the growing ferment of the Habiru and the other groups outside and inside the cities was bound to explode and bring the Canaanite civilization to an end.

The pastoral-and-farming peoples already occupied most of the land between one city and another, and each "king" felt increasingly uneasy, confined in his walled fortress and surrounded by men who were refusing to behave as vassals and who were always endangering the highways and cutting communications with the other urban centers.

Conditions were being reversed. Previously the cities had been the important centers of communication, of military and political action, of international relations and trade. Now they were becoming increasingly isolated in the sea of nomads, semi-nomads, and small agricultural bands who were filling all the empty spaces in the country.

The enemy was spread out everywhere. Even within the city walls there were serfs and slaves hostile to the king and to the nobility and willing to help those of their class. No one could be trusted any longer. The nomads and the landless were becoming stronger and more united as the challenging idea of seizing the whole country, the wealth of the towns, the rich wells, the beautiful fields owned by the princes and worked by vassals, slaves, or mercenaries, was increasingly pervading their thoughts. And the undertaking seemed ever more possible.

Perhaps it is not a pure coincidence that southern and

The site of Kadesh Naphtali overlooking the upper Jordan Valley, a strategic point during the Hebrew conquest of Canaan

eastern Palestine and the hilly country where the Patriarchs already held some land and in which they were accustomed to move freely, were the first to be conquered. Little is said in the Biblical stories about the conquest of central Palestine, but Shechem, an important town in central Palestine at the time, repeatedly served Joshua, the central hero of the conquest, as a gathering place during his military campaigns.[5] The American archaeologist George Ernest Wright has recently suggested that Shechem was a Hebrew city even before the conquest, and he is probably right.[6]

In Jordan and the Negev, large areas appear to have traditionally belonged to the Hebrews. In the Book of Judges we read that "Israel dwelt in Heshbon and her towns, and in Aroer and her towns, and in all the cities along the coasts of Arnon,

[5] Joshua 8: 30-5; 24.
[6] G. E. Wright: *Biblical Archaeology* (Philadelphia: Westminster Press; 1957), pp. 77-8.

three hundred years." [7] Jordan and the Negev were also populated by various tribes related to the Hebrews and considered
"cousins" by Biblical traditions: Ishmael, Midian, Ammon, and
Moab. These tribes probably supported in part the action of the
Israelites.

On the other hand, the coastal plains had no earlier relations with the Hebrews. They were inhabited by different peoples, and they were the last to fall into the hands of the Hebrews.

The Bible presents two main traditional versions of the conquest. One is set forth at the beginning of the Book of Judges;
according to this book, the conquest was a long process in which
each tribe conquered its own province. The other is set forth in
the Book of Joshua; according to this book, Joshua led a confederacy of tribes in a spectacular military campaign which
brought about the conquest of large parts of the country. In the
past some scholars believed that these stories contradicted each

[7] Judges 11 : 26.

A fire-blackened level that marks the end of the Canaanite culture at Beth-Shan

other, but today most agree that the one does not exclude the other and that the military campaign led by Joshua was simply an important event in a much longer struggle in which each tribe must have played a prominent role in its own region.

The earliest mention of Israel in Egyptian historical texts is on a stele erected by Pharaoh Merneptah late in the thirteenth century B.C. The ruler of Upper and Lower Egypt had just returned from one of his ever victorious military expeditions, and the dramatic text reads: "The princes are prostrate, saying: Peace! Not one arises his head among the Nine Bows. Desolation is from Tehenu; Hatti is pacified; plundered is Canaan with every evil, carried off is Askalon, seized upon is Gezer, Hanoam is made as that which does not exist, Israel is laid waste, his seed is not; Hurru is become a widow to Egypt!" [8]

Obviously by this time Israel was already a powerful political unit in Palestine. This was about the time when the tribes of Israel had entered an epic and glorious struggle, the time when Palestine became the land of the Hebrews.

"So Joshua took all that land, the hills, and all the south country, and all the land of Goshen, and the valley, and the plain, and the mountain of Israel and his valley. From Mount Halak, that goes up to Seir, to Baal-gad in the valley of Lebanon under Mount Hermon . . . and Joshua gave the land as inheritance unto Israel according to their divisions by their tribes. And the land rested from war." [9]

This is the end of the story of Palestine before the Hebrews, some 3,200 years ago, when the Hebrews entered history as a political and cultural entity.

[8] J. A. Wilson in ANET, p. 378.
[9] Joshua 11: 16–23.

CONCLUSION

Aᴛ ᴛʜᴇ sᴛᴀʀᴛ of fully recorded history, events became
identified with named individuals; heroes, saints, prophets,
witches, kings, generals, and other kinds of leaders came to control human destiny. Since then, a small number of outstanding
figures have had a tremendous influence on nations and on all
humanity. We must be grateful to those leaders who have shown
a sense of history by taking good care to let us know about their
deeds.

This historical sense of the chosen ones is gradually less evident the further we go back in time. In the Urban Age, names of
leaders are less common. This does not seem to be merely the
result of our lack of information. We know that in literate societies in a cultural stage similar to that of Canaanite Palestine, the
deeds of gods were far more interesting than those of mortal

beings. The best example is given us in the abundant Ugaritic literature.

The further we go back in time, the more the leader is identified with the human group. For the Canaanite period in Palestine we have two main sources of information: the Bible and historical texts. The Bible tells us about the Hebrews before the conquest. Their life is best portrayed by the stories of the Patriarchs. These accounts illustrate the way of life and the activities of the tribe, but we are not yet able to draw a clear picture of the personality of each individual mentioned. The three Patriarchs Abraham, Isaac, and Jacob are rather vague as individuals. Their temperament, their behavior in war and politics, and the nature of their leadership are not drawn with the clarity and fullness given to the descriptions of later figures such as Moses, Aaron, and Joshua.

Through historical texts—the most important of which are the Tell el-Amarna letters—we have learned the names of several Palestinian leaders, but we know more about their administrative work and their intrigues than about their wisdom or any of their glorious deeds. We know that some leaders did not disdain power and popularity, but most of them do not seem to have cared about posterity as much as the more sophisticated leaders of literate Egypt and Mesopotamia.

Going further back, the image of the leader fades out completely. We know only of the communal deeds of restricted human groups: city-states, tribes, confederacies. The maximal political unit frequently coincides with the main cultural one. We know the names of several of these entities: Canaanites, Hebrews, Amorites, Hyksos, Hurrites, and so forth.

These groups are identifiable archaeologically and ethnologically. Sometimes we are also fortunate enough to obtain some idea about the anthropological, or "racial," category to which they belong, but only rarely, and in vague outline, are we able to identify individuals. Only the shadows of some outstanding priests may be discerned in the existence of religious buildings of exceptional size or conception—like that discovered at Beth-Yerah—or the vague image of some autocratic dictator in huge defensive structures like those of prehistoric Jericho.

Going back in time, we are gradually and inevitably deprived of one of the great pleasures of history, the analysis of characters, and thus the privilege of loving or disliking them.

In Pre-Urban society we are confronted with the group; going further back, the group too gradually loses its identity and becomes just part of a cultural area in which groups have no apparent distinct personalities, and in which the standard of living, the means of subsistence, art, religion, and the various customs appear rather homogenized.

Throughout this book we have followed the increasing subdivision of cultures from the earliest cultures to the end of the Age of Early Farming. In the Paleolithic Age only extremely large cultural areas are detectable. In Mesolithic times smaller regions can be recognized. And in the Age of Early Farming we find very small regions showing cultural traits of their own. Following this process backward, historical action also becomes more and more disconnected and associated with increasingly large and less clearly defined entities. The minimal unit of historical action is neither the individual nor the class, nor the settlement, and not even a limited geographical region, but the cultural area, which increases in size the further we go back in time.

Our scope widens in terms of time as much as it does in terms of space. Each historical process we are able to detect is likely to have lasted years in the Age of Early Farming; generations in the Mesolithic; centuries and millennia in the Paleolithic.

We have followed man from his earliest childhood to his entrance into history. We have seen that he acquired most of his traits of character before the start of history. Physically, technologically, economically, socially, and politically, all the foundations of human nature were formed in the ages that preceded history. We have seen that the rhythm of evolution has been growing faster and faster, that every new acquisition, every new discovery, every new achievement of man has further increased the potentiality of his imagination, of his physical and mental abilities.

I chose Palestine as the region to be dissected vertically through time for two main reasons: its convenient geographical location at the crossroads of the three continents of the Old World, and the fact that except for western Europe, it is one of the few areas where prehistorical research has been flourishing intensively for the last sixty years, with the result that there have been a large number of important discoveries and an unusual amount of scientific literature has been produced. Because of Palestine's location, many general problems arise in the prehistory of the area; because of the research that has already been done, the available information is rich and varied. However, our knowledge of the prehistoric sequence of Palestine is still extremely fragmentary; prehistorical research, there as elsewhere, is still in an early stage. New excavations, new studies, and new students are needed to throw more light on the past.

SELECTED SOURCES

ONE. THE FACE OF THE LAND

Abel, F. M.: *Géographie de la Palestine.* 2 vols. Paris: Études Bibliques; 1933 and 1938.

Albright, W. F.: *The Archaeology of Palestine.* 5th ed. Baltimore: Pelican; 1960.

Barrois, A. G.: *Manuel d'archéologie biblique.* 2 vols. Paris: Picard; 1939 and 1954.

Howell, F. C.: "Upper Pleistocene Stratigraphy and Early Man in the Levant." *Proceedings of the American Philosophical Society,* Vol. CIII, No. 1 (February 1959).

Kenyon, K. M.: *Archaeology in the Holy Land.* London: Benn; 1960.

Neuville, R.: "Le Paléolithique et le Mésolithique du desert de Judée." Archives IPH, Vol. XXIV (1951).

Picard, L.: *Structure and Evolution of Palestine, with Comparative Notes on Neighboring Countries.* Jerusalem: Department of Geology, Hebrew University; 1943.

TWO. THE AGE OF HUNTING AND GATHERING

The Old Stone Age (Paleolithic)

Anati, E.: "Recherches préhistoriques au Sinai." BSPF, Vol. LV, Nos. 3–4 (1958).

Bordes, F.: "Le Paléolithique inférieur et moyen de Jabrud (Syrie) et la question du pre-Aurignacien." L'A, Vol. LIX (1955).

Ewing, J. F.: "Preliminary Note on the Excavations at the Palaeolithic Site of Ksar Akil, Republic of Lebanon." *Antiquity,* Vol. XXI (1947).

———: "Ksar Akil in 1948." *Biblica,* Vol. XXIX (1948).

Ewing, J. F.: "Ksar Akil, a Palaeolithic Site in Lebanon." BPAS, Vol. IX, No. 1 (1955).

Garrod, D. A. E.: "The Near East as a Gateway of Prehistoric Migration." *Bulletin of the American Schools of Prehistoric Research*, No. 13 (1937).

———: "Excavations at the Cave of Shukbah, Palestine, 1928." PPS, 1942, Vol. VIII.

———: "The Relation between Southwest Asia and Europe with Special Reference to the Origin of Upper Palaeolithic Blade Culture." JWH, Vol. I, No. 1 (1953).

———: "Excavations at the Mugharet Kebara, Mount Carmel, 1931: The Aurignacian Industries." PPS, 1954, Vol. XX, Pt. 2.

———: "Acheuleo-Jabroudien et 'Pre-Aurignacien' de la grotte du Taboun (Mount Carmel), étude stratigraphique et chronologique." *Quaternaria*, Vol. III (1956).

———: Notes sur le Paléolithique supérieur du Moyen Orient." BSPF, Vol. LIV, Nos. 7–8 (1957).

——— and D. M. A. Bate: *The Stone Age of Mount Carmel*. Vol. I. London: Oxford University Press; 1937.

Haller, J.: "Notes de préhistoire phénicienne: L'abri de Abou-Halka (Tripoli)." BMB, Vol. VI (1943).

Howell, F. C.: "Upper Pleistocene Stratigraphy and Early Man in the Levant." *Proceedings of the American Philosophical Society*, Vol. CIII, No. 1 (February 1959).

Köppel, R.: *Zur Urgeschichte Palästinas*. Rome: Pontificium Institutum Biblicum; 1937.

Neuville, R.: "Le Paléolithique et le Mésolithique du desert de Judée." Archives IPH, Vol. XXIV (1951).

Rhotert, H.: *Transjordanien vorgeschichtliche Forschungen*. Stuttgart; 1938.

Rust, A.: *Die Höhlenfunde von Yabrud, Syrien*. Neumünster: Wachholtz; 1950.

Stekelis, M.: "Rephaim-Baq'a: a Paleolithic Station in the Vicinity of Jerusalem." JPOS, Vol. XXI (1947).

———: "The Palaeolithic Deposits of Jisr Bnat Yaqub." BRCI, Geological Section, Vol. IX, Nos. 2–3 (1960).

———: "Villafranchian Deposits at Ubaidiya, near Kibbutz Afiqim." BRCI, Geological Section, Vol. IX, Nos. 3–4 (1960).

Turville-Petre, F.: *Researches in Prehistoric Galilee, 1925-6*. London: The British School of Archaeology in Jerusalem; 1927.

————: "Excavations in the Mugharet el-Kebarah." JRAI, Vol. LXII (1932).

Vaufrey, R.: "Paléolithique et Mésolithique Palestiniens." L'A, Vol. XLIX (1939).

Waechter, J. d'A., and V. M. Seton-Williams: "The Excavations at Wadi Dhobai, 1937–8, and the Dhobaian Industry." JPOS, Vol. XVIII (1938).

Zeuner, F. E.: "Die Gliederung des Pleistozäns und des Paläolithikums in Palästina." Geologische Rundschau, Vol. XXIX (1938).

Zumoffen, G.: "L'Age de la pierre en Phénicie." Anthropos, Vol. III (1908).

Quaternary Geo-Chronology

Avnimelech, M.: "Contribution to the Knowledge of Quaternary Oscillations of the Shore Line of Palestine." RPI, 1951.

————: "Quaternary Sediments of the Coastal Plain of Israel." BRCI, Geological Section, Vol. III, No. 11 (1952).

Bourchart, J.: "Recherches stratigraphiques sur le Pliocène et le Quaternaire du Levant." Bulletin de la Société Géologique de France, Vol. V, No. 10 (1940).

Dalloni, M.: "Sur quelques problèmes du Quaternaire méditerranéen." Bulletin de la Société Historique de l'Afrique du Nord, Vol. XLV (1954).

Dubertret, L.: "Sur le Quaternaire côtier libanais et les oscillations du niveau de la mer au Quaternaire." Comptes Rendus de l'Académie des Sciences, No. 223 (1946).

Fleisch, H.: "Depôts préhistoriques de la côte libanaise et leur place dans la chronologie basée sur le Quaternaire marin." Quaternaria, Vol. III (1956).

Garrod, D. A. E., and E. W. Gardner: "Pleistocene Coastal Deposits in Palestine." Nature, No. 135.

Picard, L.: "Géologie de la grotte de 'Oumm Qatafa." JPOS, Vol. II (1931).

————: "Inferences on the Problem of the Pleistocene Climate of Palestine and Syria Drawn from the Flora, Fauna and Stratigraphy." PPS, 1937, Vol. III.

————: Structure and Evolution of Palestine, with Comparative Notes on Neighboring Countries. Jerusalem: Department of Geology, Hebrew University; 1943.

Shalem, N.: "Attributed Climatic Changes in the Levant." Lisbon: Congress International de Géographie; 1950. Proceedings of the 2d Session.

Vaumas, E. de: "Les Terrasses d'abrasion marine de la côte libanaise." *Bulletin de la Société Royale de Géographie d'Egypte,* Vol. xxii (1947).

——: "Les Terrasses d'abrasion marine de la côte Syrienne." *Revue de Géographie Alpine,* Vol. xlii (1954).

Wright, H. E., Jr.: "Geological Setting of Ksar Akil, a Palaeolithic Site in Lebanon. Preliminary Report." JNES, Vol. x (1951).

Paleanthropology

Boule, M., and H. V. Vallois: *Fossil Men.* London: Thames and Hudson; 1957.

Buxton, L. H. D.: *The Peoples of Asia.* New York: Alfred A. Knopf; 1925.

Coon, Carleton S.: *The Races of Europe.* New York: Macmillan; 1939.

Ferenbach, D.: "Note sur un crâne brachycéphale et deux mandibules du Mésolithique d'Israel." IEJ, Vol. ix, No. 2 (1959).

——: "Le Peuplement du Proche Orient au Chalcolithique et au Bronze Ancien." IEJ, Vol. ix, No. 4 (1959).

Henckel, K. O.: "Zur Kraniologie Palästinas." *Zeitschrift für Morphologie und Anthropologie,* Vol. xxviii (1930).

Hooton, E. A.: "Report on Skeletal Remains." In E. Grant: *Ain Shems Excavations.* Vol. iv. Haverford, Pa.: Haverford College; 1939.

Howell, F. C.: "The Place of Neanderthal Man in Human Evolution." *American Journal of Physical Anthropology,* n.s., Vol. ix (1951).

——: "Upper Pleistocene Man of the Southwestern Asian Mousterian." In *Neanderthal Centenary.* Utrecht; 1958.

Hrdlička, A.: "Skeletal Remains." In P. L. O. Guy: *Megiddo Tombs.* Chicago: University of Chicago Press; 1938.

Kappers, C. V. A., and L. W. Parr: *An Introduction to the Anthropology of the Near East.* Amsterdam; 1934.

Keith, Sir A.: "A Report on the Galilee Skull." In F. Turville-Petre: *Researches in Prehistoric Galilee,* 1925–6. London: The British School of Archaeology in Jerusalem; 1927.

——: *New Discoveries Relating to the Antiquity of Man.* London: Williams and Norgate; 1931.

——: *A New Theory of Human Evolution.* London: Watts; 1948.

———— and T. D. McCown: "Mount Carmel Man. His Bearing on the Ancestry of Modern Races." In G. MacCurdy (ed.): *Early Man.* Philadelphia: Academy of Natural Sciences; 1937.

Kurth, G.: "Vorbericht über anthropologische Beobachtungen bei der Jericho Grabung." *Homo*, 1955.

Macalister, R. A. S.: "Skeletal Remains." In *The Excavations of Gezer.* Vol. I. London: Murray; 1912.

McCown, T. D.: "Fossil Men of the Mugharet es-Skhul." BASOR, No. 9 (1933).

————: "The Oldest Complete Skeletons of Man." BASOR, No. 10 (1934).

———— and Sir A. Keith: *The Stone Age of Mount Carmel.* Vol. II. London: Oxford University Press; 1939.

Neuville, R., and R. Boureau: "Squelettes palestiniens du premier âge du Bronze." *Bulletins et Mémoires de la Société Anthropologique,* 8th Series, Vol. I, Nos. 4–6 (1930).

Sauter, M. R.: "La Brachycéphalie du Proche Orient dès origines à nos jours." ASAG, Vol. XI (1945).

Seltzer, C. C.: "Contribution to the Racial Anthropology of the Near East." *Peabody Museum Papers,* Vol. XVI, Part 2 (1940).

Snow, C. E.: "The Ancient Palestinian: Skhul V Reconstruction." BASOR, No. 127 (1953).

Turville-Petre, F.: *Researches in Prehistoric Galilee,* 1925–6. London: The British School of Archaeology in Jerusalem; 1927.

Vallois, H. V.: "Les Ossements natoufiens d'Erq el-Ahmar." L'A, Vol. XLVI (1939).

————: "Neanderthals et Praesapiens." JRAI, Vol. LXXXIV (1954).

Weckler, J. E.: "The Relationships between Neanderthal Man and Homo Sapiens." AA, Vol. LVI (1954).

THREE. THE TRANSITIONAL CULTURES

The Middle Stone Age (Mesolithic)

Garrod, D. A. E.: "A New Mesolithic Industry: The Natufian of Palestine." JRAI, Vol. LXII (1932).

————: "Excavations at the Cave of Shukbah, Palestine, 1928." PPS, 1942, Vol. VIII.

————: "The Natufian Culture: The Life and Economy of a Mesolithic People in the Near East." *Proceedings of the British Academy,* Vol. XLIII (1957).

Garrod, D. A. E., and D. M. A. Bate: *The Stone Age of Mount Carmel*, Vol. I. London: Oxford University Press; 1937.

Neuville, R.: Les Débuts de l'agriculture et la faucille préhistorique en Palestine." *Antiquity*, Vol. IX (1935).

———: "Le Paléolithique et le Mésolithique du desert de Judée." Archives IPH, Vol. XXIV (1951).

Perrot, J.: "Le Mésolithique de Palestine et les récentes découvertes à Einan (Ain Mallaha)." *Antiquity and Survival*, Vol. II (1957).

———: "Excavations at Einan (Ain ·Mallaha). Preliminary Report on the 1959 Season." IEJ, Vol. X, No. 7 (1960).

Turville-Petre, F.: "Excavations in the Mugharet el-Kebarah." JRAI, Vol. LXII (1932).

Rock Pictures

Anati, E.: "Rock Engravings in the Central Negev." *Archaeology*, Vol. VIII, No. 1 (1955).

———: "Ancient Rock Engravings in the Central Negev." PEQ, Vol. LXXXII, Nos. 1–2 (1955).

———: "Les Gravures rupestres du Néguev Central." BSPF, Vol. LII, Nos. 11–12 (1956).

———: "Rock Engravings in the Jebel Ideid." PEQ, Vol. LXXXIII, Nos. 1–2 (1956).

———: "Una Scena di danza nel Negev Centrale." *Rivista di Scienze Preistoriche*, Vol. X (1956).

———: "Recherches préhistoriques au Sinai." BSPF, Vol. LV, Nos. 3–4 (1958).

———: "Les Gravures rupestres dans la région du Néguev." *Bible et Terre Sainte*, Vol. XXII (1959).

Horsfield, G.: "Arabian Prehistoric Man Revealed for the First Time: A New Group of Rock Drawings Discovered in Transjordan." ILN, June 3, 1933.

——— and N. Glueck: "Prehistoric Rock-Drawings in Trans-Jordan." AJA, Vol. XXXVII (1933).

Howe, B.: "Two Groups of Rock Engravings from the Hijaz." JNES, Vol. IX, No. 1 (1950).

Rhotert, H.: *Transjordanien vorgeschichtliche Forschungen*. Stuttgart; 1938.

FOUR. THE AGE OF EARLY FARMING

Braidwood, R. J.: "The Spread of the Village Economy in the Old World." In *Human Origins. Selected Readings*. Series II. Chicago: University of Chicago Press; 1945.

————: "A Synoptic Description of the Earliest Village-Culture Materials from the Aegean to the Indus." In *Human Origins. Selected Readings*. Series II. 2nd ed. Chicago: University of Chicago Press; 1946.

————: *The Near East and the Foundation for Civilization*. Eugene, Ore.: Condon Lectures; 1952.

————: "The Earliest Village Communities in Southwestern Asia." JWH, Vol. I (1953).

————: "Reflections on the Origin of the Village-Farming Community." In S. S. Weinberg (ed.): *The Aegean and the Near East*. Locust Valley, N.Y.: J. J. Augustin; 1957.

————: "Near Eastern Prehistory." *Science*, Vol. CXXVII (1958).

———— and B. Howe: *Prehistoric Investigations in Iraqi Kurdistan*. Studies in Ancient Oriental Civilization, No. 31. Chicago: University of Chicago Press; 1960.

———— and C. A. Reeds: "The Achievement and Early Consequences of Food-Production: A Consideration of the Archaeological and Natural-Historical Evidence." *Cold Spring Harbor Symposia on Quantitative Biology*, Vol. XXII (1957).

Childe, V. G.: *Man Makes Himself*. 2d ed. London: Watts; 1941.

————: *What Happened in History?* London: Penguin; 1942.

————: *New Light on the Most Ancient East*. 4th ed. London: Kegan Paul; 1952.

Garstang, J., and J. B. E. Garstang: *The Story of Jericho*. London: Marshall, Morgan and Scott; 1948.

Kaplan, J.: "Excavations at Wadi Rabah." IEJ, Vol. VIII, No. 3 (1958).

————: "The Neolithic Pottery of Palestine." BASOR, No. 156 (1959).

Kenyon, K. M.: *Digging Up Jericho*. London: Benn; 1957.

————: "Some Observations on the Beginning of Settlement in the Near East." JRAI, Vol. LXXXIX, No. 1 (1959).

————: *Archaeology in the Holy Land*. London: Benn; 1960.

Macdonald, E.: "Prehistoric Fara." In *Beth-Pelet*. Vol. II. London: Quaritch; 1932.

Mallon, A., R. Köppel, and R. Neuville: *Tuleilat-Ghassul*. 2 Vols. Rome: Pontificium Institutum Biblicum; 1934 and 1940.

Mellaart, J.: "The Neolithic Site of Ghrubba." ADAS, Vol. iii (1956).

Ory, J.: "A Chalcolithic Necropolis at Benei Beraq." QDAP, Vol. xii (1946).

Perrot, J.: "Le Néolithique d'Abou-Ghosh." *Syria*, Vol. xxix (1952).

————: "Excavations at Tell Abu Matar." IEJ, Vol. v, No. 1 (1955).

Prausnitz, M. W.: "The First Agricultural Settlements in Galilee." IEJ, Vol. ix, No. 3 (1959).

Seton-Williams, V. M.: Neolithic Burnished Ware in the Near East." *Iraq*, Vol. x (1948).

Stekelis, M.: "A New Neolithic Industry: The Yarmukian of Palestine." IEJ, Vol. i, No. 1 (1950).

————: "The Abu Usba Cave (Mount Carmel)." IEJ, Vol. ii, No. 1 (1952).

Sukenik, E. L.: "A Chalcolithic Necropolis at Hedera." JPOS, Vol. xviii (1937).

————: "Archaeological Investigations at 'Affula." JPOS, Vol. xxi (1948).

Tzori, N.: "Neolithic and Chalcolithic Sites in the Beth-Shan Valley." PEQ, Vol. xc (1958).

Vaux, R. de, and A. M. Steve: "Fouilles à Tell el-Farah, près de Naplouse." RB, Vols. liv–lxiv (1947–57).

FIVE. THE URBAN AGE

Albright, W. F.: "The Jordan Valley in the Bronze Age." *El Palacio* (Santa Fe), Vol. xxii (1927).

————: "The Egyptian Empire in Asia in the Twenty-first Century B.C." JPOS, Vol. viiii (1928).

————: "The Excavations of Tell Beit Mirsim." AASOR, Vols. xii–xiii (1932–3).

————: "The Chronology of a South Palestinian City. Tell el-Ajjul." AJSL, Vol. lv (1938).

————: "The Israelite Conquest of Canaan in the Light of Archaeology." BASOR, No. 74 (1939).

————: "New Light on the History of Western Asia in the Second Millennium B.C." BASOR, Nos. 77–8 (1940).

————: "New Egyptian Data on Palestine in the Patriarchal Age." BASOR, No. 81 (1941).

————: "The Land of Damascus between 1850 and 1750 B.C." BASOR, No. 83 (1941).

————: *The Archaeology of Palestine.* 5th ed. Baltimore: Pelican; 1960.

————, J. L. Kelso, and J. P. Thorley: "Early Bronze Age Pottery from Bab ed-Dra in Moab." BASOR, No. 95 (1944).

Amiran, R. B. K.: "Connections between Anatolia and Palestine in the Early Bronze Age." IEJ, Vol. II, No. 2 (1952).

————: "Tell el-Yahudiyeh Ware in Syria." IEJ, Vol. VII, No. 2 (1957).

————: "Palestine, Syria, and Cyprus in the Middle Bronze I Period." *Eretz Israel,* Vol. V (1958).

Anati, E.: "Excavations at the Cemetery of Tell Abu Hawam (1952)." Atiqot, Vol. II (1959).

Baramki, D. C.: "Ancient Cistern in the Grounds of Government House, Jerusalem." QDAP, Vol. IV (1935).

Barrois, A. G.: *Manuel d'archéologie biblique.* 2 Vols. Paris: Picard; 1939 and 1954.

Ben-Dor, I.: "A Middle Bronze Age Temple at Nahariya." QDAP, Vol. XIV (1950).

Dajani, A. K.: "A Hyksos Tomb at Kalandia." ADAJ, Vol. II (1953).

Dothan, M.: "High Loop-Handled Cups and the Relations between Mesopotamia, Palestine, and Egypt." PEQ, Vol. LXXXV (1953).

————: "Excavations at Nahariyah. Preliminary Report (Season 1954–5)." IEJ, Vol. VI, No. 1 (1956).

Dothan, T.: Review of *Lachish IV, The Bronze Age,* by Olga Tufnell *et al.* IEJ, Vol. X, No. 1 (1960).

Ehrich, R. W. (ed.): *Relative Chronology of Old World Archaeology.* Chicago: University of Chicago Press; 1954.

Engberg, R. M., and G. M. Shipton: *Notes on the Chalcolithic and Early Bronze Age Pottery of Megiddo.* Chicago: University of Chicago Press; 1934.

Evenari, M., Y. Aharoni, L. Shanen, and M. Tadmor: "The Ancient Desert Agriculture of the Negev. III: The Early Beginning." IEJ, Vol. VIII (1958).

Fitzgerald, G. M.: "The Earliest Pottery of Beth-Shan." *The Museum Journal* (Philadelphia), Vol. XXIV, No. 1 (1935).

———— and Alan Rowe: *The Four Canaanite Temples of Beth-Shan.* Philadelphia: University of Pennsylvania; 1930.

Frankfort, H.: *The Birth of Civilization in the Near East.* London: Williams and Norgate; 1951.

Garstang, J., and J. B. E. Garstang: *The Story of Jericho.* London: Marshall, Morgan and Scott; 1948.

Guillaume, A.: "The Habiru, the Hebrews and the Arabs." PEQ, Vol. LXXII (1940).

Guy, P. L. O.: *Megiddo Tombs.* Chicago: University of Chicago Press; 1938.

Heurtley, W. A.: "A Palestinian Vase Painter of the Sixteenth Century B.C." QDAP, Vol. VIII (1939).

Jack, J. W.: "New Light on the Habiru-Hebrew Question." PEQ, Vol. LXXII (1940).

Kaplan, J.: "A Cemetery of the Bronze Age Discovered near Tel Aviv Harbour." Atiqot, Vol. I (1955).

Kenyon, K. M.: *Digging Up Jericho.* London: Benn; 1957.

————: *Archaeology in the Holy Land.* London: Benn; 1960.

Loud, G.: *Megiddo II (Seasons 1935-9).* Chicago: University of Chicago Press; 1948.

Macalister, R. A. S.: *The Excavations of Gezer, 1902-5 and 1907-9.* 3 Vols. London: Murray; 1912.

Marquet-Krause, J.: *Les Fouilles de 'Ay (et-Tell), 1933-5.* 2 Vols. Paris: Institut Français d'Archéologie de Beyrouth; 1949.

Maxwell-Hyslop, R.: "Western Asiatic Shaft-Hole Axes." *Iraq,* Vol. XI, No. 1 (1949).

————: "Bronze Lugged Axes and Adze Blades from Asia." *Iraq,* Vol. XV, No. 1 (1953).

Maisler, B. (Mazar): "Cypriote Pottery at a Tomb Cave in the Vicinity of Jerusalem." AJSL, Vol. XLIX (1932).

Ory, J.: "A Bronze Age Cemetery at Dhahrat el Humraya." QDAP, Vol. XVIII (1948).

Parr, P. J.: "A Cave at Arqub el Dhahr." ADAJ, Vol. III (1956).

Petrie, W. M. F.: *Syria and Egypt from the Tell el-Amarna Letters.* London: Methuen; 1898.

————: *Ancient Gaza.* 5 Vols. London: The British School of Archaeology in Egypt; 1931-52.

Pritchard, J. B.: *Ancient Near Eastern Texts Relating to the Old Testament.* 2d ed. Princeton, N. J.: Princeton University Press; 1955.

Rowley, H. H.: "Habiru and Hebrew." PEQ, Vol. LXXIV (1942).

Seton-Williams, V. M.: "Palestinian Temples." *Iraq,* Vol. XI, No. 1 (1949).

Shipton, G. M.: *Notes on the Megiddo Pottery of Strata VI-XX.* Chicago: University of Chicago Press; 1939.

Speiser, E. A.: "Ethnic Movements in the Near East in the Second Millennium B.C. The Hurrians and Their Connection with the Habiru and the Hyksos." AASOR, Vol. XIII (1933).

Stubbings, F. H.: *Mycenaean Pottery from the Levant.* Cambridge: Cambridge University Press; 1951.

Tufnell, O.: "The Shihan Warrior." *Iraq*, Vol. XV, No. 2 (1953).

―――― *et al.: Lachish II. The Fosse Temple.* London: Oxford University Press; 1940.

―――― *et al.: Lachish IV. The Bronze Age.* London: Oxford University Press; 1958.

Tadmor, M., and M. Prausnitz: "Excavations at Rosh Hanniqra." Atiqot, Vol. II (1959).

Vaux, R. de, and A. M. Steve: "Fouilles à Tell el-Farah, près de Naplouse." RB, Vols. LIV–LXIV (1947–57).

Wright, G. E.: *The Pottery of Palestine from the Earliest Times to the End of the Early Bronze Age.* New Haven, Conn.: American School of Oriental Research; 1937.

―――― : "Epic of the Conquest." BA, Vol. III (1940).

―――― : *Biblical Archaeology.* Philadelphia: Westminster Press; 1957.

Yadin, Y., *et al.: Hazor I–II.* Jerusalem: Hebrew University; 1958–9.

INDEX

References to illustrations are given in parentheses

A NOTE ON THE TYPE

THIS BOOK is set in ELECTRA, a Linotype face de-
signed by W. A. Dwiggins (1880–1956). This face
cannot be classified as either modern or old-style. It
is not based on any historical model, nor does it
echo any particular period or style. It avoids the
extreme contrasts between thick and thin elements
that mark most modern faces, and attempts to give
a feeling of fluidity, power, and speed.

Composed by
Brown Brothers Linotypers, New York
Printed by The Murray Printing Company,
Forge Village, Massachusetts.
Bound by H. Wolff, New York.
Typography and binding design by
VINCENT TORRE

EMMANUEL ANATI was born in Florence, Italy, in 1930. He emigrated to Israel in 1945, fought in the Israeli Army in 1948–9, and then began to study archaeology at the Hebrew University in Jerusalem, where he obtained his B.A. in 1953 and his M.A. in 1955. He directed several projects for the Israel Department of Antiquities, including the excavations of the Bronze Age cemetery of Tell Abu Hawam, the excavations of Hazorea, and a survey of the Negev Desert, where he came across an area containing hitherto unknown prehistoric rock carvings in 1954. A fellowship from the French Government financed his studies in ethnology at the Sorbonne in 1956–8, leading eventually to the degree of *Docteur ès lettres* in 1960. While he was studying in France, Mr. Anati led expeditions to study prehistoric art in southern France, Spain, and Italy for the Centre National de la Recherche Scientifique, Paris. He then visited the United States and, in 1959, obtained his M.A. in anthropology and social relations from Harvard. Returning to Europe, he contributed work on prehistoric art in the Alps and Liguria. In 1960 Mr. Anati undertook a further research project in the Negev Desert on a grant from the Wenner-Gren Foundation for Anthropological Research. Since 1961 he has been preparing a comparative study of post-Paleolithic prehistoric art in Europe on a fellowship from the Bollingen Foundation. Among his publications are *La Grande Roche de Naquane* (1960) and *Camonica Valley* (1961), and he has written numerous papers on archaeology and prehistoric and primitive art for scientific journals in the United States, Europe, and Israel. His home is in Jerusalem.